£18.99

Innovative therapy:
a handbook

Open University Press
Psychotherapy Handbooks Series
Series Editor: Windy Dryden

Published titles:

Individual Therapy: A Handbook
Windy Dryden (ed.)

Integrative and Eclectic Therapy: A Handbook
Windy Dryden (ed.)

Hypnotherapy: A Handbook
Michael Heap and Windy Dryden (eds)

Couple Therapy: A Handbook
Douglas Hooper and Windy Dryden (eds)

Innovative Therapy: A Handbook
David Jones (ed.)

Child and Adolescent Therapy: A Handbook
David A. Lane and Andrew Miller (eds)

Art Therapy: A Handbook
Diane Waller and Andrea Gilroy (eds)

Innovative therapy:
a handbook

Edited by
DAVID JONES

Open University Press
Buckingham · Philadelphia

Open University Press
Celtic Court
22 Ballmoor
Buckingham
MK18 1XW

and
1900 Frost Road, Suite 101
Bristol, PA 19007, USA

First Published 1994

A catalogue record of this book is available from the British Library

ISBN 0 335 19139 8 (Pb)   0 335 19140 1 (Hb)

Library of Congress Cataloging-in-Publication Data
Innovative therapy : a handbook / edited by David Jones.
    p. cm. — (Open University Press psychotherapy handbooks
series)
    Includes bibliographical references and index.
    ISBN 0-335-19139-8 (pb)   ISBN 0-335-19140-1 (hb)
    1. Psychotherapy. I. Jones, David, 1934-   . II. Series:
Psychotherapy handbooks series.
    [DNLM: 1. Psychotherapy.   WM 420 I5885 1994]
RC480.5.I545 1994
616.89'14—dc20
DNLM/DLC   94–1682
for Library of Congress   CIP

Typeset by Colset Private Limited, Singapore
Printed in Great Britain by Biddles Limited, Guildford and King's Lynn

For Anna and Emily

By *psychotherapy* I refer to a personal relationship with a professional person in which those in distress can share and explore the underlying nature of their troubles, and possibly change some of the determinants of these through experiencing unrecognized forces in themselves.

from Sutherland, J.
'The Consultant Psychotherapist in the
National Health Service: His Role and Training.'
British Journal of Psychiatry (1968) 114: 509–15.

People who have been through it (enlightenment) tend to be described by others as simple, natural, genuine and straightforward; serene and peaceful yet alert and full of life and vitality; wise in their words and economical and effective in their actions; kind, friendly, gentle and considerate in their dealings with people, perceptive and intelligent; at ease in their bodies and at home in the world. They seem to have shed the neurotic baggage that the rest of us reluctantly carry about: anxiety, irritation, resentment, regret, guilt, meanness, greed, possessiveness, worry, confusion and the rest of the familiar catalogue. And while we look on with envy, or even disbelief, they assert that this transformation is available for all. What we see as the inevitable minuses that must come along with the plus of being alive, they see as the unwanted and unnecessary by-products of some mistakes we have made in the way we look at things.

Excerpt from *Beyond Therapy, The Impact of
Eastern Religion on Psychological Theory and
Practice* edited by Guy Claxton (1986).
Reprinted with permission of Wisdom Publications,
361 Newbury Street, Boston, Massachusetts, USA.

Contents

The editor and contributors

PETER AFFORD is a counsellor, psychotherapist and Focusing teacher. He has practised Focusing since 1985, is an accredited trainer with the Focusing Institute in Chicago and a founder member of the British Focusing Network. He works in London at St James Church, Piccadilly and in private practice in Clapham.

CAROLINE BEECH is a counsellor and groupworker and is co-director of the Eigenwelt phenomenological psychotherapy training programme in England and of the Amida project in France. She works to integrate psychology, arts and spirituality. She runs workshops on developing creativity and has a special interest in the therapy of eating issues.

DAVID BRAZIER is a practising psychotherapist and co-director of the Eigenwelt psychotherapy training programme in the north of England. His works include *A Guide to Psychodrama* and *Beyond Carl Rogers: Toward a Psychotherapy for the 21st Century*.

JULIANA BROWN grew up in western Canada. She trained in Primal Integration with William Swartley and was significantly influenced by subsequent work with Frank Lake. In 1979 she co-founded the original South London Natural Health Centre. She has been in full-time practice of Primal Integration, both group and individual work, since 1981.

DAVID CRANMER holds an honours degree in general and humanistic psychology from the University of California. He has worked with individuals and groups in a variety of mental health situations including psychiatric hospitals and short-term residential crisis programmes. He completed the first international Core Energetic training programme for professionals in August 1991. At present he supervises counsellors and therapists in Devon.

LAURA DONINGTON works in London as a psychotherapist, trainer and supervisor. She has degrees in anthropology and psychology and is a graduate and staff member of the Karuna Institute. She supervises counselling trainees at the Roehampton Institute and is a senior counsellor at the Wandsworth Cancer Support Centre.

WILLIAM EMERSON has a doctorate in psychology and has held university appointments in the USA. A past honorary fellow of the National Institute of Mental Health he has lectured extensively on pre- and perinatal psychology. His pioneering methods for treating infants and children are recognized world wide and he is the author of many publications. He practised as a psychotherapist for 25 years and is now a trainer and supervisor.

ANDREW FORRESTER currently practises in Devon as a psychotherapist, trainer and supervisor. After a social sciences degree he worked in therapeutic community and family casework for 13 years. He has trained in Gestalt Psychotherapy and Social Work and is, at present, exploring a fusion of dance, moving meditation and psychotherapy.

DAVID JONES is a graduate of the Karuna Institute. He was a lecturer in psychology at the London School of Economics, where he ran a programme in personal and professional development, and is now a psychotherapist in private practice at the Ajanta Centre, South London.

RICHARD LANG discovered the Headless Way in 1970 when he was 17. Since then he has studied it deeply and led many workshops in Britain and abroad. He is committed to sharing this work and making bridges with other approaches. He also practises as a psychotherapist, facilitates men's groups and teaches t'ai chi and meditation.

DOUGLAS MATHERS was formerly Principal Psychotherapist at the student health centre at the London School of Economics. He trained in medicine, psychology and psychiatry and then with the Psychosynthesis and Education Trust (London) where he gives supervision. He is an Associate Member of the British Association of Psychotherapists (Jungian Group) and a member of the Religious Society of Friends. He is also in private practice.

MELINDA MOORE MEIGS is a therapist in private practice in London. Her work in industry includes voicework, the process of decision-making and managing change. She originally trained and practised as a musician and singer performing throughout Europe and North America. She has given voicework workshops in the UK, Europe, the Far East and Australia. More recent training includes psychoanalytical counselling at Birkbeck College, University of London. She is a BAC accredited counsellor.

RICHARD MOWBRAY has been a full-time practitioner of Primal Integration since 1979, following training with William Swartley and further training with

Frank Lake. He has also trained in various forms of bodywork and has been a member of The Open Centre since 1979. He is the author of *The Case Against Psychotherapy Registration*.

HELEN PAYNE is completing a doctorate in psychology and is an individual and group psychotherapist (UKCP) using movement and words to facilitate change. She works as a researcher, author, consultant and trainer to organizations and universities. The leading pioneer in dance movement therapy, she is Founding-Director of The Institute for the Arts in Psychotherapy and has a private practice.

STEPHAN SCHORR-KON, a Polish-American survivor of the holocaust, died while this book was being produced. He graduated from Cambridge in English Literature and trained in cranio-sacral osteopathy and in neurolinguistic programming. He was in private practice in Cambridge and London.

CHRISTINE VALENTINE is a psychotherapist practising in Bath. She is a Tutor with the Faculty of Astrological Studies from whom she received the Astrology Gold medal in 1985. She has contributed seminars and articles on psychological astrology and is the author of *Images of the Psyche* published by Element in 1991.

WILLIAM WEST has been a freelance psychotherapist, group leader and psychotherapist trainer at Energy Stream since 1979. He works part time as a student counsellor for Sheffield Hallam University and is currently completing a doctorate exploring the cross-over from therapy into healing. He is also a spiritual healer and a Quaker.

List of figures

Introduction

DAVID JONES

This volume on innovative therapies follows the success of *Innovative Therapy in Britain* (Rowan and Dryden 1988), *Individual Therapy in Britain* (Dryden 1984) and *Individual Therapy: A Handbook* (Dryden 1990). Individual therapies include: Freudian, Jungian and Kleinian (also known as Object Relations) approaches to psychoanalysis; transactional analysis and person centred, personal construct, existential, gestalt, and behavioural psychotherapies. All of these therapies were innovative during their formative years. Today they are established as orthodox therapies, or as compatible alternatives to orthodox therapy. They are now consolidating their position rather than breaking new ground so the sense of urgency about innovation and change which they showed when they were new has declined. Some innovative therapies never get to this stage. They die out or remain, like rebirthing (Jones 1992), in the margins of acceptability.

Integration

'Integration' has become one of the main themes in discussions about therapy. There are two aspects to this. Innovations in the way therapists work used to be competitive as if one type of therapy would prove to be the only one that is beneficial. Competition still arises between practitioners but there is a growing desire to integrate different approaches, to learn from one another. In this sense innovation has become more cooperative. The other aspect of integration refers to what goes on in the client and the aim is to help clients to integrate all aspects of experience, including thought, behaviour, feelings, intuition and 'spirit' and not to emphasize the importance of just one of these at the expense of the others.

Recent innovations have focused on perinatal and birth experience, spiritual mindfulness and meditation practice, bodywork, expressive artwork and the use of ancient systems of healing. The aim is to integrate these with other therapies offered by practitioners to the public.

In the 1950s it made sense to group together a number of therapies as innovatory. They included two older therapies, Moreno's psychodrama and Assagioli's psychosynthesis which developed alongside Freudian psychoanalysis and some newer approaches including Rogers's person centred approach and encounter, Maslow's self-actualization and Perls's gestalt. These therapies differ from orthodox psychoanalysis and behaviour therapy in that they use active techniques for self-exploration such as role play, artwork, movement, voice and touch. Collectively they became known as humanistic psychotherapy and the philosophy behind them as humanistic psychology. The main humanistic therapies are described in Appendix B.

Humanistic therapy

Humanistic psychotherapies differ from psychoanalysis in a number of ways, notably in the role adopted by the therapist. Generally speaking a psychoanalyst helps patients understand their experience and behaviour in terms of reactions to events in childhood. Understanding and insight is offered in the hope that it will alter the patient's perceptions and behaviour and as a result they will start feeling better. A humanistic therapist tries to use active techniques to guide the client in an exploration of their experience, past and present, to discover its meaning for themselves and to monitor their own changes in feeling and well-being. Humanistic therapists rejected psychoanalysis because, in their view, this imposed the analyst's theoretical perspective and values on patients instead of allowing for personal exploration, growth and choice. They rejected behaviourism, based on the principles of classical and operant conditioning, as too mechanical and manipulative.

Individual hour-long sessions, held once a week or more frequently, are common in the humanistic therapies, as they are in psychoanalysis, but there is also an emphasis on weekend or longer workshops, often in a residential setting. Thirty years ago these came to be called personal growth centres or institutes, following the lead given by the Esalen Institute in California. The therapies described in this volume can be used in individual sessions but anyone who wants to discover the full potential of an innovative therapy should also attend workshops in a centre.

Rowan and Dryden (1988) point out that humanistic therapies used to have an aversion to theory. They were strongly attracted to intuition, spontaneity, bodywork and an holistic view of the individual, but not to theory. Rowan and Dryden saw this as a reaction to the tendency of psychoanalysts to develop over-elaborate and over-technical theoretical arguments, rendering the individual as a set of disembodied fragments alien from the experience of the whole person. However, therapists' attitudes are changing (Horrocks 1993). Humanistic therapists now put more emphasis than they used to on theory, including psychodynamic theory. This trend is evident in the chapters of this volume. Conversely some psychoanalysts have begun to use active approaches to therapy to help their patients use insight to bring about emotional and behavioural change.

Humanistic therapies deepened the therapeutic process by moving away from the goal of understanding towards the active exploration of experience as an integration of thought, feeling and behaviour. This created more opportunities for clients to change. The innovations described in this volume go further than that. They facilitate understanding and integration but they also offer opportunities for *transforming* the common irritations, fears and obsessions into equanimity, sympathetic joy and loving kindness. The methods of transformation owe a lot to the spiritual tradition, especially of Buddhism.

Interpretation

People who are new to therapy often have a misunderstanding about interpretation. They tell the therapist what has happened to them and how they feel and expect the therapist to respond by telling them what has caused it all and what it all means. Typically the patient recounts a dream to the therapist and expects the therapist to tell them its true meaning, revealing the unconscious motivation in the dream. This approach is like a doctor diagnosing a cause and suggesting a remedy for a patient who has discomforting symptoms. Therapy of this type leads to the criticism that it imposes the analyst's theoretical perspective and values on patients instead of allowing them personal exploration, growth and choice.

Successful psychoanalysts form tentative interpretations about meaning and offer them in such a way that the patient can choose what to make of them. It is then less likely that the patient will feel they are having the therapist's values and frame of reference imposed on them. They are developing their own.

Humanistic, active or innovatory therapists sometimes think they are not interpretative. But the way a therapist responds to a client always embodies a frame of reference and a meaning which conveys the therapist's interpretation of what the client has said or done. When a therapist asks a question about something it draws attention to the supposed importance of that thing. Statements such as 'that might be worth exploring' or 'I hear what you say and I am also hearing in your voice that you don't like it' or 'that comes across to me as like your father' are interpretative. They draw attention to something and offer a shift, sometimes just a slight shift, in the way it is being looked at, which the client can resist or accept. In this way the interpretive response of the therapist negotiates and deepens the frame of understanding which the client is using. This is true of all therapies.

Closely related to this is the question of believing in the reality of what the client says happened to them in the past. It is unwise to tell clients that what they say happened to them is a figment of their imagination. Alice Miller (1985) established this beyond any doubt. It is irrelevant whether the therapist thinks a statement by the client is acceptable as accurate history. It often is, but what is important is that the client is expressing a truth about their sense of what happened to them, their truth of what they felt and what they feel now. It is this that modern innovative therapists work with. An example concerns a woman who was angry at her father for sexually abusing her. Her therapist said she had not been sexually abused because her father made no attempt to touch her genitals. The point is that she *felt* deeply abused and in reliving incidents in her childhood with another therapist who accepted her reality she experienced the many ways in which her father had invaded her personal space and felt again his unsavoury interest in her as a sexual object which had left her feeling sexually abused although there had been no abusive physical contact.

Professionalization

Psychotherapies have proliferated in the USA, and to a lesser extent in Britain and the EC since 1950. Pilgrim (1990) has gone very thoroughly into the economic, political, social and ideological reasons for this. An important factor is the opportunity for starting a business in an entrepreneurial culture which emphasizes individual rights and achievement more than it values the individual's obligation to support the extended family or a larger national or ethnic identity. Indeed many therapists in the 1960s viewed the individual as all that mattered and viewed the family and all organisations as oppressive (Laing and Esterson 1967) and, as Holbrook (1969) pointed out they tended to blame 'society' for everything. These days there are still therapists who prefer to see themselves as living and working in a 'collective' or as part of a 'network' or 'movement' rather than as a member of an organization.

The proliferation of psychotherapies has led to two opposing tendencies. On the one hand, those which are similar have tended to form alliances in creating professional bodies. The sections of the United Kingdom Council for Psychotherapy (UKCP) reflect this. The Humanistic and Integrative Psychotherapy Section (HIPS) of the UKCP, generally speaking, contains the therapies discussed in this volume. On the other hand there has been a polarization. Practitioners want their therapy to appear distinct. The formation in March 1992 of the Association for Accredited Psychospiritual Psychotherapists (AAPP), which is recognized by the UKCP as an accrediting body, is an example of polarization. The AAPP sees itself as fundamentally different from the AHPP (Association for Humanistic Psychology Practitioners' Section), also a part of the UKCP, from which it separated. The AAPP is made up of organizations which train psychotherapists in Core Process Psychotherapy (Chapter 4) and psychosynthesis (Chapter 5).

Another trend has been for therapies to put less emphasis on activity and catharsis and to include more discussion and contemplation. A similar trend was noticed by Lewis (1989) in his study of ecstatic religions. As they develop from minority status towards being accepted as part of the majority they shed much of their ecstatic, active and cathartic behaviour.

In the 1960s concern was expressed among the public about links between the innovative therapies and organisations such as religious 'cults'. This led the British government to set up the Foster inquiry (Foster 1971) which recommended a system of registration be set up for psychotherapists. Since then there has been a move towards agreeing standards of training, supervision and codes of practice to which the proliferation of therapies has given rise. The United Kingdom Council for Psychotherapy (UKCP) is a professional organization of psychotherapists created for this purpose and an important contribution to its work has been made by a group of humanistic psychologists through the Association for Humanistic Psychology in Britain (AHPB). There is wide support for maintaining high standards of practice but some therapists are uneasy about the UKCP and its scheme for registration. They fear it will inhibit innovation and lead to overregulation.

Concern about religious 'cults' led to the founding of INFORM (Information Network Focus on Religious Movements). Based on the work of Eileen Barker, Professor of the Sociology of Religion at the London School of Economics, it provides up-to-date information about the philosophy and practices of a wide range of religious organizations and their links with psychotherapy (Barker 1989).

The structure of innovative therapies

Five areas of innovation stand out: perinatal experience, psychospiritual practice, bodywork, expressive artwork and the use of ancient systems of healing.

Perinatal experience (Chapters 2 and 3)

Until recently most psychologists assumed that psychological development began during the months after birth. During the last 20 years there has been increasing recognition of the formative effects of life in the womb. The importance of the perinatal period (before and just after birth) for psychotherapists has been convincingly illustrated by John Rowan. He refers to a case (Malan 1979) in which there are:

> clear signs of umbilical affect – in other words, the patient is remembering life in the womb, and traumatic experiences which happened there. It is all about tubes and starvation and all the rest of the phenomena which Lake (1980) describes so well. But because Malan himself has never been into this area in his own therapy, and because there is no place for this in his own theory, he is compelled to falsify it. He says that the experiences link firmly with *feeding at the breast* (his italics), and that 'any reference to an umbilical cord cannot be anything other than psychological anachronism!'
>
> (Rowan and Dryden, 1988: 289).

William Swartley's Primal Integration (Chapter 2 of this volume), is an example of an approach that integrates pre- and perinatal experience. It is also important as an example of an approach based on the philosophy of the Human Potential Movement, in which many of the innovative therapies of humanistic psychology have their origin. A central part of this philosophy is that the practitioner does not give treatment but rather facilitates a series of experiences to assist a client in their personal growth and development. The client should accept full responsibility for what they do and for what happens to them in this type of approach.

There are other approaches which also integrate perinatal experience with the present: Stan Grof's Holotropic Therapy (Grof 1988), Frank Lake's Clinical Theology (Lake 1980), Arthur Janov's Primal Therapy (Janov 1991) and William Emerson's Somatotropic Therapy (Chapter 3 of this volume) are the main examples. We can be confident that exploration of the pre- and perinatal experience will continue as an innovative area in psychotherapy and personal growth work.

Awareness and psychospiritual practice (Chapters 4 to 7)

An increasing number of therapists hold the view that therapeutic change has less to do with the type of therapy being practised and more to do with the quality of presence or a 'spiritual' aspect in the relationship between therapist and client. 'Presence' has recently been incorporated into the theory, practice and training in the spiritual therapies, notably through meditation and imagery. The aim is to develop good attention in the therapist to his or her inner process, good attention in the client to their process and good attention between the two of them.

Chapter 4 describes Core Process Psychotherapy. This is a comprehensive therapy developed over the last 20 years by Maura and Franklyn Sills at the Karuna Institute. It is a 'spiritual' therapy which means it emphasizes the development of awareness through daily meditative exercises and mindfulness in everyday life. It is based on a sophisticated theory of mind leading in practice to the development of intuition, empathy and spontaneity in the relationship between therapist and client and allows the most profound experiences of therapy to be contained within theory and yet to remain beyond words. The Core Process model of the mind is similar to the one adopted in cognitive psychology (Moorey 1990) which recognizes the importance of mental processes which lead us to create concepts and become attached to them. Core Process Therapy is also compatible with psychodynamic and humanistic ways of working with clients.

Psychosynthesis is described in Chapter 5. It concentrates on the inner life of the client, the therapist serving as an experienced traveller who follows and guides the client's process. Psychosynthesis, whose founder Assagioli was one of Freud's students, carried the importance of spiritual work during a period when it was labelled 'mystical' and rejected, caused perhaps by the erroneous Freudian belief that religion is a manifestation of neurosis. Transpersonal Therapy (Gordon-Brown and Somers 1988) is one branch of psychosynthesis which came into existence more for organizational reasons than for differences in approach.

Chapter 6 describes the system of the Headless Way, the work of Douglas Harding (1986). It provides a set of practical workshop exercises illustrating the way we create the notion of our Self and get attached to it. It is the counterpart in experiential terms of cognitive psychology's treatment of mind as a mechanism for generating concepts about ourselves and our environment so that we are able to share enough of a common reality with other people and form relationships. A Headless Way workshop helps participants sense how we structure this reality and to see that overattachment to it provides a basis for suffering.

The emphasis on awareness and the inner journey, or process, in spiritual therapy is closely linked with Chapter 7 which discusses Focusing. Focusing helps us become aware of the amalgam of thought and feeling, called the 'felt sense' which sets the tone to our experience. It can be used by therapists working with clients and can also be learned as a method for self-help. Focusing contrasts with the main self-help therapy of the 1970s, co-counselling (Evison and Horobin 1988). Whereas co-counselling generates good attention outwards by using catharsis to empty out the effects of distress so that decisions can then be made and acted on in a clear way, Focusing develops awareness of inner states and processes.

Emphasis on the body (Chapters 8 and 9)

Wilhelm Reich (1945) was a student of Freud and as a psychoanalyst pioneered the idea that our defensive strategies for coping with life lie both in our minds and in our bodies. Our beliefs and attitudes form our mental defences and our physical bearing represents these in bodily form. The way we hold ourselves gives us a characteristic posture or body armouring in which our defensiveness is held physically in our muscles. Reich listened to his patients and helped them obtain insight into the defensive nature of their attitudes and beliefs and he introduced touch, massage and physical exercises to overcome the physical defences of their body armouring. This work was taken up by two of his students Lowen (1958), whose bioenergetics has become well established, and Pierrakos (1990) whose Core Energetics, though potentially more important, is less well known.

Chapter 8 describes Pierrakos' Core Energetics. It is a system which works with the body and is compatible with spiritual therapy. Some people have difficulty with the concept of energy as an aura or field which surrounds each person and which can be worked with in therapy. I have such a difficulty for I cannot see auras. This turns out not to matter if you are working as a client or patient in this system. In a sense people like me have to suspend our disbelief for a short period of time. The rest of Pierrakos' ideas are less controversial.

Chapter 9 describes the way that the Reichian tradition is integrated with the humanistic approach to therapy.

Emphasis on expression (Chapters 10 to 12)

Most humanistic psychotherapies involve clients in artistic expression in some way but it is usually as an adjunct to the main therapeutic activity. The purpose is to allow non-verbal aspects of our minds to come into play in the transaction between therapist and client. This throws up material for discussion which can lead to insight. It also involves emotional expression which leads to change of a type which is independent of words.

Chapter 10 offers an integrated approach to therapy involving creative activity based on the philosphical approach of phenomenology. Chapter 11 describes Dance Movement Therapy. Chapter 12 describes the use of the human voice in therapy. Voicework is an example of a growing trend which combines psychodynamic ways of working with participation by the client in an activity, in this case the making of sounds.

Emphasis on ancient systems (Chapters 13 and 14)

There are a number of ancient systems which offer something to modern innovative therapy of which shamanism, paganism and astrological counselling are examples.

Shamanism (Lewis 1989; Getty 1990) in its modern form seeks to emulate the 'masters of spirits' (Lewis 1990) who practised, and to some extent still practise, as healers in preliterate societies by invoking spirits and deities. It involves rituals of healing, transition and personal development. Participants do not have to believe in the 'reality' of a world of spirits and deities. Insight and a sense of a shift in perspective can be gained by participants in shamanistic exercises irrespective of their philosophy and belief system.

Rowan (1988) describes paganism as a system for personal development which is caring about the environment of which we are a part and which sustains us. It is taught and practised largely within the domain of women's therapy.

Women's therapy seeks ways to work on power, esteem and perceptions of women, by women for women in the world as it is, largely controlled by men, often to the detriment of both. Issues about power, role, sexuality, eating, physical, verbal and sexual abuse are central to it. It emphasizes caring, holism and cooperation rather than exploitation and competition which are seen as over-emphasized in the male domain. The women's movement gave rise to therapy for women based on the techniques of the humanistic therapies and focusing on the issues which women face. A recent development is a philosophy for men's groups which explore what it is to be a man and how men should fulfil themselves in a patriarchal world. Chapter 13 describes this development.

Finally we have a chapter on astrological counselling. Many people have difficulty with astrology and I am one of them. I cannot accept astrology as a body of scientific knowledge based on repeatable observation and experiment and succeeding in making verifiable predictions. These claims of astrology seem to me to be poorly founded. However this is not what astrological counselling is primarily about. As Christine Valentine shows, it is about a language for discourse about the features of life and the characteristics of people. As a language it owes a lot to mythology and when this is combined in a therapist with sound skills of empathy, intuition and resonance it provides a frame for good therapy.

References

Barker, E. (1989) *New Religious Movements: A Practical Introduction.* London: HMSO.

Dryden, W. (1990) *Individual Therapy: A Handbook.* Milton Keynes: Open University Press.

Dryden, W. (ed.) (1984) *Individual Therapy in Britain.* London: Harper & Row.

Evison, R. and Horobin, R. (1988) Co-counselling. In J. Rowan and W. Dryden (eds) *Innovative Therapy in Britain.* Milton Keynes: Open University Press.

Foster J.G. (1971) *Enquiry into the Practice and Effects of Scientology.* London: HMSO House of Commons Report.

Getty, A. (1990) *The Goddess.* London: Thames & Hudson.

Gordon-Brown, I. and Somers, B. (1988) Transpersonal Psychotherapy. In J. Rowan and W. Dryden (eds) *Innovative Therapy in Britain.* Milton Keynes: Open University Press.

Grof, S. (1988) *The Adventure of Self Discovery*. Albany, NY: State University of New York Press.

Harding, D. (1986) *On Having No Head: Zen and the Rediscovery of the Obvious*. London: Arkana.

Holbrook, D. (1969) Madness to Blame Society, *Twentieth Century*, 2.

Horrocks, R. (1993) A fresh look at Freud, *Self & Society*, 21(2).

Janov, A. (1991) *The New Primal Scream*. London: Abacus.

Jones, A. (ed.) (1992) Rebirthing Revisited, *Self & Society*, 20(2) and (4).

Laing, R. and Esterson, A. (1967) *Sanity, Madness and the Family*. Harmondsworth: Penguin.

Lake, F. (1980) *Constricted Confusion*. Oxford: Clinical Theology Association.

Lake, F. (1986) *Clinical Theology*. London: Darton, Longman & Todd.

Lewis, I. (1989) *Ecstatic Religion*. Harmondsworth: Penguin.

Lewis, I. (1990) Shamanism: Ethnopsychiatry. *Self & Society*, 18(2).

Lowen, A. (1958) *The Language of the Body*. London: Collier Macmillan.

Malan, D.H. (1979) *Individual Psychotherapy and the Science of Psychodynamics*. London: Butterworths.

Miller, A. (1985) *Thou Shalt Not Be Aware: Society's Betrayal of the Child*. London: Pluto Press.

Moorey, S. (1990) Cognitive therapy. In Dryden, W. (ed.) *Individual Therapy: A Handbook*. Milton Keynes: Open University Press.

Pierrakos, J. (1990) *Core Energetics*. Mendocino, CA: Life Rhythm.

Pilgrim, D. (1990) British psychotherapy in context. In W. Dryden (ed.) *Individual Therapy: A Handbook*. Milton Keynes: Open University Press.

Reich, W. (1945) *Character Analysis*. New York: Orgone Institute Press.

Rowan, J. (1988) *Ordinary Ecstasy*. London: Routledge.

Rowan, J. and Dryden, W. (1988) *Innovative Therapy in Britain*. Milton Keynes: Open University Press.

PART I

Emphasis on perinatal experience

Primal Integration

JULIANA BROWN AND RICHARD MOWBRAY

Definition and historical development

Definition

Primal Integration is a very free-form type of primal work that involves an exploration of deeper levels of experience with a view to being more alive and living more authentically. It is concerned with the recovery and reintegration of split-off parts of the self and works with very early preverbal experiences from the womb, birth and infancy, as well as later experiences in a very eclectic way. The emphasis of the work is on self-direction and self-regulation and allowing spontaneous growth processes to unfold rather than on a highly structured or directed programme.

This work is undertaken in groups with minimal leader determined structure but with appropriate ground rules for safe working, as well as in individual sessions. Primal material is allowed to emerge under its own dynamic but is not directly aimed for.

Historical development

William Swartley developed the work for which he coined the term Primal Integration starting from about 1962. He summarized this development as follows:

> Primal Integration is one of a number of primally oriented human maturation techniques which have evolved during the 1970s . . . The third 'new' thing about primal techniques is the adaption I have developed for use with average, maturing adults, called Primal Integration. Primal Integration utilizes regressive techniques with average adults within an educational rather than a therapeutic framework. That is, Primal Integration rejects the authoritarian medical model of treatment, and is an education rather than a therapy . . . Primal Integration is a contribution of

the Encounter Group Movement which began on the East and West coasts of the United States during 1962, grandfathered by Maslow and Perls. Thus, Primal Integration may be viewed historically as a child of the union of regressive psychotherapy and the Encounter Movement.

(Swartley 1975)

Two historical lines of development that came together in this 'child of the union' were an increasing awareness of the importance of pre- and peri-natal experience (not least, that birth *is* an experience – that the birthing infant is capable of having an experience) and the readoption of cathartic approaches.

The first line features Rank (1929) prominently, followed by Fodor (1949, 1951) and Mott (1948) who were able to discern the importance of the birth experience largely from the interpretation of their clients' dreams. Much of the second line of development can be traced back to the influence of Wilhelm Reich (Boadella 1985) whose active, body-oriented and cathartic approach found enthusiastic support in the Human Potential Movement during the 1960s – a movement in which one of Reich's students, Fritz Perls, who developed Gestalt Therapy, played a prominent role.

Both these lines of historical development also have roots with Freud. Rank was part of his inner circle and early on Freud worked abreactively – directly with 'primary (primal) process' ('primärvorgang') – before relinquishing this approach in favour of the more rational method he named 'Psychoanalysis'.

Swartley was active in the Human Potential Movement and founded one of the first growth centres, the Center for the Whole Person, in Philadelphia in 1962 and later, the International Primal Association.

In 1970 Arthur Janov published his book, *The Primal Scream* (Janov 1970) and his Primal Therapy was subsequently undertaken by John Lennon of The Beatles resulting in widespread publicity. Swartley acknowledged Janov's influence in popularizing the re-emergence of cathartic techniques but did not have any direct contact with Janov or his Primal Therapy and developed Primal Integration independently.

Swartley's own work was rooted in his experience in the Human Potential Movement, especially with Bindrim ('peak experience' groups) and Perls, preceded by his studies at the Jung Institute, and with Assagioli amongst others. He was also a friend of the Czech psychiatrist, Stanislav Grof, who was working nearby in Baltimore with terminal cancer patients from 1967–73. They shared a common interest in primal realms, and Grof's cartography of 'inner space', derived from his work with LSD, became one of the ingredients Swartley incor-porated into his eclectic approach (Grof 1975).

Founders

William Swartley and colleagues introduced Primal Integration to the UK in 1976, only a few years before his untimely death in 1979 at the age of 52. During this period he set up and ran the training programme for practitioners in which we participated. After his death, members of the training programme including ourselves formed the Whole Person Cooperative to offer workshops in Primal Integration to the public and to organize continued professional development for ourselves. This organization lasted for two years.

Since Swartley's death we and others in the UK have been developing and evolving Primal Integration. We have integrated other influences, probably the most significant of these being the work of Francis Mott and the work of Dr Frank Lake of the Clinical Theology Association (Mott 1948, 1964; Lake 1966, 1980, 1981). Following Swartley, Lake also referred to his work as Primal Integration for a while, though his form of primal work was very different – much more structured and exclusively focused on the pre- and perinatal realm. Latterly he referred to his work as Pre- and Perinatal Integration.

Like Grof, Lake had worked with LSD before it became illegal and thereby, like Grof, could not help but become aware of the importance of birth trauma as an influence on human development. In the last few years of his life, Lake pioneered an understanding of the role of intrauterine experience and stress, in particular the importance of 'umbilical affect'. He had a particular 'feel' for existential positions of dread and affliction and his work was deeply rooted in his Christian faith.

We have been offering a comprehensive programme of Primal Integration at the Open Centre in London since 1979. Betty Hughes, who works with us regularly has made a remarkable contribution regarding the use of sandplay in a primal context. Other practitioners include John Rowan, a fellow founder member of the Whole Person Cooperative, who does individual sessions and occasional workshops. Dr Roger Moss in Devon and Dr Barbara Bapty, also in Devon, are amongst those who have continued Lake's work. The Clinical Theology Association continues to publish his literature.

Where does Primal Integration fit in?

Primal Integration is distinguished by the combination of four basic elements:

1 It is a form of personal growth work, operating within an educational rather than a medical model.
2 It recognizes the importance of very early life experiences, and acknowledges that the individual is able to remember pre- and perinatal life.
3 It works with these and other memories in abreactive as well as other ways.
4 The work takes place in an unstructured setting, which respects the unique 'unfoldment' of the individual's process, and emphasizes self-regulation and self-responsibility.

Despite an essentially independent development, Primal Integration is often confused with Arthur Janov's 'Primal Therapy' (Janov 1970, 1991) due to the similarity of names. Both approaches allow for the direct expression of primal material. However, unlike Primal Integration, Primal Therapy, offered as 'The Cure for Neurosis', is conceived very much within the medical model. It is offered as a highly structured programme based largely on an individual intensive format in contrast to Primal Integration's low structured, self-regulated set-up where intensives are usually on a group basis. Primal Integration pays due regard to the spiritual and transpersonal aspects of the primal process, and values primal joy as well as the primal 'Pain' that is Janov's sole focus.

A close relative of Primal Integration, with historical links (see above), is Grof's Holotropic Therapy (Grof 1988) combining controlled breathing, music and focused bodywork. We are in tune with the focus of his work on the spontaneous healing activity of non-ordinary states of consciousness as well as the acceptance of pre- and perinatal experience and transpersonal levels.

Central concepts

For us 'Primal' means first in time, early, but also first in importance – that which is central, core, deep. 'Integration' refers to the integration into awareness of the fruits of primal exploration, a 'gathering together', a healing, a becoming more whole. It also refers to the active application in daily life of what is being learned about oneself. This ensures that the primal work is connected, grounded and relevant. Attending to the present and keeping a balance between the need for exploring the 'past' and the need for strengthening, maintaining and developing one's sense of the 'present' form an important part of this work.

Primal Integration addresses the issue of how to live with deeper aspects of oneself in play. Often this will involve allowing unfinished traumatic experience from the womb, birth and infancy to emerge, since this is frequently what awaits when one attempts to live more deeply. However this is but one element of the more fundamental process of learning to live from one's core, from one's deeper Self, in whatever way that may be presenting at the time. Experiences from later periods in life also emerge, as well as transpersonal and mystical experiences, and creative urges.

The 'regression' that we facilitate in Primal Integration is not about going back in time, but rather about becoming aware of your *existing* state of regression – about realizing that parts of you have not grown up and moved forward into the present. In our view, most people are living in two time-scales simultaneously – past and present. Part of them will be living in the here and now. Other parts of them will be reacting to present events as though they were still 'back then', thereby confusing aspects of the present with the past.

With time, both practitioner and participant develop a sense of these two worlds. They learn to recognize signs on the surface – in feelings, language, actions, gestures and imagery that betray the presence of unconscious 'memories' that are still playing an active role in present life. It is not really accurate to refer to these as 'memories' since at this stage they are *felt* to be in the present and have yet to be appropriately reclassified as 'past', 'over' – as memory rather than current reality.

The recovery of aspects of one's *personal* history involves an opening that can also involve an expansion of one's awareness to embrace the *transpersonal*. This is particularly true of memories of pre- and perinatal experience.

Central to the practice of Primal Integration is the understanding that it is carried out under the rubric of a personal growth or educational model rather than a medical model. We do not refer to Primal Integration as a psychotherapy or therapy (or 'Primal Integration Therapy'). We are conscious that many activities that are identified by such labels (including those described in this book) would also be considered to be of a growth rather than a medical nature. However, we believe that these labels, psychotherapy and therapy, are significantly compromised by their common usage to refer to activities that are implicitly or explicitly operating within a medical model. Their use to refer to growth activities confuses the models, serves to support an already dominant model rather than promote an alternative one and distorts the expectations of people who may undertake the work. We are aware that the term 'therapy' has classical roots more in keeping with a growth model, but regard the term as having been largely co-opted by nineteenth and twentieth-century models of scientific medicine.

It is easy to forget that different models are not different realities but rather offer different perspectives on the same reality. They show you different parts of the same elephant, to borrow from the Sufi tale.

A key aspect of the medical model is the social status conferred by being defined as 'sick' or 'ill'. This is a role that carries the privilege of being allowed a partial relief from adult responsibilities (Parsons 1953). In the case of physical illness this may be entirely appropriate, however applied to psychological matters it poses problems. There are parallels between the status of being 'ill' and the status of being a child that can lead to confusion when working with processes involving 'regression'.

Under a growth model such as we are employing, the clients retain full adult responsibility for themselves – for their feelings and actions – that is not something they relinquish. They do not have the privileges of the sick role nor do they have the loss of autonomy, temporary or otherwise, that is concomitant with that role. Thus a basic requirement of those who undertake Primal Integration is that they are willing and able to accept this responsibility for themselves. We interview everyone as a matter of course to assess this.

This brings us to the principle of *self-regulation*. It has two aspects:

1 'Self-regulation' as an outer responsibility – the outer form of 'self' in the sense of adult or 'ego'. In terms of this aspect clients are responsible for abiding by the agreements they have made with the practitioners and group members. They are also responsible for being self-directed in the sense of both taking initiatives to further their growth, e.g. deciding what to 'work' on, when, how, and with whom, and for exercising a veto over the initiatives of facilitators directed at them – as allowed for in the ground rules.
2 'Self-regulation' as a form of inner guidance – where 'Self' refers to the centre of our being and 'self-regulation' involves attending to, and following the lead of inherent, spontaneous processes of development that determine what emerges into consciousness, in what order, when and how.

There are parallels here with Carl Jung's process of 'Individuation' (Jacobi 1942), Caron Kent's 'Growth Forces' (Kent 1969), Tony Crisp's notion of 'Coex' (Crisp 1987) and Wilhelm Reich's ideas about energy and motility in the body (Boadella 1985).

The cause of suffering

Suffering is part of the human condition. Experiences such as separation, loss, physical pain and death are part of life. However, some suffering does not seem commensurate with the life circumstances at the time. In our view this is often indicative of a part-emerged memory of an early traumatic situation without the context to make sense of it and without the expression necessary to integrate the experience.

The suffering referred to above assumes an ability to feel. For some people suffering means *not* being able to feel and experience – even pain. An alienation from one's feeling self can be experienced as worse than any 'feeling'. This too, often has deep roots in unintegrated traumatic experiences.

Frank Lake applied Pavlov's concept of 'transmarginal stress' to traumatic pre-, peri- and postnatal experiences and showed these could result in a splitting of the psyche (Lake 1966, 1980).

> The neurophysiological effect of trans-marginal, ultra-maximal, supra-liminal, or quite simply, unbearable stress, is, as Pavlov showed in dogs, to produce reversals in the responses to ordinary stimuli. What gave pleasure now gives pain.
>
> (Lake 1971 p36)

Lake likened this to the effect on a steel spring of stretching it beyond the limit of its elasticity. It can no longer bounce back.

Primal Integration addresses the suffering involved in these experiences but is not 'Primal *Trauma* Integration'. We believe that dealing with these types of experience should not be 'split-off' from other more joyful aspects of deep living. They should be welcomed in a setting that is inclusive of them, not exclusively focused on them.

In our view many social and political sources of suffering such as war, oppression, racism, and other forms of social injustice, have roots that extend down into primal levels and in part represent an acting out on the group level of repressed traumatic experiences from pre- and perinatal life. Lloyd de Mause (1982) has suggested that a group fantasy in which the group as a whole is regressed to the foetal level ('foetal trance state') is an active factor underlying such 'crazy' events as war.

The change process

Everyone has an inherent potential to experience processes of inner development resulting in a continuous process of 'becoming'. These processes are spontaneous and unfold in a unique way for every individual. They have their own dynamic pressure and their own pace. The question of change is one of allowing these inherent processes to function more fully. Primal Integration endeavours to offer an environment that is conducive to this.

Biological gestation and birth provide rather a good metaphor for this process of 'becoming'. You become aware of being 'pregnant' – a sense of something going on inside. Gradually you become more and more aware of its nature. It gets bigger and moves towards some sort of coming out into the world. This can be an uncomfortable process, a painful process. It may be dramatic. It may be ecstatic. Either way this is a forward and outward process.

The practitioner's role is akin to that of a midwife – albeit one inspired by Michel Odent (Odent 1984) – to encourage the client to follow the instinctive processes that will produce the natural emergence. In giving birth to aspects of oneself, even the memory of traumatic experiences – such as having been stuck during one's biological birth – will emerge naturally. Recovery of traumatic memories does not require the psychological equivalent of the obstetrical intervention that was perhaps necessary for one's survival 'back then'. One does not need to extract these experiences with forceps! As practitioners we remain midwives – midwives of consciousness – rather than obstetricians.

The 'delivery', including that of traumatic memories and 'difficult' feelings is enabled by the configuration of a contained, 'free space'. In Primal Integration, we have a high degree of structure 'around the periphery' which allows the space within to be very free. This encourages the 'structures' *within* people to become apparent, to be experienced as in their formation, and for unexpressed feelings bound up in them to be released and completed.

It seems that the intensity of the experience necessary to melt inauthentic 'structures' within people will be comparable to the intensity of the original experience from which they split off. Seldom is intellectual understanding of the relevance of these experiences enough to effect change. It seems that the 'understanding' has to run as deep as the event is significant in that person's development. The events are in a sense 'relived' at depth and in context. Important to note here, and crucial to the 'wholing' process are the differences between the original context and the present one. This time around there are resources available that were not there the first time, not least one's own 'adult'. A memory is what is being engaged rather than a present reality and it is being engaged voluntarily.

This discussion will be found wanting without also talking in terms of love. It is 'tough love' that makes up the container, attentive love that is held within it and love energy – energy for life – which emerges from it. Love contains the process. Love drives the process. Love is the process. Warmth, kindness and humour are present alongside the pain and suffering. Deep human compassion is both evoked and needed in the presence of people confronting their innermost issues.

The period after the 'birth' is one that requires attention worthy of this 'new beginning'. This is integration – welcoming and creating space for the newly recovered 'self' in one's life by giving it appropriate recognition.

Integration takes place in two stages – the integration into awareness of the formerly excluded aspects of oneself and then the practical application of these new discoveries in everyday life. Whilst the former can happen spontaneously, the latter often requires some form of active work.

The welcoming involves changes in outside life, where choices made *in the absence* of these now recovered aspects of oneself may have established social roles and patterns of living which have gathered considerable inertia. However, it is not always feasible or wise to completely change them, so there is much challenging work to be done in finding a way for the 'new self' to manifest which is meaningful and fulfilling.

This process of recovery and integration is not a 'one-off' project, but rather forms a continuous cycle of change. When it is Self-regulating, this process seems to provide for its own furtherance. The fruits of one sequence of recovery and integration provide resources for the next, continually bringing a deeper way of living into being, and a deeper way of being into living!

Goals

Put simply, the 'goal' of Primal Integration is an increase in awareness of one's Self, one's true nature, and the integration of this increased awareness into everyday life. There is no 'goal-as-end-point' envisaged but rather a path, a continuing process of becoming more authentic, a personal journey of Self-discovery.

This contrasts with approaches that posit specific end points to therapy such as the Reichian therapist's notion of a 'genital character' (Baker 1967) or Janov's Primal Therapy (Janov 1970, 1991) with its notion of 'the Cure for Neurosis' and of a 'Post-Primal' state.

Primal Integration is not an approach whose aim is problem solving or the treatment of psychological 'disorders'. What have been perceived as 'problems' frequently resolve as a result, but this is a by-product of growth, the role of such problems having been to signal one's self-estrangement and need to live more authentically. Thus its healing aspects offer a different way of 'treating' problems.

This is not a rationale for doing Primal Integration groups or individual sessions *ad infinitum*! Participation in such a setting may make it easier to attend to these growth processes and allow for a fuller expression than is often possible in society at large, but the same basic processes can occur anywhere. The Primal Integration setting is a resource to be used at times when it is helpful rather than something to 'go through'.

Rather than aspiring to achieve a 'done', 'finished', 'post-primal' state, it is in our view more relevant to learn how to live with primal process in one's life in general, to cultivate an attentive, respectful and inclusive attitude towards it, and to learn to live with it in a more creative way. In this regard we see the *way* of dealing with primal material as being an important learning experience in itself – as important as dealing with it.

Practitioners

Relationship

In Primal Integration, as Bill Swartley once said, the practitioner is the 'patient', the one who waits alongside, with patience, whilst the client is the one who does the 'work' and takes the responsibility for furthering their growth. This does not mean that the practitioner's role is a passive one, it may be very active. The role is that of a facilitator. We *do* as little as possible *for* our clients. We *do* as much as we can to maximize the possibility of them doing the work *for themselves*. This is what we seek to facilitate. Thus we make suggestions and take initiatives on the understanding that these may be taken up, discarded or ignored as the client sees fit.

The relationship between practitioner and client can feel very close, and intense at times, like a friendship, or a parent–child relationship, and although aspects of those relationships are present it is neither of them and serves a different function. The practitioner is employed by the client to help them proceed with a journey they are undertaking. The client is not in the practitioner's 'care', or taking their 'treatment'. The relationship to be cultivated is essentially one of mutual trust. Hopefully, the client has taken 'care' in choosing their helper in this important project!

The relationship is a contractual one, between adults. Each party is responsible for their own actions, experiences and feelings. The boundaries set by the simple agreements we have about commitment, financial arrangements and time-keeping serve as reminders of the 'here and now' nature of this relationship.

In addition to facilitation and the maintenance of boundaries, the practitioner is also likely at times to become a focus of both positive and negative projections. This phenomenon is not by any means restricted to the client–practitioner relationship. It will also occur amongst group members, and in either case can be worked with or weathered as appropriate.

The relationship between client and practitioner is usually face to face and any work on projections often begins that way. Touch is not excluded from the relationship unless either party chooses to veto it.

Techniques

Primal Integration is a very free-form approach that has more to do with attending to spontaneous processes of unfoldment than the application of particular techniques to effect change. More often it is a question of *not* doing things that distract from these processes. They happen of their own accord when given permission, attention and time. These three 'facilitative attitudes' are our fundamental 'techniques'.

In the group or individual setting we try to give as much time and space as possible for the primal process to manifest itself as it will. Groups are long, sessions are longer than average, and people often undertake this work on a long-term, although not necessarily regular, basis.

Time acknowledges the non-sensationalist aspect of primal work. Whilst some of what shows is loud, wild and dramatic, and seemingly 'instant', it has taken time for a person to build their ability to 'be there' for the occasion. Many of the experiences remembered and re-experienced during this work were split-off and repressed in the first instance because they were too much to bear. It is important that this time around the person is able to be more fully present, to be able to take the experience on board, to bear it and integrate it.

Permission refers to self-permission – saying 'yes' to feelings, experiences and expressions and processes that have been previously denied. The practitioners, and in the case of groups, the other group members are also saying 'yes' and provide a social support for things that are frequently denied in the wider society. There is permission to explore such things, and an invitation to express, with as few limits as possible on the form that this expression takes.

Attention to these primal processes is facilitated by being present in a setting where methods habitually used to inhibit them are minimized. Whatever their other merits, activities such as watching TV, reading, smoking, drinking, superficial social interaction, and 'keeping busy' in general are used by many people for this purpose in their lives. In the group or individual setting these are acknowledged as likely distractions. The client is also temporarily away from work and family responsibilities which require a focus on outer activities, making it easier to attend to what is going on inside.

Work in the group or individual session is bounded by a simple set of agreements and ground rules which provide for physical and psychological safety. These include an explicit form of client veto over facilitator intervention, a rule precluding violence and a rule that requires respect for confidentiality.

Groups are usually composed of a rough balance of the sexes, and are led by two or more facilitators, one of either sex.

Groups generally have two phases which alternate. The 'go-round' is a mainly verbal phase which is structured by the leaders and gives each person an opportunity to tell the group about themselves, as well as to hear everybody else's story. This is the part of the group where each member is in turn the focus for the whole group's attention. Although the format in this phase is mainly verbal, people can present their 'go' in other forms such as artwork, poetry, or song, but the primary function of the go-round is to report in and listen in and perhaps set up or find a direction for the next step rather than take the work further there and then. With groups of 18 this phase of the group takes two and a half hours or so, thus subtly developing the facilitative attitudes of patience and attentiveness in the group members!

The other phase is unstructured by the leaders and their role in this phase is to 'follow' processes emerging in individuals and in the group as a whole. We hardly ever use any whole group structures, exercises in pairs, or a 'hot seat'. Nor do we generally have exercises designed to 'raise the charge' or to evoke particular experiences, for example that of birth. The recall of such experiences is a frequent occurrence and will often be worked with in a way that includes the body, but it is not actually aimed for. We do not use any hypnotic inductions.

Group members are encouraged to experiment, explore, and find their own way. Their 'work' is to attend to what is already going on within them and to allow it to come out, drawing on the resources available, sometimes starting with what may have been clarified in a go-round, sometimes going off in a different direction entirely. Simple things can help to shift the balance in favour of the outward expression of inner processes. For example, instead of just thinking it, say it out loud. Exaggerate it. Do the opposite. Breathe.

A rich variety of resources is provided both materially and in idea form, so that each group member can find the most appropriate means of expression for their experience. Ways of working in this phase of the group include: talking, vocal expression, bodywork – massage and 'primal bodywork' – artwork, which can be painting, drawing, poetry and creative writing, music – listening or making – playing with toys and costumes, dancing, performing, dreamwork, cushion work – hitting or talking to or both – personal interaction, face-to-face eyes open work, dramatic reconstructions of situations, and even sleeping. During the unstructured phase people work simultaneously and a variety of ways of working may be occurring at the same time, resulting in a productive chaos.

A very large sandplay, tailored to the needs of Primal Integration, is also usually available in the group. This provides an effective means of reaching beyond art blocks, word blocks, voice blocks, often into a wiser, remembering self. It is an education in how one can be guided from within. It also provides a useful overview, a way to reset the perspective for someone who has become somewhat lost in one part of themselves to the neglect of the whole picture.

We find that a flexible and unstructured environment such as we have described readily allows a respect for individual pace and 'fit'. Although mostly described in terms of group work, the principles evident in the above also apply to individual sessions, bearing in mind the difference in the setting. People often work in a combination of group and individual settings.

Does it work?

Pitfalls

Most pitfalls of Primal Integration stem in some way from a state of imbalance between the process of emergence (the primal process) and the integrative process. The Self is capable of regulating this if allowed to do so by an alliance with the adult (self), and there are natural points of 'closure' that prevent consciousness being overwhelmed. Being able to allow this is in part a learned art that develops as one's adult here-and-now self learns to trust the guidance of one's Self and to trust those with whom one is working.

However, if some other part of the personality, motivated by other goals, has been allowed to take control of the endeavour, an imbalance results in which the client may for example feel swamped with primal feelings that are felt to be too much to 'digest', or lose contact with present reality in some other way. Conversely the client may experience little happening at all. This 'inner usurper' may be an inner child, a punitive parent or some other subpersonality. In the extreme this may become, to use Michael Balint's terms (Balint 1968), a 'malignant regression' rather than a 'new beginning'.

These other goals that may be pursued often involve the projection and acting out of some sort of fantasy expectations derived from the primal level. So long as these are worked with, they remain 'grist for the mill'. It is only when they become the driving force and are acted out that they pose problems. Some examples of these may be helpful by way of illustration.

One fantasy expectation that may occur is that what is on offer is a chance to rewrite one's history. The Primal Integration setting can appeal to a desire in some people to go 'back in time' to where things went wrong, and do it right this time. 'This time my needs will be met.' The fantasy is that positive experiences in the here and now can somehow be transplanted back to a time when something good was needed but was not there, hoping that the positive new experience will cancel out the negative one and make things 'all right now'. The resources offered in Primal Integration are thus used in an attempt to hide the person's true experience, much in the way a drug would be used to treat pain. This method can have a palliative effect and appeal for a while, but eventually breaks down when the truth of that person's original experience breaks through these attempts to suppress it. There will be a rude awakening and the full force of the feelings about the original situation are likely to burst forth, now directed towards whoever has now 'failed' them. The person has a choice at this point: to draw on the resources available to help them complete their experience of their past, to integrate it and be able to move on, or to seek another 'drug'.

Sometimes there is a situation in the deep feelings where 'going forward' poses the underlying threat. For example when the umbilical cord has been entwined around the neck during the birth process – so that the more one progresses the less oxygen one receives ('to grow is to die'). When in contact with this sort of memory in the feelings, safety may be sought in regression.

Some people may unwittingly attempt a repeat of how they *did* survive a situation experienced as a threat to their existence by using this as the model for the recovery of those parts of their psyche that were split off at that time. Thus an attempt may be made to act out a birth fantasy of being 'rescued' by the practitioner – seen as obstetrician. In other cases expectations deriving from primal associations with medical ('cure') or religious ('salvation') models may be the driving fantasy.

Pitfalls for the practitioner include taking on these expectations in the hope of fulfilling them as part of their own fantasy (the practitioner as 'heroic healer' or fulfiller and gratifier of primal needs) appearing to do things *for* people rather than supporting the adult to adult alliance and the sense of the present.

For the practitioner also, the intense and sometimes chaotic 'hothouse' environment involving periodic transference and expression of intense primal level emotion on a face to face basis can be very challenging – and exhausting. There is a need to pace oneself, to not overload oneself and 'burn out'. There is a need to self-regulate – it comes back to the same issue in the end.

Research

As far as we know, there has not been any objective research into Primal Integration as we have described it. Given the nature of Primal Integration, this would be rather difficult to undertake meaningfully, whilst respecting the spirit of the endeavour. The work is in a sense a subjective 'research', not the same as but akin to an artistic endeavour, a meditation or a contemplation – self 'research' – an enquiry into who one *is*.

Roger Moss has undertaken a study of Frank Lake's work by means of an 'ex post' questionnaire of participants in Lake's intensive workshops between 1979 and 1982. A preliminary report (Moss 1983), yielded a rating of clear or moderate benefit for 71.2 per cent of respondents, benefit with some negative features in a further 14.7 per cent, and 9.4 per cent reaped little or no benefit. The full report is forthcoming.

An illustration

It was not my first group. I had started coming to these weekends some months ago as well as doing some individual sessions. I started because I felt a lack of fulfilment in my life, despite my achievements.

As well as having a sense of nervous anticipation each time I came, I had begun to enjoy the groups. I wondered what this one would bring. Something always happened here, although it was never predictable. As the group assembled, I was pleased to see people I had met before and was curious about the new faces. I was especially pleased when Joe arrived, someone who had been on the weekend before last, with whom I had a particular rapport. I greeted him enthusiastically, but his greeting, though polite, seemed a little off-hand. When I listened to him in the go-round, I could see he was very preoccupied with his own things, however this little event grew in significance for me. Something had already begun to happen.

I mentioned this almost in passing in the go-round, and realized I actually felt very tense about it. I was encouraged to stay with the feelings that were coming up for me rather than try to defuse the situation, which would be my usual pattern. I resolved to do this.

During the unstructured time, I was very aware of Joe's presence in the room. I began to realize that I was convinced that Joe's 'mood' was my fault. I felt bad and horrible but I didn't know why. I felt I had to do something about it, but didn't know what. I was fearful, anticipating a blast of rage at any minute. I tried clinging to some people, which helped for a while, but I realized this only staved off the feelings temporarily. I realized how I clung to people and things in my life for the same purpose.

I lay down and allowed myself to experience the feelings I feared. My body began to shake, and then waves of fear seemed to pass through me, like a convulsion. I felt tiny, very vulnerable, and in danger of destruction. The facilitator put her hand on my belly, where the convulsions seemed to have their origin. She also placed some cushions around me, in case I should thrash out. I felt as though I was inside my mother and ought to be safe, but I wasn't. I was surrounded by fear and there were great waves of blackness coming at me from nowhere, without warning or explanation. I felt utterly powerless and terrified. I felt I was in danger of disappearing, simply ceasing to exist.

I couldn't bear this state of affairs. I attempted to exert some control over my environment by assuming that I was the cause of the problem. Though onerous, this position offered the hope of 'doing something about it' rather than just feeling intensely helpless and hopeless. So I set about my task of MAKING THINGS BETTER for Mother, a habit I carried forward in life and spread to my other relationships as if it were my destiny. As I lay there on the mattress, I felt as though all the times in my life I had acted out from this experience stood out, as if underlined in Day-Glo highlighter. Someone covered me with a blanket and gave me a teddy bear and held me for a while. I fell asleep.

There had been a lot of other things going on in the group room at the same time, which had all but faded from my awareness as I went deeper into my own exploration. As I came round now I noticed someone talking avidly to a cushion, with a couple of people with him, whom I presumed were involved in some way. Someone was having a massage, and a couple of people were painting a picture together. Someone was doing a sandplay. In the far corner, someone was making loud guttural noises. I felt drawn towards a classroom situation that was happening up one end of the room where someone was attempting to be teacher to a group of especially spirited 'youngsters'. I joined in and spent some time allowing myself to be a 'totally impossible' schoolchild, something I had never dared to be in real life, and thoroughly enjoyed it.

I felt very aware of my new discovery for the rest of the weekend. I noticed how I felt different in the room, as if I was more able to let people be, and let me BE separate from them. I was able to participate in other people's work in what felt like a very new way for me, from a position of strength and separateness rather than my desperate need to KEEP MOTHER CALM because my life depended on it.

I painted a picture of my experience and put it on the wall. Some people said it looked like something to do with the cord, but that wasn't really the point. For me, just the act of painting had been grounding.

I left the weekend feeling more able to face my own experience rather than spend a lot of effort trying to change it. Because the knowledge of the origin of one of my basic life decisions came up from so deep within me, I felt sure I would carry this through to my everyday life.

Some days later it came to me – I was born in a war zone, there was danger everywhere. My mother whilst carrying me was fearful, and my father was in danger. They were certainly preoccupied with their own things!

Comment on articles and books about Primal Integration

Unfortunately William Swartley did not publish much about Primal Integration. Swartley (1975) is the clearest written statement about the work as far as he developed it.

Lake (1980) gives the fullest statement of his views on pre- and perinatal stress, umbilical affect and the 'Maternal–Foetal Distress Syndrome'. Difficult to read because much of it is in chart form – a favourite mode for Lake, deriving from his pre-psychiatric career as a parasitologist in India – but worth the effort. Some of this material will become available in a more digestible form in Roger Moss's forthcoming book on Frank Lake's work: *In the Beginning*. Lake (1981, 1986) contain less detailed (and less graphic) statements of his views and can be used as an introduction.

Mott (1948) is: 'an analysis of the configurational involvement of birth and its relation to emergence generally' and perhaps the best introduction to the world of Francis Mott.

Stanislav Grof's original statement of his cartography of 'inner space' and the 'Basic Perinatal Matrices' is presented in Grof (1975).

Donald Lee Williams's psychological commentary on Carlos Castaneda's 'Path of Knowledge' (Williams 1981) gives as true a 'feel' for the journey involved in Primal Integration as anything else in writing that we have come across.

References

Baker, E. (1967) *Man in the Trap*. New York: Macmillan.
Balint, M. (1968) *The Basic Fault*. London: Tavistock Publications.
Boadella, D. (1985) *Wilhelm Reich: The Evolution of his Work*. (2nd edn) London: Routledge & Kegan Paul.
Crisp, T. (1987) *Mind and Movement: The Practice of COEX*. Saffron Walden: C.W. Daniel.
de Mause, L. (1982) *Foundations of Psychohistory*. New York: Creative Roots Inc.
Fodor, N. (1949) *The Search for the Beloved*. New York: University Books.
Fodor, N. (1951) *New Approaches to Dream Interpretation*. New York: University Books.
Grof, S. (1975) *Realms of the Human Unconscious*. New York: Viking Press.
Grof, S. (1988) *The Adventure of Self Discovery*. Albany, NY: State University of New York Press.
Jacobi, J. (1942) *The Psychology of C.G. Jung*. London: Routledge and Kegan Paul.
Janov, A. (1970) *The Primal Scream*. New York: Dell.
Janov, A. (1991) *The New Primal Scream*. London: Abacus.
Kent, C. (1969) *The Puzzled Body*. London: Vision Press.
Lake, F. (1966) *Clinical Theology*. London: Darton, Longman & Todd. (Abridged edition 1986.)
Lake, F. (1971) *Clinical Pastoral Care in Schizoid Reactions*. Nottingham: Clinical Theology Association.
Lake, F. (1980) *Studies in Constricted Confusion*. Nottingham: Clinical Theology Association.
Lake, F. (1981) *Tight Corners in Pastoral Counselling*. London: Darton, Longman & Todd.
Moss, R. (1983) *Frank Lake's Maternal–Foetal Distress Syndrome and Primal Integration Workshops*. Oxford: Clinical Theology Association.
Mott, F.J. (1948) *The Universal Design of Birth*. Philadelphia: David McKay.
Mott, F.J. (1964) *The Universal Design of Creation*. Edenbridge, Kent: Mark Beech.
Odent, M. (1984) *Entering the World*. London: Marion Boyars.
Parsons, T. (1953) Illness and the role of the physician. In C. Kluckhorn and H. Murray (Eds) *Personality in Nature, Society and Culture*. New York: Knopf.
Rank, O. (1929) *The Trauma of Birth*. London: Routledge and Kegan Paul.
Swartley, W. (1975) *Primal Integration*. Mays Landing, NJ: Centre for the Whole Person. (Reprinted in 1987 in *Self & Society*, XV(4).)
Williams, D.L. (1981) *Border Crossings*. Toronto: Inner City Books.

3

Somatotropic Therapy

WILLIAM R. EMERSON[1] AND
STEPHAN SCHORR-KON

Where someone, as an adult, is '*at*', is often expressed in a topological scheme, which bears remarkable correspondences to precise phases of embryonic morphology.

R.D. Laing

Definition and historical development

Definition

Somatotropic Therapy is, at its core, a somatic approach to uncovering and resolving the major topological schemas representing unresolved traumas in infants, children, and adults. Somatotropic, according to Webster, is 'the principle of organization according to which matter moves to form an object during the various stages of its existence'. During trauma, the somatic (i.e. body) system objectifies trauma in both energetic and physical forms, and the somatotropic process is a broad organization of somatic traumas which manifest in both energetic and physical form.

Somatotropic Therapy could claim ancestry in ancient shamanic healing practices found in many primitive cultures. In modern times its evolution describes an oblique trajectory from the Freudian launch pad of psychoanalysis, through the work of Jung, Reich, Rank, Assagioli, Fodor, Mott, Lake, Winnicott, Janov and Laing to the present approach.

Historical development

Classical psychoanalysis considers the life of the child from birth to age five or six, as the origin of personality. Its primary way of working is interpretive, and the reality of prenatal experience and the preverbal period have generally been excluded from the therapeutic context. Development of pre- and perinatal psychology over the last 20 years has opened up a new dimension of psychological reality which focuses precisely on the infant from conception, through birth and into the first years of life. A growing body of clinical research is beginning to establish this period as crucial in the creation of character and personality.

Otto Rank's (1929) work on birth trauma was welcomed by Freud at first, but was discarded by his circle as a potential threat to the pre-eminence of Freud's theories. One of Rank's patients was Nandor Fodor, who himself became a psychiatrist and brought his clinical attention to the formative experiences of birth (Fodor 1949). Francis Mott, a British psychiatrist and a patient of Fodor's, wrote extensively on the mythological and dream content of prenatal life (Mott 1948, 1964). Frank Lake (1966, 1980) was influenced by Mott's work, and was one of the first British psychiatrists to emphasize the effects of intrauterine life. Donald Winnicott (1975), the British psychiatrist of the Object Relations school, recognized and worked with the impact of birth on his patients, and suggested that the body retained these impacts as memories. Bill Swartley (Swartley and Maurice 1978) was the founder of the International Primal Association, introduced Primal Therapy to Britain, and considered Winnicott the real originator of Primal Therapy (Chapter 2). Winnicott supervised R.D. Laing, who explored the fundamental significance of pre- and perinatal psychology in the structure of personality.

Founders

Frank Lake and Stanislav Grof accessed pre- and perinatal material in their patients by using LSD. However, they discovered that similar effects could be obtained by using what Grof calls 'holotropic' breathing techniques. Grof, working first in Czechoslovakia, and then in the USA, observed that the 'biographical' realm, the time from birth onwards and excluding prenatal life, offered an incomplete and inadequate causal ground for the more severe psychological disturbances; he located their roots in the cataclysmic pressures experienced by the baby in the birth process. Grof (1975, 1985), in his prolific writings on the subject, explores the effects of what he calls the birth perinatal matrices or BPMs (stages in the birth process) with great power and insight. On the basis of his extensive research, he shows how academic psychiatry and psychotherapy, by excluding consideration of pre- and perinatal impacts, cannot accommodate the whole spectrum of human experience or satisfactorily retrace its roots.

Frank Lake applied the insights that Mott had delineated in his work on the pre- and perinatal significance of dreams and myths. Lake accessed the traumatic affects generated in prenatal life. He subdivided Grof's BPM 1 (the stage where the foetus gestates in the womb) into several distinct stages, and worked through the influences on the prenate of the parents' physical, emotional and psychological states from conception to birth. He coined the phrase 'toxic womb syndrome' (Lake 1966, 1981).

Grof (1975) and Laing (1976) attempted to introduce, demonstrate and explore the revolutionary realm of pre- and perinatal psychology. They presented their materials from within the fold of orthodox psychotherapy and psychiatry (or from its radical shore).

Grof's contribution to this field is immense. His description of the 'birth perinatal matrices' or BPMs and the affect relating to each, his exploration of the effects these stages have on later life, his inclusion of the somatic stratum in psychotherapy, his openness to archetypal and transpersonal realms give him a key role in this field as discoverer and disseminator.

Somatotropic Therapy evolved from 20 years of practice and experimental follow-up, done in Europe and the USA. In the late 70s in England, I (Emerson) collaborated in workshops with Frank Lake, and shared research findings with him. It was at this time that I developed my initial somatic approaches to uncover primal trauma. Focusing on the time from conception, and working through implantation and gestation to birth, I discovered ways to access the deepest and earliest pre- and perinatal traumas. Gradually, I found a precise methodology for working with infants and children to access and discharge an astonishingly wide array of traumas. In the course of my work a way of reading the face and posture as a cartography of the client's specific pre- and perinatal trauma began to emerge. Using these physical and gestural traces as indicators of the temporal origins of disturbance, I have developed ways of inducing these experiences in the therapeutic context, and thus the means to discharge the compulsive control they exert on characterological behaviour. I have also perceived that in moments of somatic disclosure during therapy, the body will take particular shapes that recapitulate embryonic development. These perceptions enable the therapist to ascertain with a great deal of precision the moment of disturbance in the client's prenatal life. I have also determined that the birth process tends to re-enact the traumas that occur from conception through implantation and gestation; and that the resolution of these earliest traumas dissipates the effects of the traumas that occur at birth.

Relationship to other therapies

Somatotropic Therapy has similarities with Primal Therapy, Primal Integration (Chapter 2), Core Process Psychotherapy (Chapter 4), Reichian breathwork (Chapter 9), Biosynthesis, Holotropic breathwork (Grof), Trance Regression (Cheek), Polarity Therapy, and Cranio-sacral Therapy. It differs from some of these in the kinds of somatic techniques and prenatal techniques, as well as depth of access and compatibility with infants and children. Somatotropic Therapy, in common with most therapies similar to it, puts as great an emphasis on integration as on the process of uncovering and experiencing unconscious material. It recognizes that integration does not take place automatically, but must be painstakingly woven into the real life fabric of the client's life.

Central concepts

One of the central concepts in this field is the notion that mind pre-exists the nervous system; that there is a level at which the *conceptus* is aware of essential qualities of feeling present in its inception; that this awareness records its struggles to survive the hazards of implantation, the history of its gestation and the detailed drama of its birth, at an energetic and cellular level. Prenatal awareness, perceptiveness and intelligence is currently under intense review, with the inception of these processes starting earlier than heretofore imagined (Chamberlain 1988). From this perspective, it follows that the intrauterine strategies devised to ensure the prenate's survival, and protect it from the potential spectrum of indifference or rejection on, or soon after its embodiment in the womb, develop into aspects of the construct of the self.

Strategies and survival learnings, by necessity rapidly adopted, carry with them powerful implications about self-value and worth. Lack of acknowledgement of pregnancy may raise doubts about the right to exist. Outright psychological rejection may create attitudes of worthlessness, inadequacy, impotence and so on. It may also be one of the contributing factors in miscarriages. Medical drugs, substance abuses, unaddressed anxieties, or external trauma in the life of parents will in most cases be 'taken on' by the foetus. This is what I call participatory trauma, where unborn children participate in the biological and psychological experiences of their mothers (and indirectly their fathers). Frank Lake referred to participatory trauma as the 'toxic womb syndrome'. We marinate in the shadow (i.e. the denied aspects of the unconscious) of our parents.

The basic stratum of the personality, and the associated underlying belief systems which hold it in place, derive from a number of factors: the shadow aspects of parents; the same unresolved elements in the lives of grandparents (the ovum from which the mother sprang was already formed at 11 weeks gestation in the maternal grandmother); a commensurate and immeasurable twine of psychogenetic ancestral memories; the prenate's own 'baggage' from preconception; the experience of the conception itself, the phenomenology of implantation, and the whole duration of the gestation period, all together form layers of affect in this self-forging process.

Most irregularities in the birthing process appear to derive from unresolved conflicts in the lives of the parents, relating to themselves, to each other, to their parents, or to their attitude about the infant. They may also be a recapitulation of the mother's own birth history; she may unconsciously be acting out disturbances which occurred to her through her mother's affects and process while giving birth. These irregularities express themselves in such issues as prematurity, breech births, fast births, long labours, cord complications and birthing positions. Each of these irregularities, as well as a number of medical interventions such as anaesthetization, Caesarian section, forceps, inductions and incubations will leave profound and detectable characterological traces in the behaviours of the recipients. They are all amenable to treatment through regressive and integrative work.

Three further key concepts in this model are regression, catharsis and integration. They are touched on here, and developed as part of the change process in the following section. Regression means to go back in time, to uncover memories of experiences which were formative (either positive or negative), and to release any unresolved, blocked or negative affects associated with these experiences. Catharsis is the major process of release, usually involving intense emotional discharge: crying, raging, moaning, sobbing, grieving and so on. The deeper the catharsis, the more likely that core aspects of the psyche will be touched at the level of transformational and/or spiritual energies. By transformational energies we refer to the essential energies which connect us to the Self, energies which we can access through meditation, or other spiritual disciplines.

In the context of Somatotropic Therapy, individuals and their styles of healing are deeply respected. Both cathartic and transformational processes, which interact and support one another are accommodated in this work. Some individuals heal primarily through catharsis, others through transformation and others through a combination of both. Ultimately, when trauma is healed, the transformational process becomes integrated into the psyche, and available in a way that was previously unimaginable.

Integration acknowledges that certain affects (called secondary, as compared to primary processes) accompany traumatic or ecstatic experiences and that these secondary processes need to be identified and dealt with in order for the individual to be free from them. In somatotropic terminology, traumatic experiences are the primary processes which impact the individual somatically.

But traumatic experiences enfold a number of secondary processes as well, and these co-occur with trauma and remain as established parameters of trauma. The secondary processes are, in and of themselves, capable of impacting the personality and development of individuals, even after traumatic experiences have been catharted. An example has to do with trauma posture. Through close observation of children going through traumatic experiences, we have found that certain postures tend to be associated with trauma. These postures remain as somatic memories, and reside as embodied shapes throughout life, until the foundation trauma is resolved and until the postures are identified and repatterned.

These postures support what is called response-produced emotion. The postures themselves, once crystallized in the body, create the same traumatic feelings that the cathartic process releases. This can be experienced directly, albeit in a minor way, by creating a fist, for example, and holding it for a long period of time. Angry feelings are likely to emerge. In this sense, postures (and other secondary processes) create a replicating supply of traumatic energy, and this replicating energy is not resolved until the secondary processes are acknowledged and repatterned. The depth of Somatotropic Therapy accesses these secondary processes and allows them to be altered in a way which is consistent with the basic nature of the individual, and with the energies of the higher Self.

As trauma and their secondary affects are resolved, the tenets of the old belief systems begin to shift and loosen their grip on dysfunctional facets of the personality. New choices become available and awareness starts to grow exponentially. This has outcomes which were hitherto unthought of or unheard of. This is because the process of resolving trauma requires a systematic approach incorporating a spectrum of levels of integration. When this resolution is attained, the result is the spontaneous emergence of the true Self, and simultaneous contact with the psyche at the most profound level, unencumbered by coaxial, coexistent presence of traumatic memories or energies. This brings with it the capacity for the unfolding of full human potential. Ultimately, the quintessential outcome is contact with one's essential being, unencumbered by traumatic and/or conditioned experience.

The cause of suffering

We have implicitly indicated that lack of awareness causes suffering, which is highly consistent with the Buddhist concept of ignorance. This lack of awareness has two aspects. The first is repression or forgetting, wherein unresolved suffering resides in the unconscious, out of awareness. In order to be externalized and healed, unconscious material forces itself into conscious experience, forces itself into awareness in dreams, symptoms or behaviour, causing suffering in the here and now.

The second aspect refers to a historical disregard of prenatal consciousness from the time of conception onwards. So long as we refuse to acknowledge the consciousness of the prenate, we cannot make the protective discrimination between what we as parents are feeling as compared to our feelings for and toward infants in the womb. This lack of awareness has also affected us when we absorbed the shadow aspects of our parents, grandparents and so on through the generations. Unawareness of the generational nature of consciousness keeps our patterns of suffering and blindness in place; through it we maintain the seemingly endless repetitions of behaviours which are reactive, governed by fear, grasping and aggressive.

By acknowledging the budding and determining consciousness of children in the womb, we can make discrete differences between our own state and the state of children that we are welcoming into the world. This knowledge ushers in the opportunity to make profound changes in the cycle of ignorance; we can prepare the ground for the seed of new awareness. By relating consciously and lovingly to prenates, we create the potentiality of a new dynamic. The new being can be acknowledged and made welcome. A prenatal bond is forged between prenate, mother and father, probably helping to ease the birth process.

In this relationship paradigm, the mother and father deepen their feelings for each other and for prenates. They also promote, in themselves and each other, a greater sense of responsibility towards each other, the baby and the birthing process. In so doing, they learn to challenge the unquestioned authority and power of the medical profession, which frequently treats pregnancy as illness. Thus a positive ecology of loving awareness can take the place of perpetual cycles of ignorance, in which growing babies are perceived as unfeeling objects. The knowledge that newly conceived infants and neonates are conscious beings can and will have growing effects on babies, parents and the world. It will help to ensure our survival as a species, in a web of interdependency throughout the planet.

The change process

As traumas are uncovered, habitual behaviour patterns become more visible and their compulsive components begin to lose their power. Thus dysfunctions decrease, life becomes more harmonious and balanced. Personal success and happiness seem much more attainable; relationships tend to flow more smoothly; work gets easier. But these are just the superficial changes. More significant are the shifts which have to do with one's relationship to the inner Self. In psycho-analysis, therapeutic progress occurs when the ego relates to the world in realistic terms, when the ego subjects itself to reality. In Somatotropic Therapy, however, the ego becomes subject to the inner core of being, to the influences of the higher Self.

The change process can be divided into several major areas, all of which are readily discernible from the central concepts, outlined above. First of all, individuals must be regressed so that unresolved trauma can be uncovered and confronted. Regressive experiences usually occur according to thematic patterns, and it is important to collect all the major experiences which fit a common theme. For example, one young woman uncovered birth trauma, where she was trapped for a long period of time. Subsequent to this, she uncovered entrapment in other life experiences: she was locked in a closet by her brother for six hours; she was trapped in an automobile as a result of a car accident when she was 11 years old; she was forcefully held during sexual abuse by a neighbour; and she was enmeshed in a long-term romance when she was a teenager. Once all these experiences were uncovered and catharted, the integra-tional process began.

Integrational processes usually cover the following five areas.

Connections

In the course of the therapy we examine the connections and parallels between regressive experiences and current patterns of perceiving and relating to oneself and the world. We explore ways in which the presenting systems derive from those fundamentally formative experiences. For example, in the case of a person delivered by Caesarian section, intense feelings are likely about doing things in their own way and in their own time, and not being pushed or rushed; there might be latent expectations that others would help them complete projects.

Decisions and conclusions

Through close observation of infants and children, it has been established that unresolved traumas are spontaneously and unconsciously keyed into the linguistic system at about the age of three years or earlier. Stated differently, in the prever-bal stage, traumas remain in the unconscious as diffuse feeling states and their effects cannot be cognitively interpreted. It is only with the onset of language that these states are encoded.

In the encoding process several things occur:

1 the traumas and their effects can be interpreted,
2 the quality of the language learning will affect the interpretation and attach to it,
3 the traumas become more deeply engraved in the psyche, and
4 once entered into the linguistic neurology, the cognitive process can trigger and activate them at any point in life.

So, for example, as the baby gets stuck in stage one of birth, where immense pressures force it towards the cervix before dilation, it reacts experientially, either by remaining in the pushing state (hypertonic), or by giving up and going flaccid (hypotonic). In the verbal phase, but still at the level of the unconscious, what develops is either the decisive encoded message: 'under pressure, I struggle through'; or 'under pressure, I give up'. These newly articulated decisions will feed into the belief system, becoming more enduring perceptions.

The subtlety or crudeness of these perceptions will be influenced by the degree of complexity of the language skills the child acquires. If language development is sparse, or illogical, interpretations and decisions will be of the same calibre, while if the development is rich and varied, the descriptions and decisions will be rich and varied. As the child in the above example grows up, pressures on its system will then activate one of the two reactions noted, in degrees of subtlety or crudeness that depend on the linguistic skills acquired during the period of primary language learning.

Belief systems

Perhaps the most crucial and important of the secondary processes are belief systems. To understand these, one must comprehend what is meant by prenatal consciousness. Prenatal consciousness has recently manifested from Spirit, and is aware of any and all circumstances which surround its major waking experiences. Prenatal consciousness is also a particular kind of consciousness which involves a non-verbal awareness of the events surrounding traumas. It is somatic in nature, and has the capacity to register experiences and feelings of the prenate, or to register experiences in the womb surround, i.e. the mother and her spatial/emotional field. Along with these experiences, belief systems form.

Belief systems might best be described as the domain of non-cognitive and unarticulated 'knowings' which form during pre- and perinatal life, particularly during stress, trauma or ecstasy. They embody a primal, preverbal set of perceptions about the nature of life, the world and the parents. The memory traces of these belief systems are constantly available, and when language begins to form, they are spontaneously filtered through language, and adopt linguistic models appropriate to their experiences.

Because belief systems form the deepest strata of the mind, they form the underpinning for all cognitions and thoughts. Their impact on the psyche is like a mental tincture, so pervasive and constant that it is barely noticeable, but affecting the colour and tone of everything. Belief systems are non-verbal, and are omnipresent in the cellular, tissue and postural organization. They influence one's perceptions and relationships to the world, far beyond the realm of cognition and language. This was illustrated by one of my (Emerson) patients, Peter, who was attempting to break through a block that he had with women, an 'intimacy barrier' as he called it.

Peter's belief system
Peter's trauma postures and trauma tonicities were diagnosed, and he was regressed via activating these postural and tonic patterns. He immediately

contacted an experience at five months of gestation, where his maternal uncle was dying from alcoholism. Highly embarrassed, his mother sent the uncle to a distant treatment institution, where no one would know him. But it was too late, his liver would no longer function, and he soon died. His mother was grief stricken and depressed for several months, even contemplating suicide (although no attempts were made).

Peter uncovered these memories, and also uncovered rage at his mother for hiding the uncle's alcoholism, for abandoning the uncle, and for her self-indulgent depression (after all, he was the wonderful prenate who would soon be born). His rage poured out, as well as his mother's embarrassment about alcoholism (he recognized that he wasn't at all embarrassed, but that his mother's energetic relationship to alcohol had got into him).

His belief systems were also activated through somatic means, and as is common, he exhibited non-verbal but intense feeling states. He was quickly able to image the belief systems, and uncover the corresponding language system which formed at 19 months. His belief systems were that he was no good, that his mother didn't want him around, that other men were more important than him, and that mother-women couldn't be trusted. With regard to the latter, it was interesting that he never chose nurturing women (i.e. nurturing in a motherly sense), because the belief system was a somatic tincture which implied that he couldn't trust them. So he was constantly 'hungry' and 'untouched' in heterosexual relationships.

Another belief system involved 'hangovers'. He frequently had prenatal and non-verbal feeling states that paralleled his perceptions of the uncle's hangovers . . . his belief was that he, like his uncle, must be 'hung over' because both were rejected (his 'hangovers' were culturally unbiased, and were uniquely his, involving cold feet, cold nose and gut aches). He was totally shocked that he held these beliefs, and while his external relationship to other women and alcohol would have changed with his cathartic work, his inner relationship to women and alcohol would not have changed without the work on this substratum and would have emerged as shadow material in any intimate heterosexual relationship.

Belief systems hold incredible power, power that frequently needs to be brought into awareness and changed.

Proaction and counteraction

Most dysfunctional behaviours will spontaneously change when belief systems are uncovered and repatterned, because the basic primary energy underlying the behaviour, its deepest underpinning, has been unfastened. However, a few will not, either because they have become independent and ego-attached, or because they serve some other purpose outside the belief system. In such cases, clients are asked to specify behaviours which are opposite to those that are dysfunctional (counteraction), and behaviours which will bring them what they really need (proaction). These behaviours are then adopted, and regular evaluations with support partners or therapists assist them to become firmly rooted.

Somatotropic treatment

During intense experiences of any kind (positive, ecstatic, or traumatic), the body enacts certain tonicities, certain postures and particular movements. When the experiences are overwhelming, the tonicities, postures and movements are unable to be processed by the nervous system and reside in the deeper layers of somatic consciousness until the psyche is ready to confront and integrate the experiences. The tonicities, postures and movements can easily be observed and accessed at any time, with permission.

I (Emerson) discovered these somatic principles when I was 16 years old, quite by accident. I was working the night shift at a restaurant. I was alone and was cleaning up after closing hours. I heard a terrible crash outside the back door, and rushed out to find that a car had run headlong into a tree. I opened the car door to see if I could help the driver. Her head had crashed into the steering wheel, which had smashed several of her front teeth into her tongue. She was in shock, but would periodically turn her head to the left and slightly up, while moving it toward the steering wheel. Each time she did so, she moved into reverberations of terror and pain. She continued to repeat these movements every two or three minutes, interspersed with periods of silence, when she was in deep shock.

When she was recovering in the hospital, and talking about the accident, her head and upper body would, quite unconsciously, go into the same postures and movements, and at these times, she would become emotional and feel the physical and psychological pain of her accident. Following her hospitalization, these movements became less and less obvious, more and more subtle, but continued into her life following the hospitalization.

I've since observed the same phenomenon time and again, with people going through various kinds of traumas, from skiing and car accidents to physical abuse, sexual abuse, birth and other traumas. The psyche not only stores the cognitive memory of traumatic events, but also stores the memory of accompanying tonic patterns, postures and movements that were linked with it. Through close observation, I have come to find that, if trauma is pre- or perinatal, these tonic patterns, postures, and movements actually contain the trauma and hold the memory. In contrast, post-verbal memories may not be contained by somatic patterns, but are contained by the central nervous system as cognitive memories. The exception is that postverbal traumas may be contained by the somatic processes mentioned above, if they also re-enact or symbolically represent prior pre- or perinatal traumas.

It has been interesting to note that catharsis alone, without the somatic interventions of Somatotropic Therapy or other body-oriented approaches, frequently fails to release the somatic holding of traumas. When catharsis without somatic technique is finished, the tonic patterns, trauma postures and trauma movements still remain and when activated, arouse the depth of primal pain that was associated with the original impact. This suggests that trauma is not only a central nervous system memory, but a somatic memory as well. To resolve trauma completely, both need to be dealt with and somatic memories take primacy, i.e. if somatic processes are dealt with, then both somatic release and cathartic release of trauma take place. If trauma is released emotionally, without the appropriate bodywork, then only a portion of unresolved trauma will be dealt with.

Tonic patterns, postures and movements associated with trauma reside within the energy system and for related and postverbal events, in the central nervous system as well, and are called somatic memories. Tonic patterns, postures and movements surround all events, but they do not become imprinted as somatic memories unless trauma occurs. Specialists in hypnosis say that traumas and stress induce trance states in which the traumatized person is highly suggestible and unconsciously takes in whatever is happening at the time of stress or trauma.

Tonic patterns, posture and related movements are three major elements of trauma that are imprinted at the time of a traumatic event. None of them is imprinted unless there is a high degree of stress or trauma, in which case they become relatively permanent aspects of the person.

One can observe this process very clearly in newborn babies, all of whom have cranial moulding (i.e. specific cranial shape) and patterns of movement after birth. This is entirely normal, since the head must adjust its shape in order to come through the birth canal. However, one can observe vast differences in the extent to which moulding recovers and this depends on the duration and degree of birth trauma. Conversely, one can observe, when treating birth trauma in babies, that heads spontaneously return to 'normal' as birth traumas are resolved. However, the process of normalization decreases with age. As babies age, heads are less likely to return to normal unless specific interventions such as craniosacral therapy are also utilized. This is because of adhesions which form between tissue and bone, as the ageing process progresses, fixating the trauma postures of birth.

It should be mentioned that the postures and movements associated with trauma do not adhere in their actual physical state, but remain in what are called representational states. Representational states are mini-representations of the actual trauma postures and trauma movements. So, for example, if a shoulder were pulled back 10 degrees from its normal position during trauma, and this were the actual trauma posture, the representational state or representational posture might be only one degree out of true. However, during life events which are symbolic of the trauma, or which are similar in some way to the trauma, the representational posture contains all the electromyographical and neural impulses that make up the trauma posture itself, except that the impulses are of lower intensity.

When individuals are regressed to traumas, these representational states intensify and approximate the trauma postures themselves. In a majority of cases, Somatotropic Therapy is required in order to resolve trauma postures and trauma movements. Furthermore, in working with infants and children, or with adults who have difficulty accessing traumas, I (Emerson) found that somatotropic treatment was the easiest, the most reliable and the most thorough way of accessing unresolved trauma. In its most basic form somatotropic treatment engages the trauma tonicities, the trauma postures and the trauma movements and these greatly facilitate the uncovering and the somatic integration of trauma. Since the body holds preverbal memories in this way, contact with the traumatic processes induces a complete, deep and thorough release of traumatic memories. Furthermore, engaging the somatic processes spontaneously allows the body to integrate the experiences and to find a neutral ground in which trauma-free postures and movements can be initiated.

An example: Seven year old Johnny had a conventional trauma posture, i.e. his right hip was higher, right leg shorter, right shoulder lower and there was cranial compression on the right side, resulting in a cranial syndrome called *side bending rotation*. This is a common postural pattern found in unresolved birth trauma. By slowly and progressively placing Johnny into these postures and by increasingly engaging the cranial and tonic patterns, he proceeded to uncover his birth trauma and at the same time resolved the emotional and somatic bases for it. When his body returned to its normal state, repatterning processes were initiated to provide him with an optimal basis for free and harmonious functioning.

When the body can be entirely released from its somatic trauma, it is possible to realize deeper states of meditation and deeper states of consciousness. So one of the subtle outcomes of this work is that clients are able to function better in life and are also able to develop spiritually. The spiritual process cannot progress until the traumatic aspects, the shadow aspects of the person are dealt with, a conclusion that Freud and Jung both came to and which became an underlying basis for Jungian psychoanalysis.

Practitioners

Role of the therapist in working with adults

The facilitator is active in promoting regressions, in promoting somatic and verbal techniques to uncover trauma. It is essential to know various approaches to regression and to conduct them in cooperative and collaborative relationships with clients. It is not necessary for therapists to apprehend what clients are experiencing, but rather to let clients report what is happening. A prerequisite in the therapist is an ability and willingness to be open at the level of the heart and to respond with genuine empathy and compassion to the emerging content.

This prerequisite is not to do with technique, but rather with a state of mind and heart. As the client uncovers and discharges trauma, it is the therapist's state of empathy, compassion and objectivity which most dynamically promotes the healing process. Once the traumatic experiences and their reverberations are uncovered and catharted, the facilitator takes on an educational role, sharing with the client various integrational procedures and guiding the client through these in a supportive way.

Role of the therapist in working with infants and children

The therapist performs three primary functions: to contain the reality of the trauma, to hold it with compassion and love, and to facilitate its expression and integration. With infants the therapist acts as the baby's advocate and/or means of articulation. He or she will voice the baby's traumatic feelings, which may or may not include feelings about the medical staff, medical procedures, the birth, the mother, the father and/or the siblings.

The practitioner gains acceptance from the baby as well as the parents before initiating or continuing any technique and also explains to the parents what he or she is doing and encourages them to allow the baby to express what it is feeling. In that role, the therapist is also mediator between the baby and its feelings and perceptions of the world. Through a thorough understanding of the pre- and perinatal stages and the somatic topology of the baby, the therapist broadly reconstructs and reflects the history of the birth from conception onward. The therapist contains and mirrors the prenatal biography and by voicing the baby's feelings, gives them a substance of equal stature to the parents. This process demonstrates the acute consciousness of the baby and, in that respect alone, significantly improves and/or deepens the quality of relationship between the baby and the parents.

In this process, the parents may access some of their own birth material. While it may be vital for them to work with it to facilitate their parenting abilities, or to assist in their babies' release of participatory trauma (babies frequently hold the trauma of their parents), the therapist maintains clear boundaries between the babies' material and the parents' and between the times that babies work and parents work. One or preferably both parents are required to be present during sessions, as it is their level of love and empathy that is responsible for the ultimate healing bond. With children the facilitator is initially a friend or peer. The child is engaged at its age level with playfulness and loving respect. After deep contact is made the roles will move between friend, playmate, advocate, observer and adult, shifting as required and sometimes overlaid, depending on which of the many games or techniques are being employed. Parents are required to attend sessions, because it is their love and the depth of their actual or potential empathy that is most healing for children.

Sequences in Somatotropic Therapy

Phase 1
In working with babies, as with children, the first phase or step is to establish rapport with the baby and its parents. But in the case of babies, this requirement is magnified: it is the essence of the field of communication between therapists, babies and parents which is at the heart of the treatment process. The essential and underlying presupposition is that the babies are sentient and capable of precise communication. This becomes swiftly obvious to those who learn to fine-tune their responses and proprioception. Frequently, release from pain occurs simultaneously with babies' perceptions that they are being heard, seen and felt, perhaps for the first time.

Once deep contact has been established, the practitioner makes an initial scrutiny of baby's face, head, facial shape and body, observing postures and movements which embody the birth schema. In this way evidence of the trauma's impacts begin to emerge. Communication with parents to ascertain and confirm participatory trauma is also evaluated. Examples of participatory trauma are prenatal disturbances such as moving house, a death in the family, financial crises, injuries, accidents, wars, relational upsets, dubious or negative feelings about the conception or the pregnancy and so on. The parents are then joined in articulating these events and contacting their feelings about the distressing events. The potential impacts on their children are also discussed.

Parents are then guided in making extremely clear distinctions between their own feelings and reactions and their babies' feelings and reactions. Once these distinctions are grasped, they need to be articulated by the parents in the presence of the baby and the distinctions owned. This articulating process is often a powerful catalyst for the baby, who frequently responds to what is being verbalized by crying, screaming or other actions through which it will demonstrate and release its memory of the traumatic experiences and work through the effects of the participatory trauma. This process will often precipitate major changes in the baby's behaviour and its relationship to the parents.

Phase 2

The second phase focuses heavily on observation of the bones and tissue structures of the face and head which were impacted by birth pressures. In rare cases where trauma does not occur during birth, the visible effects of these impacts will spontaneously resolve within a few hours or days. As the vast majority of births, however, contain traumatic elements, each stage of birth leaves very specific indications of traumatic stress on the head and facial features of the individual baby. It is here that precise and detailed knowledge of the pre- and perinatal birth stages and their subdivisions are required, as well as a knowledge of the traumas and feelings associated with each stage. This is where babies' traumas are accessed, as distinct from participatory trauma. In addition to the facial features, the visual cues and the cranial/bodily indications mentioned above, the whole skeletal–muscular structure carries the signature of the birth trauma. These are evaluated by palpation, using what is called 'near touch', in which the baby is palpated off the body, feeling for indications of trauma in the energy field around the impacted areas. When the 'energy memories' are thus located and the hands connect with these leaks, the baby begins to respond, either giving permission for the work to continue, even though it is often painful, or clearly indicating that the work should stop.

An essential element of this work is its procedure under the control of the baby. This cannot be stressed too heavily. The baby in this process is engaged; it is informed that it will be in charge of the cathartic process, which it can stop at any time. When such a contract is made, the work can take place. The baby will often endure bouts of relived pain of some intensity and, between rests, will often guide the practitioner's hand to the areas which require work and adjustment. The skin on the head, neck or body may occasionally change colour and/or temperature, or it may swell. These are all clear signals of the physical impact of birth trauma retained at an energetic, cellular or tissue level in the body.

Phase 3

It is in this third phase that the deepest aspects of the trauma are uncovered. This is accomplished by a process called birth-simulating massage (BSM – a copyrighted term), a technique which focuses on the infant cranium and shoulders. In order to do BSM practitioners must first have knowledge of the journey of the cranium through the pelvis and all the places of conjunct where maternal pelvis and infant cranium meet. These journeys are reproduced by practitioners, utilizing their hands to simulate the precise movement of the head through the maternal pelvis, thereby simulating the birth and uncovering the deepest aspects of birth trauma. The contact, now using direct touch to simulate the birthing, releases the memories and the traumas they embody. During this process the other approaches already discussed are also used simultaneously. The essence of this work, birth-simulating massage, resonates all through the work with children and adults, since it forms the basis for the surest, most precise and deepest contact with unresolved trauma.

Management and technique

In times of resting the baby can turn to the mother for the breast, for comfort, for love and for reassurance. Dramatic changes in behaviour, posture, eating, crying, sleeping and relating usually occur quite early in this work, sometimes after several sessions. The length of treatment depends on the number and degree of prenatal traumas, the seriousness of birth trauma and the length of the mother's labour. As a rule of thumb, four times the length of labour are required for the full course of treatment. If the only trauma is birth trauma, the average number of sessions required to complete treatment is 12.

One of the immense benefits of resolving birth traumas in infants is that the traumas are dealt with and dissipated before they have a chance to be crystallized into the verbal realm, where their hold otherwise becomes much more tenacious. With children, as with babies, empathic communication and rapport must be deeply established before work can commence. With children, the array of techniques is much more extensive and complex. It involves prenatal games, conception games, birth games, sand tray work, bodywork, cranio-sacral therapy, artwork, guided imagery and regression through contact with somatic processes, as described above. (Winnicott called a child's re-enactment of this journey 'serpentation'.) The training for this aspect of the work is the most rigorous, as it is the most complex. The work is used with children from the time of language development and right into adolescence.

In working with adults a number of regressive techniques are used, including guided imagery, birth simulation, verbal regression, trauma postures, tonic energizing and de-energizing, birth-simulating massage, trauma movement and others. The work is usually done in group settings, where the focused dynamic energy of the group amplifies the potentiality for regressive journeying and the potency of integrative work. Emphasis is once again laid on the need for a therapeutic support system when this work is undertaken. So deep and powerful are the contents encountered, so much alienation is indigenous to the process of trauma, that loving and skilled support are requisite for dealing with and resolving traumas. Once deep regressions have taken place, the door opens for an entirely new dimension of work to take place. The client can (and should) return to their own therapist, who need not be a specialist in this work. Provided that the therapist can comfortably allow and accommodate intense somatic and emotional expressiveness and, provided that she or he is alive to the need for keeping the client's attention on the somatic reality they will re-experience in their work following the first regression, deep and rapid progress will be made.

Does it work?

> The quintessential possibility of regressive therapy is spiritual opening and the emergence of a volitional relationship with one's higher Self.
>
> W.R. Emerson

From 1964 to 1974, I (Emerson) conducted over 8,000 hours of intense and ongoing regression sessions with adults. Profound changes in clients were observed and these observations invited the possibility of beginning treatment much earlier, with infants and children. The hope was that, by starting treatment early, the development of adult symptoms could be prevented and the treatment process could be completed more efficiently. In 1974 I began to develop therapeutic approaches and to conduct exploratory treatment of pre- and perinatal trauma in infants and children. This work was followed up to determine the long and short range outcomes of therapy. The treatment of infants and children was evaluated in terms of a pre-test/post-test model, using changes in presenting symptoms as well as standard questionnaires to evaluate therapeutic effectiveness. A control group (infants and children who were referred for, but did not receive, treatment) was also included for purposes of comparison.

Therapeutic outcomes with infants and children

One of the major successes of the experimental work with infants and children was the development of a broad range of therapeutic techniques. These were successfully used to deal with traumas ranging from conception to Oedipal conflicts at age five.

The work with infants and children indicated that, not only could they be treated, but they could be treated far more effectively and economically than adults (in terms of time and outcomes). Infants and children required an average of only 12 sessions to discharge birth traumas and their work yielded a broader and deeper range of outcomes than adults. There were significant changes in the treatment group, but not in the control group, on ten dimensions:

1 resolution of presenting symptoms;
2 resolution of somatic symptoms;
3 prevention of potential symptoms (follow-up has been 18 years to date);
4 degree of emotional maturity;
5 extent of mutuality and empathy;
6 degree and type of non-aggressiveness;
7 degree of self-awareness and ability to communicate;
8 level of individuation;

9 manifestation of unique human potential (passion and ability in unique talents and skills); and
10 connection with the Self.

Several comments about these outcomes are warranted. With regard to somatic symptoms, it was common to find reversals or remissions in various paediatric diseases. In most cases psychosomatic disease patterns resolved; occasionally other paediatric illnesses (such as bronchitis, asthma, dermatitis, colitis and others) also responded to psychotherapeutic treatment. In addition, temperamental behaviours in infants were very responsive to treatment: 'fussiness', extensive crying, breast-feeding difficulties, nocturnal or frequent waking, irritability, hyperactivity and lethargy were often rectified. In several dramatic cases, autism and attachment disorders responded to treatment. Learning disabilities, developmental delays and emotional handicaps in children would often show marked improvements.

The most universal outcome, and one which was not anticipated, had to do with transpersonal phenomena, or Self-manifestations. Treated infants and children were significantly more adept on dimensions of the Self. The Self refers to qualities that have been called 'magical' by Pearce (1980) and 'radiant' by Armstrong (1985). In addition, a number of treated infants and children had transpersonal experiences, e.g. visions, peak experiences, meditative phenomenology, conversations with God, clairvoyant experiences etc. (either during or following completion of treatment). None of the children in the 'comparison group' had such experiences. This finding is significant since there is considerable debate within transpersonal psychology about the possibility of transpersonal experiences occurring prior to full ego development. Contrary to consensus opinion, the data reported in this chapter suggest that transpersonality occurs prior to full ego development.

There was another unexpected finding, having to do with human potential. During or shortly after the resolution of trauma, there were dramatic expressions of unique human potential, vivid manifestations of passionate interests, talents and abilities. The somatotropic treatment process appeared to open the psyche to considerable depths, where the seeds of human potential reside. When there were no unresolved traumas to obscure their expression, latent talents and abilities surged into consciousness, where they could be acknowledged and acted upon. Because of this, treated children were more likely than untreated children to have 'found themselves', to have identified their unique qualities, frequently without parental support or encouragement.

For example, one three year old boy completed his trauma resolution and immediately began to exercise a passion for balls. He played with balls for two hours each day, on his own and with much talent and enthusiasm. His parents were academically oriented, had never engaged in sports and were very surprised by the focus and intensity of his new interest. Their boy grew up to be an exceptional athlete. A three year old girl first began to express an interest in sewing as she was resolving major traumas, ended up selling tapestries at the age of five and was an accomplished artist by the age of 10.

The list of exceptional characteristics is long: a four year old reading fluently;

a three year old painting landscapes with oils; and a five year old repairing electrical equipment with no training or modelling. These activities were self-chosen and pursued with a degree of concentration and attention that did not require parental initiation, encouragement or praise (although all these were appreciated by children). Furthermore, these specialized areas of interest accompanied a breadth of development in other endeavours: children were well-rounded and competent in academic and social areas.

Therapeutic outcomes with adults

During research with infants and children approaches were discovered which made major contributions to work with adults. These approaches elicited deeper and more accurate contact with regressive content and gave access to transformational material in ways that had previously not been possible. Results with adults were similar to the results with infants and children, although the full range of outcomes (mentioned above) were rarely attained. For example, human potential (in adults) was only actualized in about 50 per cent of cases over a five year follow-up period and in 70 per cent of cases over a 10 year period. This was because many adults found it difficult to make life changes which were consistent with their newly-found human potential.

Case study

The following case shows how Somatotropic Therapy heals trauma and facilitates the emergence of human potential. The case involves a 30 year old woman who completed 12 years of psychotherapy, none of which included regression techniques. An interview revealed that she suffered from anorexia, low self-esteem, claustrophobia, depression, career frustration and highly unsatisfying relationships. Career frustration was fuelled by the feeling that she couldn't get anywhere in her career, despite the fact that she was making rapid rises up the corporate ladder, far exceeding her male counterparts. Her depression centred around her inability to consummate intimate and satisfying relationships with men. Every man she had been in relationships with exhibited varying degrees of weakness, dependence, narcissism and irresponsibility. She said, 'I keep hoping that they will be responsible, strong and independent. But no, they don't pursue jobs or keep commitments and they want to be taken care of all the time. I seek men and end up with little boys.'

Her initial regressions involved prenatal memories about her older sibling (a brother) and were facilitated by trauma-postures and tonic-energizing of tissue memories. She discovered that while she was *in utero* her brother took all of her parents' time and attention. He felt very threatened by her presence and did not want her to live. She felt totally rejected by him, dominated by him and 'short-changed' by the parents' attention to him. (Many unborn children have psychical relationships with their born siblings. This case, and many other cases like it, have underscored my opinion that prenates need protection, attention and love, and parents should plan children so that the healthy but primary narcissism of a birthed child does not overlap the gestation of an expected child.)

Her memories were very intellectual and trauma postures were essential in helping her to uncover and feel the pain of her unmet needs and her rage at and distrust of her brother. She discovered that her continual choices of 'little boys' instead of men were recapitulations (i.e. repetitions) of her relationship with her brother, who took all and gave little. At the same time, she was frightened of 'strong men' for a related reason; if they were strong they might be able to take from her. Her birth regressions were facilitated by trauma postures and birth-simulating massage.

She discovered the terror she had felt when the doctor, in an attempt to save her mother from tearing, had pushed and held her back. She associated this feeling with the way she felt about the men in her corporation. She was subsequently able to see her own progress and to see her male colleagues' support of her. She experienced her endogenous depression, which stemmed from being stuck for 36 hours and unable to progress. She said,

> I realize now that I've always been depressed, I just didn't know it. I thought everybody felt that way. The hopelessness and helplessness I felt during my birth were the same feelings I carried to my work and my male relationships.

Her depression gradually lifted and as an added bonus she discovered that her eating problems, particularly anorexia, were a recapitulation of her emotional starvation while *in utero*.

When asked to summarize her therapeutic experiences she said:

> I'd done it all, every therapy imaginable, but I still couldn't be close. Then I started regression therapy with William Emerson. He did what he called 'reading my cranium and soma-postures'. He then guided me into some postures that felt very unusual and quite uncomfortable emotionally. Feelings began to come and I was in the middle of an experience. It was very intense, almost overwhelming, but at the same time it felt right, it was my gestation experiences with my brother. He took all the attention that I needed and I almost starved to death emotionally. For many sessions I had different memories and feelings. Then I found some postures and Dr Emerson did some cranial stroking which brought up the most amazingly strong feelings I'd ever felt. They were my birth feelings and I was totally stuck, just jammed up and totally hopeless. I was really depressed in there. After many months of feeling my womb despair and my depression, I began to feel deeply quiet. I noticed almost immediately that my capacity for intimacy had changed. Never before had I really felt a hug, or been able to engage in deep eye contact. I can see 'little boys' from a mile away and I stay away. I'm beginning to date men who are self-reliant and it's scary but exciting. I've been having strong images of myself and daydreams, which I never before had. I see myself doing things I would love to do but could never consider doing. Mostly they are images of horses, of owning and racing horses. Gradually, by working with belief systems, I was able to let go of limiting beliefs and to acknowledge my deep longing to own and race horses. I have since left my corporate job, except to act as an occasional

consultant for them and embarked on a highly successful and exciting career, training and racing horses. My life is totally transformed.

Pitfalls

The client needs to be in a safe therapeutic support system, such as ongoing therapy. Then the regressive process is contained in a way that honours the clients' processes and defences. When clients regress they frequently enter deep, altered states of consciousness in which they can filter what material, emerging from deeper levels, they are prepared to work with. The more that clients are in control of the process, the deeper they can progress, because control and safety are intricately intertwined.

The regressive process must be conducted in a way which respects the boundaries and capacities of clients. If the process does not empower clients, if it does not honour their boundaries and capacities, then there may be pitfalls. In such cases the major problems are that clients are unable to access deeper memories; they are only able to access screen (i.e. protective) memories; they are unable to remember the regressive experiences and/or their life is disrupted by the power of the emerging content which intrudes in dreams and during waking consciousness, making work and concentration difficult.

These problems are more likely to occur with certain clinical syndromes, namely those involving borderline personality disorders, hysterical and conversion disorders and psychotic disorders. Special regressive procedures are necessary for individuals with multiple personality disorders, dissociative personality disorders and schizoid disorders, particularly schizo-affective types.

Note

1 This chapter is dedicated to my dear friend and colleague Stephan Schorr-Kon who wrote this chapter with me. He died unexpectedly on 31 December 1992.

Further reading

Emerson (1987) describes the use of Somatotropic Therapy with infants and summarizes my research on treatment outcomes.

Emerson (1989) describes the basic parameters of psychotherapy for infants and children. Fundamental techniques are discussed and research results from 15 years of development and evaluation are summarized.

Grof (1975) summarizes his pioneering research over an 18 year period, exploring the phenomenology of birth, the nature of schizophrenia and interactive dimensions such as art, religion, personality dynamics and the treatment of emotional disorders through regressive experience.

Lake, F. (1966) (abridged 1986). The 1966 edition is preferable and outlines in entirety Dr Lake's findings from regression therapy over a 20 year period and its implications for theology.

Sills (1990) is a thorough introduction to a system of energy medicine which can be utilized for the uncovering and treatment of trauma. The concepts and techniques may be most useful to those in the somatic professions, such as chiropractors, cranial osteopaths, nurses, body workers, midwives and massage therapists who wish to uncover and resolve traumatic memories in the body. Many of the techniques are similar to and compatible with the integrational techniques utilized in Somatotropic Therapy.

Ward (1987) describes the stages and content of prenatal development and how the work may be applied to infants and children.

References

Armstrong, T. (1985) *The Radiant Child*. Wheaton, IL: Theosophical Publication House.

Chamberlain, D. (1988) *Babies Remember Birth*. Los Angeles, CA: Tarcher.

Emerson, W. (1987) Primal Therapy with infants, *Aesthema*, 7, The International Primal Association.

Emerson, W. (1989) Psychotherapy with Infants and Children, *Pre- and Peri-Natal Psychology*, 3(3).

Fodor, N. (1949) *The Search for the Beloved*. New York: University Books.

Grof, S. (1975) *Realms of the Human Unconscious*. London: Souvenir Press.

Grof, S. (1985) *Beyond the Brain*. Albany, NY: State University of New York Press.

Laing, R.D. (1976) *The Voice of Experience*. London: Pantheon.

Lake, F. (1966) *Clinical Theology*. London: Darton, Longman & Todd.

Lake, F. (1980) *Studies in Constricted Confusion*. Oxford: Clinical Theology Association.

Lake, F. (1981) *Tight Corners in Pastoral Counselling*. London: Darton, Longman & Todd.

Mott, F. (1948) *The Universal Design of Birth*. Philadelphia: David McKay.

Mott, F. (1964) *The Universal Design of Creation*. Edenbridge, Kent: Mark Beech.

Pearce, J.C. (1980) *Magical Child*. New York: Bantam Books.

Rank, O. (1929) *The Trauma of Birth*. London: Routledge.

Sills, F. (1990) *The Polarity Process*. London: Element Books.

Swartley, W. and Maurice, J. (1978) The birth of primals in wartime Britain, *Self & Society*, 6(7).

Ward, S. (1987) Infant and child birth refacilitation. The work of Dr William Emerson, *Self & Society* 15(2).

Winnicott, D.W. (1975) Primary maternal preoccupation, *Through Paediatrics to Psychoanalysis*. London: Hogarth Press.

PART II

Emphasis on awareness and the 'spiritual'

4

Core Process Psychotherapy

LAURA DONINGTON

Definition and historical development

Definition

Core Process Psychotherapy is an exploration of how we are in our present experience, and how this expresses the past conditioning and conditions of our lives. A depth awareness of what is happening in the present moment is used to explore our inner process. This awareness encompasses our energies, sensations, feelings, mental processes and their expressions in the body. The aim is not to alter our experience but to sense how we relate to it, so that it becomes possible to move with greater creativity and flexibility in our lives. Core Process work is based on an understanding that within the conscious mind there is a deeper wisdom that moves naturally towards healing. Integration and freedom come from insight into the ways in which we hold on to our suffering, and from a deeper connection with the openness, compassion and wisdom at the heart of human experience.

Historical development

Core Process Psychotherapy has been developed over the last 20 years. It incorporates a wide range of concepts and skills that have been developed in the West, but the conceptual framework, the focus on awareness and presence in the work, derive from a Buddhist perspective, though the work itself requires no special commitment to Buddhism.

The approach was deeply influenced by the innovative work done in the 1960s and 1970s, which built on the work of Freud and Wilhelm Reich on ways of working with patterning in the body, and the healing and integrative effect of working with emotional and cognitive patterning. Major influences include Alexander Lowen and later post-Reichian therapists (Chapter 9, this volume) in their exploration of psychoemotional patterning in the body; Fritz Perls and others who developed Gestalt practice; and Stan Grof and Bill Swartley (discussed in Chapter

2) and William Emerson (Chapter 3) in their work with very early forms of patterning around womb and birth experiences.

The insights of psychoanalysis, analytic psychology and Object Relations Theory were acknowledged as important accounts of aspects of cognitive functioning and the developmental process. The emphasis on the inherent movement towards growth as expressed within humanistic psychology by Maslow, Rogers and others, and within Jungian psychology, was also taken up in the work.

These approaches, and the skills and techniques developed within them have been deployed within the framework of Buddhist psychology (Trungpa 1973, 1975).

Buddhism as a spiritual practice is based on a deep understanding of the processes of consciousness which challenges many western assumptions (Walsh and Vaughan 1980; Welwood 1983; Claxton 1986). While western psychology has been much influenced by attempts to develop models of the structure of mind within the framework of objective science, Buddhist psychology comes from a very different philosophical tradition based on the introspective practice of mindfulness. Rather than seeking intellectual understanding, or developing the 'self-conscious' awareness of the ego, this draws on deeper levels of unconditioned awareness to penetrate the processes involved in the arising of consciousness itself.

'Conscious mind' is seen as a manifestation of a process of 'taking form' which is expressed also in our physical form, our emotions, and our perceptions. These are all aspects of personality, which is the expression in the moment of past conditioning. Bringing attention to the shaping process itself opens up the possibility of letting go of this conditioned 'self', releasing the creative and spiritual energies of the 'unconscious mind', and connecting with our deeper potential for pure awareness, compassion and love. In Core Process work, this understanding, and ways of working distilled from Buddhist awareness practice, have been integrated with western practice to form the basis of a practical psychotherapy.

Founders

Core Process Psychotherapy was developed by Maura Sills, who was born and educated in Edinburgh, Scotland. She came into psychotherapy through occupational therapy, specializing in psychiatry and working with drug addicts. She taught in universities in England and the USA, and later ran a therapeutic community for former psychiatric patients. During the 1970s she trained in England in Post-Reichian and Gestalt Therapies, and did intensive training at the Esalen Institute in California.

During this time she was also exploring the eastern spiritual traditions. She became a Buddhist nun under the Most Venerable Taungpulu Sayadaw of Burma, and trained in Buddhist studies and meditation practices. This profoundly affected her outlook on therapeutic process, and her work moved towards a synthesis, which became known as Core Process Psychotherapy.

In 1979 she was joined by Franklyn Sills, who brought a deep knowledge of Buddhist psychology and bodywork therapies to the work. He was a Buddhist monk with the same teacher, and had training in western and Ayurvedic medicine, Polarity Therapy and Cranio-sacral Therapy. They founded the

Karuna Institute in 1980, and together have been developing ways of integrating the psychotherapeutic and spiritual aspects of the work. The Karuna Institute offers training, groups and workshops in Core Process Psychotherapy and related forms of healing.

Where does Core Process Psychotherapy fit in?

In terms of contemporary psychotherapeutic approaches, Core Process Psychotherapy is humanistic, integrative, transpersonal and psychospiritual. The emphasis is on facilitating and releasing the client's own potential for healing. Experience which goes beyond the personal and historical is seen as central to the healing process. The approach is integrative not just in bringing together different ways of working but more fundamentally in that it works towards an integration of levels and states of consciousness, in the belief that *awareness in the present is inherently integrative and healing*. The approach is psychospiritual in that it recognizes the inherent freedom and openness of the human condition, and offers a coherent account of how we can move with this awareness in our everyday lives.

This understanding of the healing potential of the human psyche contrasts with the Freudian notion of the 'unconscious' as inherently disruptive, and is closer to the Jungian view, in which the movement towards growth rests within the psyche itself, and the Self is more about the ability to 'know the moment'. In this view, which also has resonances within existential psychology and phenomenology (Spinelli 1989; van Deurzen-Smith 1990 and Chapter 10, this volume), exploration of personal process eventually leads to the awareness that there is no 'identity' to be found, but only the process of 'becoming', at the centre of which is our essential state of being.

Core Process Psychotherapy works by bringing awareness to the way we are holding on to our past experience in the present moment. In Core Process terms, personality is not seen as 'fixed', but as the expression of a process of 'becoming' which is happening all the time, and which reflects our personal history in that it is patterned by the circumstances and conditioning of our lives. Western theories of personality are understood as ways of describing the conditioning process. Ego development is seen as the process of learning to take fixed positions in relation to our experience.

Core Process Psychotherapy shares theoretical ground with existential and phenomenological approaches which focus on how we perceive our experience. The idea of 'self as conditioned' is shared also with Behaviourist Psychology (O'Sullivan 1990), and with Object Relations Theory (Klein 1987; Cashdan 1988). However, unlike these primarily cognitive approaches, Core Process work is truly holistic and integrative in that all aspects of process and levels of consciousness are explored. It is not specifically 'body-orientated' but incorporates ways of working with the body. The patterning that manifests in the body is no different in this respect from cognitive or emotional patterning – these are all manifestations of a unitary process. Healing takes place through deep awareness of how we are experiencing ourselves in all levels of our being.

In terms of practice, the work focuses on what is arising in the present moment, on 'being with' rather than 'doing', on comprehending 'how' rather than 'why'. In this it is similar to other Process Psychotherapies such as Existential Psychotherapy, Birth Process Therapies, and other humanistic and integrative forms. The particular emphasis given to the role of awareness in healing and transformation gives a centrality to ways of working deriving from eastern mindfulness practice, and ways of working deriving from western approaches also, in effect become ways of facilitating the client's awareness of particular layers or aspects of process (Welwood 1983).

The Core Process 'model' of personality process is not a developmental model, but is about *how we are in our present experience*. There is also a developmental model of personality in the work, derived from prenatal and birth psychology, Object Relations Theory, and Post-Reichian psychology, but the practical work is based on an understanding of the process of becoming who we are in the present moment.

In Core Process work both client and therapist work with awareness of their inner process in the present, and as it manifests in the therapeutic relationship. This links the work with more recent psychodynamic and analytic exploration of transference and counter-transference. In Core Process work this is extended to include the subtle interactions associated with very early preverbal and perinatal experience.

Core Process Psychotherapy not only integrates different therapeutic approaches, but also works towards integrating different levels of consciousness. By learning to experience ourselves more fully, we can tap into deeper levels of unconditioned awareness and discover how we hold on to our past experience in the present. Healing happens naturally as we integrate these levels of awareness into our way of being in the world.

Central concepts

Core Process Psychotherapy is based on the premise that we are *essentially free* – that the core of our sense of 'self' is a state of being which is open and boundless. In Buddhist terms, at the heart of human experience is the already enlightened mind.

Through our conditioning, this very important aspect of 'being here', this sense of the freedom inherent in every moment, becomes atrophied and is usually missed in our experience of ordinary life. Most of the time we are moving from unaware attachment to certain positions in relation to the world, from beliefs about 'who I am' and 'how things are' which colour and shape our experience both internally and externally, sometimes in quite subtle ways. It is our conditioned 'personality structure' and our attachment to it that restricts our potential for fulfilment, compassion, wisdom and joy. Core Process work is an exploration of how we cut ourselves off from this natural state of awareness, so that we can rediscover a sense of it for ourselves.

The Core Process 'model' of personality process is about how we are in our present experience. There is also a developmental model of personality in the work, which is based on an understanding of how our patterning is influenced by the conditions of our lives from the very circumstances of our coming into being onwards: the primary experiences around conception and implantation, gestation and birth give rise to some of the deepest conditioning which patterns much of how we meet subsequent experience in the world, together with the held consciousness of archetypal and intergenerational material. This primary patterning provides the matrix for later experience, and the secondary patterning which is built up out of our relations with significant others in our lives from birth onwards, and the developmental task of separation and individuation. Our earliest patterning is overlaid by the defensive strategies we develop to help us survive and protect the sense of our inner being, and the emotional and somatic forms we take as a manifestation of these.

This developmental understanding is an important part of the conceptual framework, but the practical work is based on an understanding of the process of becoming who we are in the present moment. 'Personality' is seen as the endpoint of a continuous process of 'becoming' which is active in every moment of our lives and which can be experienced in the immediacy of the present moment. By accessing our awareness of process, by opening up and softening into more layers of our immediate experience, we begin to experience this *as* a process and allow our awareness of our underlying core state to expand, so that there is a sense of spaciousness even in the middle of desperate feelings. The work is based on the understanding that awareness *in itself* is transformative and healing. Healing happens not by 'making changes' but from recognizing the depths of our inherent freedom.

In our immediate experience, we start with pure awareness, open-heartedness and receptivity. But when an object impinges on our field of awareness – an internal event, a memory or an image, or an external object or event – we move instantly to reaction based on our tendencies and past experience. We start recognizing, making associations, identifying with the inner or outer object of our awareness. Feelings, needs and desires become attached, and we start to move towards or away from the experience. We become caught up in our reactions, we identify with them, label them and build up a sense of ourselves on the basis of them, believing that 'I am this person who experiences, feels and reacts in this way'. We sense our past experience and reactions to be who we are in the present, and in defending this position we limit our potential for appropriate, spontaneous response.

The Core Process model

The Core is that unconditioned state inherent in every human being, our essential state of 'Being', the source of our aliveness and well-being, and sense of relatedness. It is the experience of wholeness, without attachment to self-image or ego process, without movement towards or away from objects. It is a pure, open and expansive awareness in the present, which manifests as peace, compassion, loving kindness and sympathetic joy – qualities that arise naturally when there is no rigidity or self-view in the moment. This inherent state of 'Core' permeates all that we become if we allow ourselves to attend to it. It is not achieved by striving, which is linked to ego process.

Core Process is the movement from this inherent core state towards a sense of separateness. It is the process by which we tend to shape our personality into a unique form with which we identify and through which we see the world, out of which a sense of separate self or 'ego' arises. It is the movement from essential openness, to the conditioned response of personality, which becomes defended and reactive.

There are several 'layers' in this process. The first layer around the Core is 'subtle energetic' – the open expansiveness of unconditioned awareness is drawn by the energy of the moment so that it is no longer neutral. This layer is full of 'tendencies and urges', like a pulsating or vibrating 'sea' of desires, urges, movement. In here are the held energies of our past experience, and the subtle conditioning from which the basic urge to take form, to be here in this world arises. It holds our developmental tendencies, our archetypal patterning, the imprints of prenatal and birth processes and later experiences, and the basic drives of life. As we get older, our energy becomes more locked into habitual patterns of response.

Around this layer, a secondary process of perceptual filtering arises, so that our immediate experience is sensed through those tendencies and urges. Responses and reactions arise which are not grounded in the present, but are an expression of those past experiences and tendencies.

Within these layers of tendency and perception, our experience takes on *feeling tones*. This is the realm of the 'felt sense' (Chapter 7), a subtle realm of feelings before definable emotions, thoughts or physical sensations arise, within which subtle feelings 'about' an object begin to be given a shape and to be sensed in the body. These are the layers of *impression*, within which we sense the world through our conditioning; impressions arise based on that perception, and a sense of ego-shape begins to form in relation to present experience.

From this we move towards the layer of *expression*. The movement of process becomes solidified, identified, and attached to an object, so that it is experienced as a particular emotion or behavioural impulse in relation to that object – 'I hate my boss', 'There is no one there for me'. From this we quickly move towards expression and activity in the world. Thoughts, sensations, emotions and actions arise which, though felt to be in direct response to the present situation, are more about perceptions and feelings carried over from the past.

It is this outermost layer of expression that we most identify with, and is the most resistant to change. It becomes the shape through which we meet the world. It includes those aspects of ourselves with which we feel most comfortable, which Jung called our 'persona'. It also contains our reactions to our impulses, and the repression of those parts of ourselves that we don't much like, which Jung called the 'shadow'. In this layer we have made many judgements about which of our 'shapes' are acceptable or unacceptable, and much energy becomes bound up in this inner conflict. The strong identifications we have in this layer mask our experience of process and block our experience of the Core. Having lost touch with the process of creating it, we sense ourselves to *be* this shape or position, and become bound up in reacting to defend it. We forget that we are free, and resist the experience of life itself. In this way, we 'create' our sense of ourselves in every moment.

An important aim in the work is to create some space between experience and

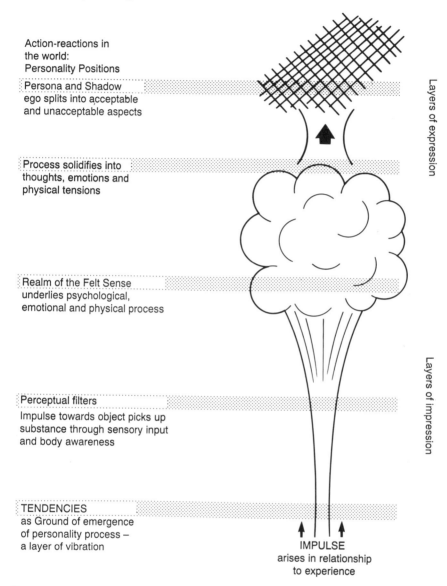

Action-reactions in
the world:
Personality Positions

Persona and Shadow
ego splits into acceptable
and unacceptable aspects

Layers of expression

Process solidifies into
thoughts, emotions and
physical tensions

Realm of the Felt Sense
underlies psychological,
emotional and physical process

Perceptual filters
Impulse towards object picks up
substance through sensory input
and body awareness

Layers of impression

TENDENCIES
as Ground of emergence
of personality process –
a layer of vibration

IMPULSE
arises in relationship
to experience

Figure 4.1 Personality shape forms in relationship to experience

reaction, and open to expanded possibilities, by bringing awareness to this process of taking form. This is done by simply paying deep attention, without judgement or attachment, to whatever is arising in the present moment. As we bring
awareness to process, *it slows down*. Through this we become more aware of 'where
we are coming from' in our encounter with the world, and can move more skilfully
and creatively to meet it. This happens naturally as we integrate deeper levels of
awareness into our way of being in the world, and appreciate the essential
freedom at the heart of our experience.

The cause of suffering

In both East and West, the 'ego' or self is considered the central organizing principle of how we relate to the world. In much of western psychology, suffering is seen as the result of damaged ego formation, and the model of health is that of a well-functioning ego system. Buddhist psychology goes beyond this to describe the process whereby the ego itself causes suffering by taking up all our space, and drawing our attention away from our deeper, unconditioned experience of ourselves. In this way, 'ego mind' cuts us off from the source of our creative energies and sense of aliveness, from our core state which is already integrated and free.

A healthy personal ego is important as a base from which to move out into the world, and work may be needed to strengthen ego-functioning, to build up self-esteem and a sense of personal boundaries. But the ego is a construction of human consciousness. It is simply the way in which we have learnt to divide up and perceive the world. In Buddhist terms, it is our tendency to believe in and identify with the desires and conflicts related to this perceived 'world', to react from this, that is the origin of the neurotic mind and our loss of sense of well-being. Suffering (like joy) is part of the universal human condition, but personal suffering comes not from the world, rather from how we relate to it. We become who we have learnt to be and a prime cause of suffering is our attachment to this conditioned sense of self and to our habitual ways of dealing with the world.

When we explore our process, we begin to experience the deeper reality that what we sense to be our 'self' is only a continuous movement of mental, emotional and physical processes. This can open to a sense of expanded possibility, a feeling of spaciousness within all of our experience, a sense of participation in a much larger and interconnected consciousness. This experience is deeply integrative and healing. Yet in order to open up to it, we need fully to experience our personal self, and discover how we create much of our suffering. It is only through exploring this 'self-process' with compassion and acceptance that we can appreciate the deeper potential and inherent freedom within it.

The change process

The Core Process Model assumes that inherent in all of us is a basic movement towards truth – an underlying movement of awareness which is by its nature healing and transformative, but which can become blocked, locked in or 'solidified' by our attachment to or identification with aspects of process as somehow fixed or 'real' ('I am angry', or 'I am bad').

In Core Process Psychotherapy we don't attempt to alter our experience, but we explore how we relate to that experience. It is by opening ourselves up more fully to the present moment that we come to experience our process as a movement rather than as a fixed ego or 'self'. The more that process is experienced as movement, the less investment there is in particular manifestations of that process, so the less judgement there is, the less repression and conflict. The more I let my identifications and attachments go, the more my awareness of core expands to fill up the whole of my process, so that even when there is movement and craziness in other layers there is an awareness of something underneath all this that gives a sense of space.

True healing is only possible to the extent that we can be present without judgement in our immediate experience. It is this process of allowing and letting go, and expanding our awareness of process that is integrative and healing. Transformation happens by letting things be as they are, by being open to my experience of how things are, not by trying to understand things or move things on, or change them or hide them.

If sadness comes up, I do not immediately seek for an object or cause, but I wait with that feeling, allowing it to be there and fill up as much of my being as I can tolerate in that moment, rather than suppressing it, or distracting myself by moving into reaction, or doing. In staying with it I might notice other layers – perhaps an underlying anger or fear. Maybe it will feel familiar and I will feel the echo of some situation I have been in at some point in my life. I may reconnect with that earlier pain and the held charge of that, I will recognize how I dealt with it then and how I am holding on to that pattern right now, in my body, in my judgements, in what I am not allowing myself to feel.

Being present to my experience and fully allowing it is transformative. Becoming aware of how I am stopping myself from being fully here in the moment, how I am closing myself off is an essential part of the work. This means starting from how I am experiencing and reacting right now, and developing the ability to stay with things as they are, experiencing the energetic charge that has become attached to those particular forms, and how I am holding on to them – and through this developing a realization of how I create my way of being in the world.

This can be painful and difficult, because it also entails letting go of habitual defences, and my idea of myself, which I have spent a lifetime building up. That self-image, even if it includes a lot of negative judgements of myself or of others, or is full of pain, has been built up in a particular way for good reason. It represents the way in which I have survived in a world which was not giving me all that I needed, or which was experienced as life-threatening or dangerous. But this has often been achieved at the cost of a degree of withdrawal and contraction, of separation from my deeper sense of myself. Maybe I have learnt to think of myself as unlovable to protect myself from a mother who couldn't love me, or to be angry with myself rather than hate my father. Letting this go means re-experiencing the pain of those early deprivations, assaults or traumas as I reconnect with those split-off or hidden parts of myself. Then there is the existential pain of no longer knowing 'who I am', the pain of which has been described as a sort of death – the death of the ego.

But through this core awareness becomes available, allowing clarity, insight and love to arise. This encounter with the deepest sense of self can penetrate the underlying patterns of fear and suffering, and open up the possibility of things being different, of letting go of my attachment to this conditioned sense of 'who I am', and reconnecting with the underlying sense of well-being. As held patterns are released, so my experience of myself becomes integrated, freely moving and whole.

The therapeutic process involves a depth of present awareness and the trust that awareness is in itself transformative and integrative. This involves allowing ourselves to be present in our arising experience so that the various levels and expressions of ego begin to be experienced as a unitary and integrated process. My experience of self becomes more integrated, and there is greater congruency in my beliefs, thoughts, feelings and physical process. A deeper sense of truth can then naturally arise. From this I can move more freely and creatively in my life, and be in relationship with true open-heartedness.

Therapeutic goals

The task is defined by the client's present experience as it arises within the therapeutic encounter. Part of the work is to help the client deepen their awareness of their arising experience and to sense the potential for freedom within that experience. Most clients come because they are locked into ways of being in the world which are not giving them what they need, or involve denying some important part of themselves. The therapeutic goal is to facilitate awareness of how we create and hold on to these patterns so that a sense of new possibilities begins to emerge – to loosen the hold of the reactive mind and move towards greater creativity.

The aim of the work is to open to the present moment to allow this to happen. Just as meditation is a means of giving the mind more space by simply observing without judgement what the mind is doing, in Core Process work the aim is to give space to arising process within which the client can learn to be more present and notice how she is relating to her immediate experience. The work holds open the possibility of resting in the present moment and truly seeing things as they are. In this state of awareness, there is a natural arising of compassion and love, with the possibility of expressing greater spontaneity and joy.

There may be tasks that need to be completed before the client can let a pattern go and move into other ways of relating to her experience, but this is not a matter of rigid stages or developmental sequence, because all of a client's experience is encompassed in each moment. The client will take the work to whatever level there is the motivation for in that moment, so long as the therapist is open to those possibilities and can give space to the client for this.

While the aim may be to work towards letting go of aspects of ego-identity, the therapeutic task may also involve working with ego-process and ego-boundaries to enable the client to build up 'witness consciousness' and grow a stronger sense of a separate adult self. Clients may need to work with emotional or physical expression of repressed aspects of themselves and with their 'objects' so that they can get to know 'what is there' that they are holding on to but not allowing themselves to know or to feel. Different skills are used to help the client to access more layers of 'what is happening for me right now', but the purpose is always to facilitate the client's awareness in the moment. It is this that opens up the possibility of change.

Bringing awareness to how I am in the world is a step towards spiritual growth, and the work can lead to deep spiritual insight, but this is not set up as a specific aim. Psychotherapy aims only to release the client into a fuller sense of their aliveness in the world. It is life that is the spiritual journey, and psychotherapy is only a small part of this.

Unlike some transpersonal therapies, and some meditation practices, there is no investment in 'higher' realms of consciousness. Unlike some humanistic approaches, there is no investment in 'feeling good'. Even with awareness, process still arises (in fact awareness and process arise simultaneously) – the freedom comes from not becoming attached to it or identified with it. The aim is not to rise above or alter our human experience, but through fully allowing and being present to it, to feel it as a manifestation of a universal process through which we can feel a deep connection with the human condition beyond our own personal experience, and the inherent freedom of the core.

Practitioners

Relationships

It is through relationship that we learn who we are. The relationship between client and therapist lies at the heart of Core Process work, and creates the conditions within which healing can happen. It is a powerful resource which remains as an alive connection even when transferential material is present, difficult feelings are being experienced, or disturbed and damaged messages are being conveyed. The depth of contact creates the space within which clients can explore their inner process, and discover the conditions they place on themselves to keep things as they are.

The quality of presence – the quality of 'being there' in body, thoughts and feelings – is fundamental. The deepest work occurs if both client and therapist can be 'in the present moment' – not reacting to some part of the experience, but allowing the fullness of it to be felt. The work is a joint awareness practice where both client and therapist work with awareness of their inner process in the present and as it manifests in the therapeutic relationship.

The therapist has a very receptive position, open to being vulnerable and receiving at all levels. The intention is to remain open to the whole of what the client is communicating (and knowing when it is not possible to do this), with the therapist following her own process while staying focused on the client. This involves ways of listening, and a quality of attention that allows a special quality of relating to arise. It means listening from the fullness of my human condition to the fullness of another's. The therapist is there with her own personality, her bodily senses and reactions, not moving from these but making the fullest use of them in experiencing the client, sensing all the time which aspects of what is happening reflect her own resistance, and which are reflections or embodiments (felt in the body) of the client's arising experience, recognizing that sometimes it is not possible to 'know'.

The extent to which the therapist can be open to the client reflects the extent to which she is open to and able to tolerate her own experience. The more deeply she has explored her own process and found her own inner space, the more she can keep the space open for another person, let herself be vulnerable to their reality, and receive them with love.

This openness and presence makes possible a special way of listening, a quality of attention, which creates the ground and space for the work. It involves listening, being affected, and continuing to listen, trusting there is wise mind even in madness. If nothing else is getting in the way, the therapist can become so open to what is happening for the client that the duality of experience dissolves, and there is only the deep relatedness of compassion.

This way of relating creates the conditions within which the client can share their deepest experience of themselves – to bring into the light what has been held in the dark, to accept what was unacceptable, to be with what seemed unbearable, and to know that this is not all there is. The felt and known presence of the 'other' who is able to be with the client without judgement in their deepest experience of themselves is a profoundly healing experience out of which the client can discover a new way of being with their own experience of themselves.

Techniques

In Core Process work, the client is encouraged to bring a continuity of awareness to their arising experience. The therapist's role is to facilitate and encourage the client's own exploration of their process, and to interfere with this as little as possible. The task is not to 'make sense' of it but to discover what is stopping the client (or therapist) from following that process, from being present to their own experience. To the extent that process is moving freely, the person will move towards their truth and begin to sense how all aspects of their experience interrelate.

The therapist has to be prepared to meet the client without knowing what she will 'do', leaving the focus of the work to emerge from the client's immediate experience in the moment. The task is to follow the client, encouraging her to stay open to what is happening, and how it is happening. The key questions are: what is your experience right now? how is it for you? what is happening for you? what are you doing with that right now? It also means paying attention to what is not happening, to aspects of the client's experience that are being suppressed or denied: what is happening in my body? how does that feel? how am I judging myself? what am I choosing to pay attention to or to avoid?

Clients are helped to gain access to their inner process by focusing on whatever is arising for them, in whatever way this is manifesting for them in that moment. This might be through sensations, feelings, through cognitive and mental process, fantasy or imagination, or through the body. Different people tend towards particular 'modes' of experiencing themselves, and any of these can be a way into process, though as our sense of 'identity' is so bound up in how we think and feel about things, learning to access what is happening in the body or at the less fixed level of the 'felt sense' or subtle energy allows a greater sense of movement and possibility of change. The therapist will work with the client's most familiar mode of access, but this may be expanded to facilitate an exploration of less familiar modes, which can open up new layers of experience, and bring deeper awareness.

The focus is on what is happening in the here and now, but each arising moment carries also all of the past that still has energy locked up in it. In fact, the past can only be worked on as it is now – which is not exactly as it was then. For a start, there is an adult who can survive, even though it doesn't feel like it. The adult part may feel very small, or not present at all, in which case the task is to give it room to grow. This may mean that the therapist has to 'hold' the client's awareness for a while, 'hold' the knowledge that this is not all there is, while letting the client experience as much as she or he can tolerate right now, and discover how she or he can pull back, take it a step at a time, not be over-whelmed, until it becomes possible to face the original pain, and see it for what it is. It is the therapist's ability to bring the work into the present, to focus on how the past is being experienced in the moment, that allows a shift in the old patterns and opens the possibility of something new.

A wide range of techniques are used to deepen and hold the client into the work. Ways of working deriving from eastern meditation and body awareness practice are used to develop mindfulness, to focus attention and develop open-heartedness, to bring our attention to deeper levels of experience. One of the most important of these is following breath. This simple but powerful technique is a way of quietening the mind, and bringing awareness into the body, connecting with the level of the 'felt sense' (Chapter 7, this volume) and subtle body. The client learns to use this as a way of deepening the work or slowing it down if it feels overwhelming. Similarly, 'patient pausing' is a way of waiting with par-ticular sensations or feelings so that the full energetic charge of them can be felt and allowed to dissipate. (These ways of working are distilled from awareness practices but meditation itself has a different focus. A practice such as Vipassana meditation or Kum Nye can be a useful adjunct to the work, providing the form for exploring a deeper awareness of the core but it is not used in the therapy session itself.)

Skills deriving from western practice are also used – techniques deriving from Gestalt work to encourage awareness of inner dialogue and repressed aspects of the personality (subpersonalities), bioenergetic exercises or subtle bodywork to enhance awareness of holding patterns in the body, the use of *focusing* to deepen the client's attention. Cathartic work is useful in releasing old patterns of emotional holding, and interpretations may be offered as a way of framing the client's experience. The client may be encouraged to explore her or his inner pro-cess through active imagination or visualization, working with dream material or 'past life' consciousness, or using regression work to explore the held con-sciousness of experiences around conception, gestation and birth. The work will include discovering the distorting impact of unmet needs, and the conditioning effects of past experience manifesting in the relationship between client and therapist as transference and counter-transference. Many of the techniques and skills described in other chapters of this book are used as an integral part of the work. These are seen as ways of working with different layers and manifestations of personality process.

However, particular techniques are brought into the work only as a direct response to the client's process – evoked by the nature of what is arising in that moment, and the therapist's engagement with that process. Underlying the use of any of these ways of working is the fundamental attitude of reverence and respect for the client's process. Technique is far less important than the cultiva-tion and practice of openness to the client's experience.

It is this that provides the basis for two of the most important aspects of the therapeutic encounter: *resonance* and *reflection*. These are not techniques as such, but are an expression of the quality of therapeutic presence. Resonance is like an echo taking place in the therapist's experience as she works with the client. It is not the same as the client's experience, but a reverberation of it. The therapist's own depth of present experience enables her to resonate with the feelings, sensations, energies and other qualities manifesting in the client's work. The client's experience is deeply felt by the therapist but not taken on as her own.

Reflection is the way the therapist mirrors or offers back her experience of the client to aid a deeper exploration of process. It is not intended as a perfectly accurate reflection, but is offered with the therapist's own subjectivity accessible and knowable to the client.

Resonance and reflection involve an active process of connecting into the client's experience with awareness, taking in as much as possible of what the client is bringing, and offering it back in a way that the client can use, so the possibility of a different reality begins to emerge.

The work does not preclude the therapist being directive at times, so long as this is a deep response to the client's process and recognized as such by the client. The process may involve the therapist working against the client's patterns to exaggerate them, resisting the client's implicit demands in order to intensify them, or supporting the client so that they can let go of some of the need to 'hold on'. These are all offered as ways of allowing the client to move towards a greater awareness of what is 'in there' for them in that moment.

One important aspect of Core Process work is the way in which it incorporates ways of working directly with the body as a way of accessing process. Physical touch is used as a means of reflecting and mirroring what is happening energetically or physically in the body. This usually means using light touch or intentional holding (not always necessitating physical contact, but working with the energetic field) to enhance awareness of physical patterning (tension, blocking, holding), and allow physical process to unfold. The therapist may work against a particular pattern of holding to exaggerate the resistance and make it more strongly felt, or work with it to support the process and allow the body to 'hand over' some of the function of that holding, to soften and release the held pattern.

These modes of touch are exactly equivalent in intention and purpose to ways of working involving verbal or other interventions. Like these, they are evoked as a deeply intuitive response to the client's process, and used with full awareness of intention. Physical touch often carries a particular loading, and direct body work will not be appropriate for some clients, at least in early stages of the work, though working less directly with body awareness may still be possible. For others it will be the most important 'way in', and a major focus for the work. Release of held patterns as they manifest in muscular rigidities and energetic contraction in the body is an important element in the work of integrating and transforming deep underlying patterns, and accessing a deeper awareness of the Core.

Does it work?

Pitfalls

'Following process' is a very permissive and gentle way of working, but it is also extremely powerful, and can release enormous charge as it penetrates the client's resistances. One potential pitfall can be simply to underestimate the depth of the work. It is important that clients don't feel overwhelmed by opening up threatening territory or unravelling defensive structures too quickly. Defences are there for good reason. It is sometimes necessary to slow the work down, and work at the edge of the resistance in order to explore and discover the purpose it serves. Some clients encounter a deep existential and psychospiritual crisis as old certainties are abandoned.

For the client, it is important that the therapist does nothing to impede their work, but it is also essential that the therapist is 'visible', that there is someone 'there' to relate to. If the therapist gets too closely into the client's process too soon, the client may feel in some way quite abandoned. It is essential that the therapist meets the client where she or he is coming from, spending time in building up the relationship to provide a framework for the client's work. The therapist needs to learn the client's language, but must also find ways of communicating her or his reality to the client. The client may need to learn how to use the therapeutic encounter, and to trust that there is someone there for them. For clients with little or no experience of ever having been listened to or respected for their separate reality, or who have little awareness or ability to reflect on their experience, the basic task is still the same – to reflect and mirror their reality in terms they can understand, to offer a safe setting in which they can begin to experience themselves more deeply, and develop their own awareness.

The emphasis on following process, on staying with the client's experience rather than moving from technique, theory, or cognitive understanding is sometimes taken to mean the therapist has a passive role, or that there is something 'wrong' about using structured or 'doing' ways of working. In fact the work involves a very active role for the therapist, but the expectation of simply staying open to the client remains central even when more structured techniques are brought into the work in response to the client's process.

A potential pitfall of psychospiritual work is the tendency to retreat into a 'spiritual' space as a means of avoiding painful and difficult feelings. This is a pitfall also sometimes encountered by people who are exploring spiritual growth through meditation or other spiritual practices. In fact, for some the spiritual task may be to find a way of being more fully 'in the world'. This may mean at some point having to 'do the work' of psychotherapy, with the full experience of being human that this involves. It is a matter of letting the day to day become sacred by allowing its fullness to impact on me rather than seeking the sacred somewhere set apart from the world.

Case study

This is an account of some particularly powerful sessions in which deep insight arose. The client had previous experience of psychotherapy and was training to

become a psychotherapist. Considerable follow-up work was needed to consolidate and integrate the work. The client was born in 1947, the elder of two sons
in a working-class family. His schooling was basic but he went back into education
and graduated in Philosophy aged 30. He developed a successful business career
which ended in disillusionment. He suffered a serious psychological crisis which
took him into Zen training, Psychodynamic Therapy and humanistic growth
work. He began professional training at the Karuna Institute in 1990.

Revealing the mask

As I went through the doors into the institute our group leader appeared in
the corridor. I tried to catch her eye but she seemed to look past me as she
greeted a fellow trainee. Instantaneously I seethed with anger. I felt
unrecognized, a nobody. When she turned to greet me I smiled and said a
soft hello, hiding my anger. For the rest of that weekend I felt intensely confused and aggressive, until finally our group leader reflected her feeling that
I had been disconnected during the weekend.

Days later, experiencing violent, hateful thoughts towards the group
leader, filling me with guilt and despair, I went to my therapist determined
to rationalize these issues. Our session began with breathwork, opening to
a presence, which gave me a sense of peaceful relief from the angst. Then,
in a volcanic uprush, my rage broke out and I launched a savage attack on
those I thought responsible for my pain. My therapist remained silent, but
as I looked at her I froze with fear. Encouraging me to stay with my breath
she asked me what was happening right now. I began to weep. She put her
hand on my shoulder and the weeping intensified – I cannot recall having
wept so bitterly in all my life. My words seemed to rise from a place that
wasn't part of me. I felt like a small boy, and as I searched to understand
where all this was coming from, my therapist reflected 'You didn't let the
group leader know that you'd felt she had ignored you.' This resonated as
if I had unconsciously known it all along, and memories of my mother arose.

The breathwork had displaced my tendency to rationalize away from feelings and shifted awareness into my body, which led to a crucial insight.
Frightened that my feelings would lead to rejection, I had disconnected from
reality and engaged my mask. Coming to awareness of this unconscious
process as an experience, as opposed to theoretical understanding, was
deeply transformative. I felt the depth of the transferential material at work.
My traumatized child was calling.

The next session began with breathwork and further bodywork:

As my therapist touched my feet I froze. I panicked as my field of vision
narrowed and my breath became shallower. She encouraged me to stay with
my breath and not verbalize – something was trying to break out. My body
writhed, my tongue twisted, and I felt helpless and terrified. Then I looked
towards the wall and saw the side of a cot, and with this came a blissful
feeling of loving warmth and safety. Experiencing this depth of contact,
trust and safety opened up a new space for me in which there was an

instantaneous shift from terror to bliss. From this experience the insights flooded in. I saw that I had lived my life in defensive reactions to real human contact which was as intolerable for me as it was for my parents. My response was to split off from real contact and my feelings, project the intolerable parts, then defend myself from them with aggression and power play. I had abandoned my heart because the love I needed so much was terrifying. This left me feeling abandoned, unrecognized, depressed and psychologically unwell.

Emerging from isolation into relationship with my therapist was fearful and dangerous for me. It was the quality of her skilled presence holding me in a safe place which enabled me to go beyond reactive defences and re-experience deep traumas. Healing work flowed from this, providing new space from which to view my process as one of change, and break free of the rigid patterns in which my life had been stuck. Breathwork and subtle bodywork accessed unconscious material which gave rise to transformation and a renewed sense of being. Opening to the Core, the unconditioned heart in relationship with my therapist has been one of the most powerful experiences of my life.

Research

Whilst no objective research has been done on the outcomes of Core Process Psychotherapy as such, there is a considerable and growing body of research on the physical, perceptual and emotional effects of the meditative practices such as those used in Core Process work. Some of these studies are summarized in Goleman (1988). West (1990) is a more detailed account of recent research. Material is also available on the psychotherapeutic tools used in humanistic therapies, which also form part of the Core Process approach. These studies show positive patterns of response in the reduction of anxiety and other unhealthy mind states, and an increase in positive psychological states.

However, the question comes out of a western 'scientific' paradigm, which looks to independent or 'objective' evidence that can only be at one remove from the reality it purports to measure. Core Process Psychotherapy also recognizes and values the science of inner observation which is the profound basis for Buddhist psychology. In the end, whether or not Core Process Psychotherapy 'works' rests with the subjective value which is the client's living experience of well-being.

Acknowledgement

I would like to give grateful acknowledgement to Franklyn and Maura Sills and to Tom Greaves for their help in preparing this chapter.

Comment on the literature

Other than Donington (1989) there is nothing published specifically on Core Process Psychotherapy. However, a number of excellent books are directly relevant to the work.

Welwood (1983) is a collection of essays by therapists and meditation teachers on the relationship between spiritual practice and therapy, and the nature of psychotherapeutic process.

Claxton (1986) consists of essays by psychologists and psychotherapists on the relationship between spiritual traditions and western psychology, and the application of these ideas in psychotherapy and in everyday life.

Walsh and Vaughan (1980) is another collection which includes some more specific discussion about the nature of conscious mind in meditation and psychology.

Bugenthal (1978) gives a lively and readable account of Process Psychotherapy.

Goldstein (1976) is a good introduction to meditation.

Trungpa (1973, 1975) are more substantial accounts of Buddhist psychology.

References

Bugenthal, J. (1978) *Psychotherapy and Process: The Fundamentals of an Existential-Humanistic Approach*. New York: Random House.

Cashdan, S. (1988) *Object Relations Therapy*. London: Norton.

Claxton, G. (ed.) (1986) *Beyond Therapy: The Impact of Eastern Religions on Psychological Theory and Practice*. London: Wisdom.

Donington, L. (1989) What is Core Process Psychotherapy? *Self & Society*, 17(8).

Goldstein, J. (1976) *The Experience of Insight*. Boston, MA: Shambala.

Goleman, D. (1988) *The Meditative Mind*. Los Angeles, CA: Tarcher.

Klein, J. (1987) *Our Need for Others and its Roots in Infancy*. London: Tavistock Publications.

O'Sullivan, G. (1990) Behaviour Therapy. In W. Dryden (ed.) *Individual Therapy: A Handbook*. Milton Keynes: Open University Press.

Spinelli, E. (1989) *The Interpreted World: An Introduction to Phenomenological Psychology*. London: Sage.

Trungpa, C. (1973) *Cutting Through Spiritual Materialism*. Boston, MA: Shambala.

Trungpa, C. (1975) *Glimpses of Abhidharma* Boston, MA: Shambala.

van Deurzen-Smith, E. (1990) Existential Therapy. In W. Dryden (ed.) *Individual Therapy: A Handbook*. Milton Keynes: Open University Press.

Walsh, R. and Vaughan, F. (eds) (1980) *Beyond Ego: Transpersonal Dimensions in Psychotherapy*. Los Angeles, CA: Tarcher.

Welwood, J. (ed.) (1983) *Awakening The Heart: East/West Approaches to Psychotherapy and the Healing Relationship*. Boston, MA: Shambala.

West, M. (1990) *The Psychology of Meditation*. Milton Keynes: Open University Press.

5

Psychosynthesis

DOUGLAS MATHERS

Definition and historical development

Definition

Psychosynthesis focuses on the development of human potential. Classical and contemporary ideas from eastern and western psychology merge; the place of spiritual values in human life is emphasized; intuition, inspiration and creative insight are valued. The theoretical model, supported by a coherent system of practical techniques, benefits people who seek life's meaning and purpose, enhancing relationships and creativity. Individuals are encouraged to see themselves within a social matrix. Psychosynthesis is not just about counselling. It has applications in many areas: education, business management (e.g. team building), creative arts and sport (e.g. The Inner Game approach to tennis and skiing resemble psychosynthesis).

Founder and historical development

Psychosynthesis originated with the Italian psychiatrist and psychoanalyst Roberto Assagioli (1888–1974). Born in Venice to an upper middle-class Jewish family he studied classics and languages before taking up medicine at Florence University in 1906. His mother, a theosophist, encouraged his lifelong interest in mysticism. He was also a keen mountaineer. He learnt psychiatry at the Burghölzli in Zurich with Bleuler and Jung and was a member of their psychoanalytic study group. Freud expected him to bear the torch for psychoanalysis in Italy. However, Assagioli felt there were limitations to Freud's model, and developed his own. His critique of psychoanalysis was the subject of his MD thesis in 1910 which outlined the principles of psychosynthesis for the first time.

During the First World War he worked as a doctor. Afterwards, he started an institute for psychotherapy in Rome. Libertarian political views led to imprisonment by Mussolini, followed by flight and hiding in the countryside. When peace came after World War II he resumed practice. His ideas were fed by contacts with many thinkers, including Keyserling, Frankl and Desoille – the originator of the Guided Daydream. The first Institute of Psychosynthesis opened in Florence in 1961.

Assagioli visited Britain regularly from the early 1920s. Colleagues in Great Britain started two centres in London, now the Psychosynthesis and Education Trust and the Institute of Psychosynthesis. Thriving training centres exist in over 50 countries, including the USA, Canada, France, Holland and Switzerland. New schools are beginning too, for instance, in Sweden, Germany and Austria.

Relationship to other therapies

Assagioli (1965) intended to extend psychoanalysis, working with the unconscious through the past to explore inner conflict, towards synthesis in the psyche: to reconstruct the analysed parts into a whole personality. He didn't aim to displace either psychiatry or psychoanalysis, rather, to complement them. He knew the value of thoroughly understanding the past and acknowledged the importance of transference, though he preferred not to work with it overtly. Psychosynthesis' goal is to allow the development of a personality capable of continually under-standing more of itself, in harmony with its environment. This personality is not a perfect individual, but one able to work towards self-knowledge, with less need of neurotic defences: goals similar to the Individuation process, as described by Jung. At the basis is a spiritual perspective, which Assagioli felt missing in psychoanalysis. This belief, still held by psychosynthesis practitioners, may have been truer when Freud and Jung were alive, in conflict, and Assagioli was in Jung's camp. For, as in all fields of human inquiry, younger practitioners tend to amplify differences with the 'parent' as a way of marking out territory for themselves.

Psychosynthesis presently aligns with the Human Potential Movement (Drury 1989), part of the 'new age'; indeed, it is included as a new religious movement in Professor Barker's (1989) guide to those groups, along with other growth therapies. This may be at the expense of its medical and analytic origins, and makes acceptance by conventional practitioners difficult. This is unfortunate as, in practice, psychosynthesis has more in common with cognitive and behavioural therapies than is often supposed.

There is a concentration on active, practical and pragmatic strategies. A down to earth problem solving approach is encouraged, whilst holding a spiritual perspective – a 'bifocal vision'. Methods are freely borrowed from Gestalt Therapy, Transactional Analysis, Psychodrama and also from the Human Potential Movement. 'Being with' the unconscious and sharing pain in develop-ing transference and counter-transference are less well understood within psychosynthesis.

In his pamphlet on Jung, Assagioli (1967) says that, for him, the word 'unconscious' is an adjective. Perhaps this is a fundamental point of difference between psychosynthesis and psychoanalysis, for to analysts and analytical psychologists the unconscious is a noun. Presently in the UK there are few links with medical practitioners, but many to 'alternatives'; psychosynthesists may be trained or interested in, say, astrology (Chapter 14), aromatherapy

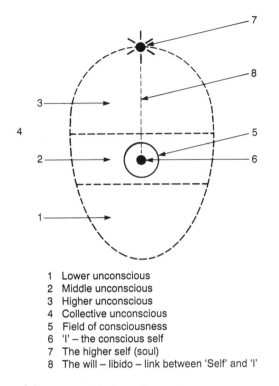

1 Lower unconscious
2 Middle unconscious
3 Higher unconscious
4 Collective unconscious
5 Field of consciousness
6 'I' – the conscious self
7 The higher self (soul)
8 The will – libido – link between 'Self' and 'I'

Figure 5.1 A map of the person: The 'egg diagram'

or acupuncture and tend to be unhappy with orthodox psychiatric views of emotional distress.

Central concepts

Assagioli summarized his theory in what is affectionately known as the 'Egg Diagram' (Figure 5.1). It is important to remember a map is not the same as the territory, and any theory is not 'the truth', though it may contain some truth. The diagram resembles Freud's early topographical models of the psyche with conscious, preconscious and unconscious. There are similarities to Jung's ideas concerning personal and collective unconscious. In the diagram, the lines are dotted to indicate exchange between the different areas. As one grows, greater exchange between conscious and unconscious occurs, and the 'field of consciousness' becomes relatively larger.

Assagioli divided the unconscious into four parts: lower, middle and higher and the collective unconscious. The terms 'lower' and 'higher' have connotations ('higher' could imply 'better') – but the model is not intended to convey moral judgements.

The lower unconscious (1) resembles Freud's id: a realm of instinctual drives, out of which may arise compulsions and other neuroses. It can be seen as referring

to childhood, to 'unfinished business', our psychological past. The middle unconscious (2) is akin to Freud's preconscious, a store of recent, easily recalled
experiences, our psychological present. The higher unconscious (3) is the source
of insight, of altruistic impulses, of creativity. Abstract qualities such as truth, love
and power belong here, spiritual experiences may originate here. It represents an
individual's potential, our psychological future. Pathological distortions in
actualizing this potential may take psychotic forms, such as omnipotent delusions.

The collective unconscious (4) contains common human experience, evolved
through the ages, such as myths, fairy tales and symbols recurring in related
forms through the centuries and across cultures.

The field of consciousness (5) describes what we are aware of at a particular
instant – right now, the words on this page are (hopefully!) in your field of
consciousness. At the centre of the field of consciousness is the 'I' (6). From this
position in the middle unconscious the individual observes the rest of the
personality.

The higher self (7), which mystics might call the divine essence, can be thought
of as existing both within and outside time. It is drawn half in and half out of the
psyche to emphasize its continuity with the spiritual world. The Will (8), the link
between the Self and the I, resembles Jung's concept of the libido. It is a central
psychic function linking spirit and matter. Development of the Will increases
the ability to make choices.

An important difference between psychosynthesis and other psychotherapies
is the former's emphasis on the Will's crucial function for the personality. It is
the way things are carried out. For example, in buying a car, a skilful Will
researches the best buy, whereas an impulsive Will leads to an impulsive, and
probably regretted, buy. Assagioli described a detailed procedure for developing
Will, outlined below in the section on technique.

View of personality

Assagioli believed a personality contained six basic functions: thought, intuition,
impulse, sensation, feeling and imagination (see Figure 5.2). Here he differs
from Jung, who described only four. The functions are expressed through the
modes of body, feelings and mind. Individuals tend to have an identification with
the physical, emotional or mental mode, according to which is most developed.
For example, readers may be mentally identified, having developed minds
through academic work. Others who are creative, such as artists, tend to identify
with their feelings: athletes identify with their bodies. Each group's experience of
the world tends to be different because of their preference for a different perceptual function. Psychosynthesis aims to develop the less used functions within an
individual; creating a harmonized personality, giving us more choices about the
way we act.

Subpersonalities

In addition to the six functions, Assagioli described the psyche as containing
'subpersonalities'. These are like the sociological concept of role, or transactional

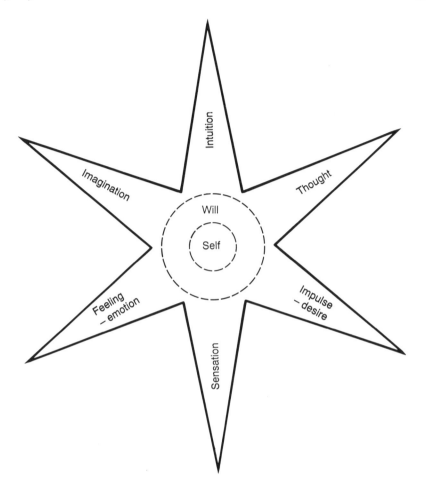

Figure 5.2 A map of the functions of the personality: The 'star diagram'

analysis's idea of parts in ourselves (parent, adult, child). They often occur as polar opposites: mystic and pragmatist, critic and frightened child. Assagioli considered them to be small personalities contained inside a larger one, each with its own physical, emotional and mental life. The idea is very similar to Redfearn (1985) and Rowan (1991), though they arose independently.

Examples of three subpersonalities coexisting in one person might be strict parent, sober professional and wild adolescent. It is easy to see the latter two could conflict, having different needs and world views. To solve their conflict they need to recognize each other and see they are not the whole person. Psychosynthesis believes we are controlled by our unconscious identifications, so when identified with the adolescent, the individual has no choice but to act as it dictates.

We begin to have control when we can see this as if from without; that is, when we can disidentify. When disidentified from a pair of conflicting subpersonalities something can be done about the conflict, such as agreeing to 'time share' resources. Resolution may be a long process, indeed sometimes it may be impossible. But a start can be made, a truce declared. Here, the individual might move from identification with the adolescent to the position of the 'I', which can arbitrate and make choices.

Unlike Freud's notion of the ego, beset by the id and the superego, the 'I' is capable of coordinating and regulating conflicting parts and their needs. Its capacity to organize is related to its connection to the Self, by means of the Will. It is not a subpersonality itself and is not driven by their demands.

The cause of suffering

Assagioli gave the purpose of psychosynthesis as harmonization and integration into one functioning whole of all the qualities and functions of an individual, of mind, body and feelings – self-realization. Suffering arises when the connection between the 'I' and the Self is imperfect; if the 'I' cannot organize the personality then the 'eggshell' is too weak and the individual is flooded – possessed, obsessed, overwhelmed. Over-identification with particular conscious attitudes leads to forgetting or repressing the rest of the personality. We can be trapped by oppressive psychological patterns beyond our control called chronic life patterns.

These correspond to the Jungian idea of a *complex* and are usually located in particular subpersonalities, or traceable to particular early relationships. If the Will is not developed adequately enough to express the Self within the limits of a given personality, neurotic conflicts predominate. If the distinction between the Self and the 'I' breaks down, and the 'I' is flooded with transpersonal material, psychotic problems occur.

Moreover, each quality is capable of distortion. Love can be distorted into possessiveness, power into the wish to dominate, truth into fanaticism. Assagioli believed these distortions also occur in the collective psyche, and he had reason to know the effect of this on himself during both the First World War and his imprisonment by Mussolini.

The change process

Distress in everyday life with its attendant pain brings people to work on themselves. Any change process must start with enough self-knowledge, insight, in the client to recognize things need to change. Some psychosynthesists call themselves 'guides' rather than therapists, emphasizing the positive, exploratory nature of their work, which is not primarily concerned with pathology. They aim to help the client develop already inherent abilities to journey in their own inner world with ease and confidence.

Change starts with an initial phase of opening a relationship to the inner world of feelings, memories, and images. This can be done by inviting the client to write an autobiography: reconnecting to the past, to things forgotten, either because they are too painful to experience, or because family and society do not value them.

This analytic work comes first, enabling discovery of parts with competing and contradictory aims; subpersonalities. A next step might be the development of detachment, called 'disidentification'. By this, we allow ourselves to discover our true centre, or I. There can be an experience of inner freedom, a perception of how we really are – of what we may be. Thus patterns causing problems are discovered, described and then there is an attempt at disidentification. To go further requires mobilization of the Will.

The middle phase of therapy emphasizes strengthening the sense of I. The guide models this by a non-judgemental, accepting and compassionate attitude. The guide may suggest to the client 'just being'. This is not a meditation as such, but simply being still and observing what is happening, without immediately judging or getting into an internal dialogue – usually an internal argument. At this point mobilization of the Will can be encouraged. The Will, as connection between I and Self, gives access to the transpersonal.

The transpersonal

Literally, this means 'beyond the personal'. To those with no spiritual orientation, this can be taken as maintaining profound respect for the uniqueness of an Other. Buddhists might say 'seeing the Buddha nature'; Christians, seeing that of God in every human. At a personal level, this awareness – think of it as a sense of proportion, myself in relation to humankind – can help us identify the next step to take in our lives. The concept is similar to Maslow's idea of self-actualization; the transpersonal is the driving force towards self-actualizing, towards individuation.

Awareness of purpose fluctuates, loss of this awareness is like depression: existential despair. In the absence of conscious awareness of our Will, there is frequently identification with a victim subpersonality. We become people to whom things are done, rather than autonomous agents.

Assagioli described the Will as having four aspects: strength, goodwill, skilful and transpersonal will. The first is powerful, the second, compassionate, the third, mediates and the fourth gives spiritual insight within which the others operate. Each aspect has particular qualities: energy, concentration, determination, persistence, initiative and organization. A conscious act of Will involves discovering the emerging purpose, deliberating, affirming, planning and executing.

For example, in writing this, the purpose is sharing knowledge; the intention is a clear account of psychosynthesis – other motivations include money (not a lot!) and the pleasure of seeing my name printed; deliberation meant reviewing knowledge, did I know enough to write this? Affirmation is committing to finish by a given date, planning is the rough drafting and execution is sitting at the word processor – and doing it!

The final stage of the change process is of course never reached – the potential of any individual is limitless. However, work with a guide is finite. Work usually takes at least a year, sometimes three, rarely longer. Psychosynthesis can be used for time limited goal directed therapy. Examples might be helping a student deal with exam related anxiety, or enabling a battered wife to decide not to return to an abusing husband. Whatever the original goal, the guide will regularly review the work, encouraging the client to assess progress. The client usually decides exactly when to end.

The end of the work is reached when we feel our presenting issue has been adequately addressed, when we stop seeing ourselves as someone in need. Ending always needs careful working through, and there are inevitably incomplete issues. There is a natural progression here: imagine going over the painful ground first with a bulldozer to clear a path, then with a spade to get ready to plant seeds. It may or may not be necessary for the guide to stick around until the seeds grow, or for the ground to be gone over again with a comb.

If ending is being discussed the guide will not open up new areas, but will look at how the work done might apply to as yet untouched areas in the client's life. They may have solved a problem about career, but relationships are still a mess. The guide is careful to avoid premature endings. If the client has got a sense of their future direction, is integrating back into society and showing the beginning of capacity for intuitive vision, with the return of a sense of wonder, then ending is likely to go well.

The whole process is designed to leave the client feeling part of the larger whole, connected again to the transpersonal. This is often ignored by other psychological approaches, but psychosynthesis believes this has a vitalizing effect on the rest of the personality. The capacity to be open to transpersonal experiences, to moments of joy and wonder is seen as essential for maintaining well-being.

Though transpersonal experiences are positive in themselves they can be a source of problems if a person is not well enough prepared or mature enough to handle them. There is also a pathology of the sublime.

The desire for autonomy, to become an individual, to affirm one's self in the world has to be complementary to the tendency to harmonize, to be part of the larger whole, to interrelate with others. There has to be a good balance between individuative and integrative needs.

Therapeutic goals

Increasing awareness of the psyche's content and activity, both personal and transpersonal, provides a client with the chance to take more responsibility for their own growth. With awareness comes the ability to be responsible for the neurotic parts too; the goal is a more harmonized psyche, and increased inner freedom – a lifetime's work! However the techniques once internalized can continue to be used long after therapy finishes.

Practitioners

Relationship

As in any other method of counselling or psychotherapy the relationship between the guide and client is an essential part of the change process. This can be illustrated using the concepts outlined above.

The guide first of all ensures a safe and containing setting is provided, with, like the 'egg', clear and well defined boundaries. In much of the initial phase of work, the guide is modelling the 'I' through being warm, empathic and understanding, accepting the client in a positive and non-judgemental way. The guide could be thought of as holding the Self of the client, facilitating expression of the parts they can't yet see. They may have the task of advocacy on behalf of a repressed subpersonality, they will almost certainly have to review continually the client's emerging history and use this to revise their initial plan for the work.

Psychosynthesis, in keeping with its place in the Human Potential Movement, assumes both client and guide to be on an equal footing. The guide has more theoretical knowledge and experience of inner psychological landscapes than the client. Guides provide a framework within which a problem can be understood. This means building trust, giving a base for new coping strategies to be learnt. Sessions are usually weekly, sometimes fortnightly, rarely more frequently. The client provides the will, motivation and direction of the process.

Difficulties originating in the past emerge in the transference between client and guide. This may not be worked with explicitly. Often, projective techniques will be used to make the past experience 'live' in the session, giving the client the opportunity to take responsibility for dealing with how that affects their relationship to the guide.

Assagioli preferred to work around transference, rather than in it, so it does not take the central place it has in psychoanalysis. However, psychosynthesis clearly describes similar defensive strategies to analysis: denial, splitting, projection. These appear both in relation to recalling historical events, and in the emergence of the transpersonal. For example, some clients rationalize away spiritual experiences, split them off and attribute them to the charismatic gifts of the guide, or to the therapeutic model itself. Guides, through their own therapy, become aware of how they use these mechanisms, and become alert to them in their clients.

Techniques

Methods described here may be familiar to cognitive, behavioural and Gestalt therapists. The use of an autobiography has already been mentioned; usually clients are encouraged to keep a psychological workbook in which they can record the events of their psychological journey. This encourages learning to recognize and value inner experiences.

Many active techniques can be used, though sometimes few will be; in certain cases they are contra-indicated. For example, those recovering from a psychotic episode do not necessarily benefit from guided imagery as it can recall and rekindle the original psychotic experience. Different techniques can be used at different stages in the process. For simplicity, these are described in three groups, corresponding roughly to the order in which they might be used.

Projective techniques aid recall of deeply buried, unconscious, historical material using mental imagery. These indirect, symbolic processes need detailed interpretation and grounding. *Integrative techniques*, which help in assimilation of unconscious material include some drawn from Gestalt Therapy.

Behavioural techniques may be used to help the client practically apply what has been learnt.

Projective exercises access the Unconscious. They can be simple, as in asking the client to do free drawing or creative writing, or complex, as in active imagination and guided imagery. For example, an inner dialogue (a particular form of imagery) consists in suggesting the client talk to a helpful inner partner about a problem. The guide asks the client to relax, close their eyes and breathe deeply. They suggest visualizing a being who knows and loves the client – perhaps a guardian angel, or a wise old being. Perhaps a longer, slower visualization, or a series of graded exercises will be used. Typically, this might take the form of a journey – a walk through a meadow or a climb up a mountain. As in any projective method, the images can themselves become objects for analysis; both content and form can provide valuable clues to unconscious patterns.

Images tend to take on a life of their own. They may be invited to interact, to make their own synthesis. They can be interpreted as in dream interpretation, by asking for associations, by amplification, by completion. Interestingly, these techniques can help those who are unaware of their dreams to become so; this can be valuable in working with depression. The use of dream diaries is encouraged.

Symbols can be evoked directly; if a particular quality is emerging, say power, the guide may invite the client to allow an image to appear – a sword, a power station. These images can be analysed, their historical origin understood, and their higher potential explored. Symbols are believed to originate in the Unconscious. They carry archetypal qualities. Notice this is not the same as Jung's idea of Archetypes; in psychosynthesis Archetype means a spiritual quality, in this case power, freed from the normal value judgements. Power can be used for good as well as evil; the sword to cut through as well as kill, the power station to warm as well as pollute.

The second, integrative group, often involve Gestalt exercises. The guide might choose to give direct feedback about body language. If the client is irritated, but not recognizing it, the guide might say, 'I see you tap your foot, I wonder if your foot has something to say?' – The guide may have the idea that the foot wants to express anger at this point. Or, the guide knows the client can't talk to an abusing parent. A second chair may be used, and the client asked to imagine the parent on the chair. They then say what they need to say to the parent, imagined on the chair. If they can, they may be invited to sit in the chair, become the parent and reply.

This can be repeated over several sessions, allowing the completion of unfinished business, of incomplete Gestalts. Psychosynthesis also uses a 'third chair'; an observing part of the client – the nearest they can imagine to their higher Self – may be invited to comment on what is going on in the other two chairs, and suggest which archetypal quality is trying to emerge. It may be distorted love, as in those sexually abused, or distorted beauty, as in the child who is so idealized they can never be themselves. This kind of work helps clarify the origin of chronic life patterns. After their recognition, a disidentification exercise might be followed by an identification with the Self exercise.

For example, if there is conflict between an adolescent and a professional subpersonality, disidentification would consist of describing one part, then saying, 'and I am not just this'. A Gestalt technique of sitting one part in a chair and having a dialogue with it, or getting one part to draw the other, or imagining one part taking the other on a difficult journey might be used in addition. Then a 'third chair' could provide a place to review what needs to happen next, to let both subpersonalities co-exist.

Techniques for exploring life purposes, such as imagining a journey to find a treasure, although exploring the Unconscious are also integrative. The adolescent may need a quest, the professional may need reminding of the deeper meaning in how they first chose their profession. Meditation is another bridging technique. A reflective meditation involves thinking deeply about a problem, trying to find as many meanings to it as possible. A receptive meditation involves allowing a symbol to emerge for the problem, rather than using cognitive processes.

Behavioural techniques include evoking and developing desired qualities, perhaps suggesting practical exercises to develop the Will. The stages of an act of Will have been outlined above. This can be very similar to Behaviour Therapy, with its careful assessment of the 'when, where, and how often' of a problem, and construction of pragmatic strategies to deal with it. How it may be sabotaged is usually examined too!

Strengthening Will might involve specific exercises done as homework between sessions – someone who disliked their body might develop a plan to get themselves to go swimming. The key point is not ending up in the pool but learning they can have control over something previously seen as inevitable, in this case, being unfit.

Important as understanding all of these methods is to the practising guide, it is even more important to have a sense of when to use them and when to be patient. In learning to guide clients towards the creative use of pain, crisis and failure, Assagioli stressed repeatedly the importance of reality testing – not as a way of pushing people more into their pain, but to help move towards a transpersonal view of acceptance. Simply, the crisis is showing us a truth not only about ourselves but about humanity, and our part in it.

Psychosynthesis seeks to develop capacities for clear and direct communication, empathic skill and emotional sensitivity in its practitioners. It is this overlapping of pragmatically dealing with crises and at the same time recognizing their spiritual significance which is its hallmark.

In the end, psychosynthesis is not so much about techniques as about letting nature take its course. Perhaps this is true of its place in the field of psychology too. It is not so much another school with a unique vision, more a place in which integration between different schools might be attempted.

Does it work?

Pitfalls

Psychosynthesis sees itself as a distinctive form of psychotherapy, as well as a philosophical theory of wide application. The lack of a clear boundary between therapy and a theory of personal growth can have several problems for therapists.

A wish to be distinct may have prevented recognition of the many overlaps with cognitive, behavioural and other psychotherapies, including family therapy. Valuable opportunities for sharing skills have been missed. There is distrust of psychoanalysis and analytic concepts, especially transference and counter-transference, though this is changing. The wish to see the good can lead to a failure to recognize the bad and the ugly.

Psychosynthesis is not especially oriented towards working with psychopathology, and has more to say to the healthy, or 'healthily neurotic', yet it has difficulties in working out who such people are. Therapists can get into difficulties when they do not recognize pathology, take on clients who are too disturbed and then wonder why the client leaves, or gets worse – and they feel a failure. Poor understanding of transference and counter-transference can mean that the therapist finds it hard to accept the validity of their own malign feelings toward the client. Guides often have difficulty with hate in the counter-transference, and there can be problems with boundary keeping. Supervision is undervalued. Burn-out is commoner than it needs to be.

Like psychoanalysis, splitting amongst and within the training organizations is common, in both cases due more to personality clashes and career ambition than real theoretical differences. However, this tends to be denied.

For the client, a goal directed approach can be experienced as persecutory. The real impulse in the guide to do good can lead to over-activity, piling in with more and more techniques when sitting still, doing nothing and just being for a few months would achieve far more. This is exemplified in not addressing transference issues directly, but shunting them off into imagery or chair work. Guides can collude unconsciously with the client's wish to deny their neurosis; after all it sounds better to have a spiritual crisis than to be just another neurotic. Most guides will not attempt to work with those who are psychotic, but they have problems recognizing borderline personalities. This is a pity, for the ego strengthening techniques, especially work with the Will, can be valuable for such people if therapy takes place under careful supervision.

Perhaps all of these pitfalls stem from one thing: Assagioli's use of the word 'unconscious' as an adjective. This would matter less if there were not a tendency for the word to be used as a disparaging adjective, as in 'I went unconscious', when one has done something stupid. It may be comforting to see a psychotic breakdown as a 'transpersonal experience', though it may not be compassionate. Emphasizing personal growth and human potential is like building a beautiful house. Unless the foundations are solid, it will simply fall down again afterwards. Assagioli was first a doctor, then an analyst and finally evolved psychosynthesis. Perhaps this breadth of skills, or at least an awareness of the validity of these skills would help the whole psychosynthetic project to be better grounded.

Research

There has been little or no use of 'objective' scientific research within this tradition; there are no short or long term outcome studies, no comparative work relating it to other therapies, no systematic analysis of process. Sometimes research is seen as 'old age' nineteenth-century scientific materialism, best left behind. However, in Italy, the home of psychosynthesis, much thoughtful case reporting and discussion of theoretical issues is published in the journal *Psyche*. This work bears comparison with analytic journals, and shows that Assagioli's vision has been considerably advanced.

Case study

Ben is a 24 year old Canadian student who completed a BA there 18 months before starting his PhD. He came because he was 'stuck' – unable to write. This began three months earlier, and had reached a stage at which he felt his physical health was affected. He had lots of vague aches and pains, could not sleep well and was beginning to lose weight. He had stopped working out. He feared he was going crazy.

Ben wore a ripped vest over track suit bottoms, his black shoulder length hair needed washing and he smelt of nicotine. His girlfriend was threatening to leave him. He feared he was gay: 'I've lost whoever it is I was', he said. I noticed he tended to apologize continuously, as if expecting me to be critical of everything about him. He'd start describing how he felt, then run out of words and cry with frustration. His eagerness to please reminded me of an unhappy seven year old rather than a graduate.

The initial stage of working together allowed Ben to feel safe enough to keep coming, and to talk about his inner world. Diagnostically, he was depressed and experiencing an identity crisis – in psychosynthesis terms, a crisis of meaning and purpose. His primary identification is with his body: in dress, exercise and tendency to somatize. I was puzzled about why he wanted a PhD, especially when he spoke of his love of the outdoors – when visualizing his 'ideal self' five years hence, he gave a glowing picture of being a lumberjack, his vacation job.

His grandfather emigrated to Canada from Armenia after the Turkish holocaust. His father was a successful drama teacher, grandiose, polygamous and very academically ambitious for his son. His mother was Scots Canadian, a dreamy and detached soul who drank too much. We could have focused on his relationship to his parents at this point, assuming he was doing the degree to get his father's approval. Ben recognized that a scholarship to study in the UK had done just that, and now he was sabotaging himself.

His homosexual fantasies may have been based in a wish to rebel against his father's adulterous abandonment of his mother, or to escape his girlfriend, who wanted to get married and have children. Allowing his history to emerge and allowing Ben space to reflect on it is part of 'trusting the process', the most fundamental part of the psychosynthetic attitude. Again, it would have been easy at this point to suggest a Gestalt based piece of 'chair work': getting Ben to dialogue with the angry adolescent part of himself, the part that studied long hours when he wanted to be outdoors, but there seemed to be more.

He talked as though he were an only child, yet in the first interview he had mentioned 'being a big brother'. In a later session I said, 'As an only child, maybe . . .' and he interrupted, 'Oh no, I had a little sister but she died when she was four of cancer . . . when I was seven', then he broke down and wept. He had come to see me two weeks after his sister would have had her twenty-first birthday.

Ben felt terribly guilty about her death. After it both his parents became unavailable. His mother needed medication for depression; his father needed his first extramarital affair. We used guided imagery to 'talk to' his sister. This very movingly allowed him to start a process of mourning which had been frozen inside since childhood.

He cried a great deal as he recognized much of his life had been spent trying to repair his family. He had taken on both his father's wish for him to excel and be macho and his mother's wish for him to replace his sister. Ben took six months off and took a job labouring.

In this period he decided to start living with his girlfriend. He used me as an 'idealized parent' at first, who was willing to listen. Idealization gave way to anger when I did not tell him what to do, especially about his thesis, and his depression lifted. He joined an environmental group who valued his research skills, which motivated him to complete his thesis. He found a worthwhile channel for his anger working with them to 'save the planet'.

Further reading

Roberto Assagioli's (1965) book *Psychosynthesis* is a pioneering theoretical text and is regarded as difficult to read because of Assagioli's somewhat terse style. It is a book to be read very slowly, to allow time for the ideas to unpack.

Molly Brown's (1983) book is a well written and illustrated guidebook, with clear examples of the commoner psychosynthetic exercises. Perhaps a bit too 'West Coast' for Europeans.

Piero Ferrucci (1990) is the leading Italian practitioner of psychosynthesis. His book goes more deeply into the developmental potential of psychosynthesis and is strongly recommended.

Jean Hardy's (1987) book is a scholarly tracing of the origins of the ideas found in psychosynthesis, which shows how it attempts to bridge the split in the Western mind between spirit and matter.

Diana Whitmore's (1991) book is an excellent, clear and practical manual, using case examples to illustrate the whole process from initial interview to ending, and showing appropriate application of the techniques. As useful for potential clients as for practising counsellors, probably the best book to start with.

References

Assagioli, R. (1965) *Psychosynthesis*. London: Turnstone Press.
Assagioli, R. (1967) *Jung and Psychosynthesis*. New York: Psychosynthesis Research Foundation.

Barker, E. (1989) *New Religious Movements: A Practical Introduction.* London: HMSO.

Brown, M. (1983) *The Unfolding Self – Psychosynthesis and Counselling.* Los Angeles, CA: Psychosynthesis Press.

Drury, N. (1989) *The Elements of Human Potential.* London: Element Books.

Ferrucci, P. (1990) *What We May Be.* London: Aquarian Press.

Hardy, J. (1987) *A Psychology with a Soul: Psychosynthesis in Evolutionary Context.* London: Routledge and Kegan Paul.

Redfearn, J. (1985) *My Self, My Many Selves.* London: Library of Analytical Psychology.

Rowan, J. (1991) *Subpersonalities.* London: Routledge.

Whitmore, D. (1991) *Psychosynthesis Counselling in Action.* London: Sage Publications.

6

The Headless Way

RICHARD LANG

Definition and historical development

Definition

The Headless Way is a contemporary, science-inspired model of humanity's place in the universe and a demythologized, transcultural 'way' of liberation. It demonstrates that all things, including ourselves, consist of layers of appearances surrounding a 'central reality' – a mandala or onion-like structure. It claims that this 'central reality' (which has no limitations) has generally been repressed from awareness, but is accessible to direct observation in oneself, and offers a series of 'experiments' or awareness exercises for seeing who you really are. This seeing is at the same time an ongoing meditation or therapy that can be practised anywhere (Lang 1994).

Historical development

The Headless Way has its immediate roots in the work of Douglas Harding, an English philosopher born at the beginning of the twentieth century. Harding's work is rooted in the western scientific tradition. Modern science, conceived in the Renaissance by people like Galileo, was a reaction against the speculative logic of the medieval schoolmen and their reliance on 'revealed truth'. Science turned instead to the evidence of the senses in its search for truth. Harding extended this same method by turning it around on himself. Pursuing the question 'who am I?' he looked at himself to *experience* who he was at centre rather than trying to work it out by *thinking*.

Within this western tradition Harding's work is fertilized by many different sources. Amongst these are A.N. Whitehead (1926), in particular his concept of 'the fallacy of simple location', and William James (1961). A drawing by Ernst Mach, the German philosopher, helped trigger Harding's actual seeing of 'who he really was', whilst the work of the German philosopher Fechner inspired his vision of the living earth. More generally Harding's work embraces the ideas of

Darwin, Einstein, Freud and Jung, weaving them together into a new model of our place in the universe.

Seeing who you are also connects with a much wider and older tradition of enquiry and awareness – that of the mystics of every culture. In their own ways saints and seers have looked into the centre of themselves and found who they really are. Within the Christian tradition the great medieval theologian Meister Eckhart spoke about his identity with God, as did Catherine of Genoa, St John of the Cross, Ruysbroeck and many others, not the least of which was Christ himself. Following the Buddha, the great Zen masters of China and Japan saw into their own true nature, the void which was their original face. Lao Tzu and Chuang Tzu, the fathers of Taoism, sing the praises of the wordless source. In Hinduism the Upanishads, Ramana Maharshi, Anandamayi Ma, Nisargadatta Maharaj and others speak of the Self within all beings, whilst in Islam there is Rumi, the great Persian poet and seer, Kabir and many others. The western poets Traherne, Blake, Emily Dickinson and Rilke write in their own ways about their true identity. Seeing who you are embraces this ancient tradition, continuing and developing it in a contemporary transcultural form.

Founders in Britain

Douglas Harding was born in Suffolk in 1909 into a strict fundamentalist Christian sect, but left the sect at 21 to find out about life for himself (as well as to become an architect). Curiosity and an ambition to write philosophy led him in the 1930s to formulating an onion-like model of the self – many layers surrounding a central but mysterious reality. The question which became uppermost in his mind was: What is at the centre of all the layers? or Who am I really? His 'realization' of the nature of his own centre occurred in India during the Second World War, inspiring his book *The Hierarchy of Heaven and Earth*, a major work of western philosophy prefaced by C.S. Lewis and first published in 1952.

Subsequently Harding wrote more books (including *On Having No Head*) and in the 1960s and 70s developed awareness exercises or 'experiments' for 'seeing who you really are'. Audio and video tapes have followed, a tool kit, a three-dimensional 'youniverse model', a magazine, and an annual 'gathering' that is internationally attended. At the age of 85 Harding continues to lead workshops all over the world. He has influenced thousands of people, and there are now many who are using the experiments and developing their own style of work.

Relationship to other therapies

The Headless Way grows out of Douglas Harding's enquiry into the nature of his own identity. The techniques used have been developed to guide people in this same direction; they have evolved as ways of testing the 'hypothesis' that at centre you are not who you appear to be to others. This approach links theoretically with the 'new physics' of Fritjof Capra (1975) and David Bohm (1980).

In turn this connects with the Buddhist system of philosophy and practice which evolves from seeing that underneath all our ideas, feelings and actions there is no 'self' – nothing solid and lasting. However, the Headless Way's claim that our true identity is available now, and for everyone, differs from approaches that see 'enlightenment' as only for the few, and probably not in this lifetime.

The perspective of the Headless Way links with many ideas popular today. This includes Jung's idea of the collective layers of the mind and the need to integrate the Self into our daily lives; the idea in Systems Theory that we cannot look at our lives in isolation from our environment; the unity of mind and body that Reich explored; the sense of wholeness that some 'new age' philosophy expounds (Louise Hay (1991) for example); the awareness in Transactional Analysis of unconscious game-playing (Harding identified the Face Game as the basic game).

Practical links have already been made with Dance Therapy (see Chapter 11, this volume) and t'ai chi – the sense of stillness at the heart of movement; voice therapy (see Chapter 12) – awareness of the silent source of sound; creative art therapy (see Chapter 10) – creating from 'nothing'; meditation (see Chapter 4) – letting go of identity, and many more. In general, the Headless Way differs from therapies that see the Self as a fixed thing (to be manipulated) rather than a process. And it specifically acknowledges in the midst of our lives the presence of unbounded and whole awareness.

Central concepts

The cause of suffering

At the root of all our suffering is our identification with our human self to the exclusion of our real Self. This process of identification is, however, part of growing up. In our first months we were all wide open to the world and our true nature. But we gradually named and divided up our original wholeness, taking parts of it and calling them 'me', and naming the rest 'not-me' (though the boundary between these is always changing).

It is not that this identification is 'wrong'. In a way it is necessary and creative. But the overlooking of our true identity is a hole right at the heart of our lives. Deep down we know something is wrong. Life isn't quite right – and at the end is death. Where is the meaning in it all?

I believe Jung said that after we reach middle age our main need is spiritual meaning. We have found out who we are as individuals and it isn't enough. We begin to look for something bigger, deeper. We may not know this. We may drink or take drugs to fill that frightening emptiness inside. We may work obsessively to convince others, and therefore ourselves, that we exist and are valuable. But this behaviour only betrays our insecurity. The loss of our true nature drives us in many ways.

Who am I?

How we live is interwoven with and based on how we see ourselves. Headlessness re-evaluates our identity in a modern light.

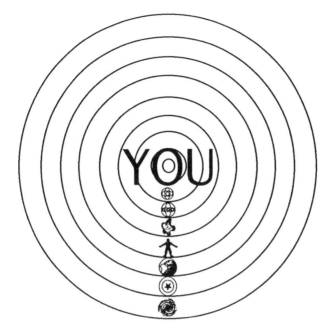

Figure 6.1   The onion-like structure of self (body and mind)

What and who we are depends on distance

Our appearance depends on the range of the observer. From a few feet we look human, but closer to we are cells, molecules, atoms, electrons, particles and so on, down to practically nothing. Further away our human appearance is absorbed by the landscape, the planet, the universe.

The onion-like structure of self (body and mind)

The overall structure of these appearances is an onion-like system of layers surrounding an undetectable centre. These layers are hierarchically organized with the status of each layer dependent on its distance from the centre. (These layers of appearance are actually what others perceive us to be – they exist out there in the observer's perception and are reflected back to us.) Knowledge about these layers is gained through scientific investigation. Biology for example focuses on the close cellular layer, archaeology on the historical beginnings of the human layer, astronomy on the anatomy and behaviour of planetary, stellar and galactic layers. In fact the various layers of appearance or body (cellular, individual, collective, planetary, universal, etc.) correspond to the various levels of mind. We identify with being individual human beings, but not all the time. Sometimes we think, feel and act for our family, country, religion or race and even identify with the whole planet. At other times we seem to shrink to the pain of a toothache. In expansive moods we embrace everything

Figure 6.2 The headless body

in our sympathies, and at the opposite extreme we just want to stop the world and get off.

The headless body and the centre

What and who are we at *the centre* of all these layers? Since you alone are at your centre, you are the only one with authority to describe it. What do you see of yourself at zero distance? I will speak for myself. Looking down I find my own body and legs, arms and torso, but no head! Above my shoulders I see two blurs I call my nose, and there are tickles, aches and warmths, but nothing else. Only empty, boundless, aware 'space'. Looking out from this empty space I find it occupied: with my headless body, this page, other people, houses, clouds, the stars beyond, and with my thoughts and feelings about these things. My world, from the distant galaxies to a blur I call my nose, has at centre nobody at all. Not even a 'mind'. I am uncontained and at large.

First person and third person identity

These terms signify two different but complementary aspects of identity: who/what we are for others, at a distance, which is *third person identity*, and who/what we are for ourselves, at zero distance, which is *first person identity*. The difference between these two aspects is total (consequently they fit together

perfectly, like a hand in a glove). Third person is peripheral, a regional manifestation, whereas first person is central, the source of that manifestation. Third
person is human, complete with a head like other people, whereas first person is
headless, the spiritual core of our humanity. Third person is just one thing in the
world, separate from other things, whereas first person is 'space' for the world,
or no-thing full of everything. Third person is mortal, first person unborn and
undying.

Face to no-face, the first person view of relationship

For others I am face to face with people and separate from them. This is the view
of me as third person. As first person however I am face to 'no-face' with people.
If I am looking at you I have your face in my field of vision and not my own – and
you have mine. I am you – I am 'capacity' for you. This is called trading (or
exchanging) faces. It takes time for this insight to sink in and affect our lives –
interpersonally, internationally, environmentally – but whenever we see into our
'facelessness' we deepen it.

Three stages of individual development

1 As babies we are faceless. We have not yet understood nor even seen what and
  who we are in appearance – the small baby that others see. Our mind/body is
  at large. We are the undefined centre of everything – without knowing any
  other way of being.
2 As adults we overlook our original faceless condition, shifting focus almost fully
  to our third person identity. We identify with our face, body, feelings, mind,
  name, family, country and everything else we associate with ourselves. In effect
  we repress first personhood. Most adults reach and, up till now, remain in this
  stage.
3 The seer is the potential third stage. Here we are conscious of both our projected self-image in the world and the centre of being from which that image
  arises. This is conscious third and first personhood combined – the acceptance
  and living of a paradox. Having a head for others I am someone in the world.
  Headless for myself I am 'space' for the world.

Three stages in the evolution of humanity

Humanity's evolution as a species corresponds broadly to the stages of individual
development. The first preself-conscious stage of early humanity corresponds
with the faceless infant. We identified with the tribe, with nature. We did not see
ourselves as particularly separate from 'others' and the world. Consciousness was
shared with every river, tree, mountain, animal, star. It was a living universe.
In the second stage of self-consciousness we think of ourselves as a species distinct
and separate from other species. We are separate sparks of consciousness in a
largely dead universe. Such a view is at the root of the wars and exploitation which
now threaten life on this planet. This stage corresponds with the second phase of
individual development. Perhaps we are now moving from this stage into the

next. This new consciousness has been heralded in the past by the great spiritual teachers of humanity – men and women who have awoken to who they really are. In a sense they were early mutations in consciousness, making the leap from iden- tifying with only one level – the human one – to identification with the centre – which embraces all levels (including the human). Consciousness, no longer imagined as confined inside the human layer, inside our heads and brains, is realized as belonging to the whole universe. There are strong indications that increasing numbers of people on the planet are now embracing this third stage.

The change process

Therapeutic goals

The aim of seeing who you really are is steady awareness of the first person point of view. However this 'goal' has a double-sided nature. On the one hand, though it is the centre of all one's identities, all the layers of body and mind, when it is reached it turns out to be no goal at all. In itself the centre, or who you really are, has no substance. There is nothing to it, nothing to aim for.

On the other hand there is a journey involved, away from the centre and then back again. This is a process of growth, an experience of change and transforma- tion. We can look now in more detail at this process of forgetting who we are, rediscovering it, and then integrating it into our everyday lives.

Becoming a person

Conception and life in the womb is an individual world in the making, but even after birth, during the first few weeks and months, for ourselves we are undefined. We are no-thing and everything, a centreless edgeless awareness 'around which' all revolves. Faceless and at large we are 'space' for the world. Growing up is the journey into becoming something, becoming a person: peripheral, mortal, alone. We move away from our original state of oneness into separateness.

Acknowledging the repressed true self

In our adult life we have learned to repress our no-thingness, our true nature – the 'original face we had before our parents were born' as Zen puts it. Perhaps unconsciously we feel threatened by it. On first seeing into their no-thingness people sometimes talk about feeling invisible, of disappearing. It can feel strange and even frightening. The embrace of this shadow, this repressed 'split off' part of ourselves, is the concern of seeing. It is an expansion of the area of attention to include our original Self, and the integrating of this into our individual understanding of things. As the prodigal son found on his return to the father's house, home, the place we have never really left, is seen with fresh eyes after the journey away from it.

Integrating the true self

This transformation in consciousness is 'achieved' simply by attention to one's absence or first personhood. It is not an additional 'thing' brought into awareness, a perception of something new or even old, but a letting go of all ideas of who one is. It is growth by ungrowth, a surrender to formlessness, a death into no-thingness which is simultaneously a rebirth into all. The integration of this 'awareness' into one's life is a day by day, year by year, unending process. At first people often feel as though this seeing comes in flashes. Gradually, however, it becomes steadier, sometimes in the foreground of consciousness, other times in the background. This process of stabilization may be what D.T. Suzuki (1970), writing about Zen, meant by 'the long maturing of the sacred womb'. The bird flying home to God has a long and demanding journey. Yet the paradox is, by simply looking at God the bird is home now, for the face it beholds is its own.

What are some of the specific changes we might expect *en route* to the place we never left, to who we really are?

Specific changes

People who become aware of their headlessness sometimes describe a veil being removed from between them and the world. They are 'out of the way' and the world is revealed in all its physical beauty. The body too is rediscovered. Body sensations, now felt in the bodyless space of awareness, are released from their imaginary prison. There is a feeling of expansion, a communing with people, creatures and things as if you are clothed in them. Sounds are clearer, colours look brighter, tunnel vision is replaced by a more panoramic awareness. There is a new sense of space and clarity. One woman exclaimed in a workshop that she 'felt like a lighthouse'. Herrigel (1960), writing about the experience of satori in Zen, spoke of the world being bathed in the light of the void. The world seen from the void is a different world from the one seen only from the perspective of the limited self. It is experienced at no distance, as oneself. It is real, not imagined.

With this goes a new sense of peace and freedom of mind, a letting go of identification with all the feelings, images, and thoughts that flow through one's being. Underneath the changing emotional weather a steadiness is perceived. Mind feels big, an aspect of the world as much as of oneself. It is as if the gate to the source were lifted completely off its hinges to reveal the mind – or no-mind – behind the universe wide open and thinking and acting through one. There is a sense of endless creativity within, a feeling of abundant inner wealth. Alongside this people gradually discover a sense of inner confidence that rests not on human achievements but on the presence of who one really is. What could inspire greater trust and sense of worth in the long run than realizing one's true identity to be the source? As the Buddha said, 'I alone am the Honoured One above and below the heavens'. He was talking about his true identity, not his human one.

Letting go of growth

Such change and transformation is not, however, always experienced, or experienced to the same degree in everyone. Sometimes it all seems to vanish and we are left empty-handed. But nothing has really gone wrong when this happens. Such loss of 'results' is part of the process of transformation too, and makes room for new growth. What is really unlosable, ever-available and reliable, is the awareness which always underlies particular experiences, remaining after they have come and gone. It can be trusted to give and take at just the right moment.

Practitioners

Role relationship

On one level the workshop facilitator is a guide. He or she is familiar with the techniques or 'experiments' and uses them in a workshop to guide people's attention to who they really are. At the same time the facilitator teaches, presenting a new perspective involving new ideas. Often headlessness stimulates many questions which need addressing.

One of the best ways to address these questions is through the experiments. In other words, to refer back to the person's own experience. The facilitator evokes awareness and understanding by encouraging each person's unique response rather than feeding in answers.

In addition the leader models headlessness for people. This does not mean following any kind of preconceived pattern of behaviour. It simply means practising headlessness oneself. This is absolutely essential for the facilitator, whatever other role he or she is playing at any point. Such modelling is 'infectious', a transaction with others. When the facilitator is consciously faceless it encourages others to be faceless too.

Occasionally someone in a workshop feels frightened by headlessness. The tendency here is for that person to lose sight of who they are and to identify with the feelings and images about it. The facilitator's role is to remain present with that person and, depending on the time available, to give space for feelings to be expressed. At the same time it is vital for facilitators not to lose sight of being headless themselves. This offers the 'client' a bridge back to their own still centre and the awareness that their own being is bigger than these particular feelings.

In fact headlessness is the awareness that one is in no role whatsoever for oneself. Only in relationship with others does one take on roles – and then drop them. This awareness helps facilitators, and indeed anyone, respond with a minimum of defensiveness to the roles in which others put them.

Underneath these changing roles the essence of the relationship is one of equality, for headlessness celebrates that 'place' where we are identical. From this point of view 'giver' and 'receiver' are the same, sharing experience and learning from one another.

Figure 6.3 'Pointing Here'

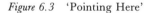

Techniques

The key practical methods used in a workshop are the 'experiments'. These are a series of awareness exercises which focus attention on first person identity, making clear the difference between this and third person identity.

In principle people need only do one experiment to see who they are, and often people say that they 'got the point' from the very first one. However experiencing a number of them opens up different perspectives. It helps clarify and deepen understanding and can be profoundly moving.

There are a few dozen experiments, about a dozen of which are better known than others. These can be divided up depending on how many people are needed. Those that can be done on one's own include 'Pointing Here', 'The Card', 'Spinning' and 'The Single Eye'. Those needing two people include 'The Paper Bag', 'Face to No-Face', 'The Clear Pool', 'Onion-peeling' and 'Creating from Nothing'. (In the first two a mirror can replace the other person.) For larger groups of people there are 'The No-Head Circle', 'The Unclassifiable', 'The Machine', 'The Storehouse', 'Tree of Life', 'Losing Shape and Gaining Shape' and others. 'The Closed-Eye' experiment is done with any number.

'Pointing Here' can be done on one's own. It involves looking first at things you can see, then at you, the looker! The aim is to see yourself as you are for yourself, as first person. The best way to understand is to do it. Point your finger at something in front of you. (Pointing is to help focus attention, especially in the final part of the experiment.) Say you point at a chair, then notice its colour, size, opacity, distance. Point at your shoe. Notice its shape, texture, condition. Moving closer, point at your torso. Observe how you look from this angle and distance. Finally, point to where others see your face, the place you are looking

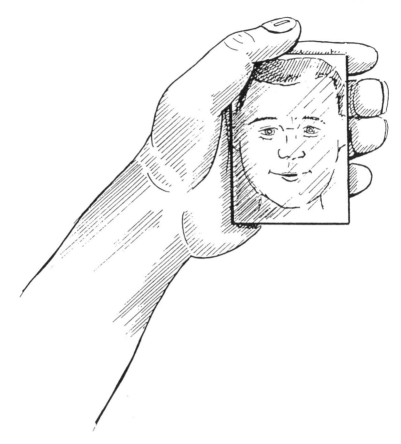

Figure 6.4 'The Mirror' experiment

out of, and observe what you *actually see* – not what you *expect to see*. Any colour or shape here, at no distance? Any eyes, cheeks, or mouth? Any face? If you are doing this alongside someone else, look at the difference between them pointing (at a head) and you pointing (at no-head). This is the difference between third person and first person.

'What about the mirror? I can see my face there.' This question inevitably arises. It is explored in 'The Card' experiment and more simply by looking in a mirror and seeing *where* your face is. Is it above your shoulders or in the mirror? For that face there to be here you would have to imagine moving it from there to here, turning it round and making it bigger! Bring your mirror towards you and see how your face blurs, disappearing on contact. Your face belongs out there, in the mirror and where others are in receipt of it, not here. This experiment illustrates that you are not the same at centre as who/what you appear to be at a distance.

Relationship and identity with others is explored in the 'Face to No-Face' experiment. This involves two people. Sit opposite someone and notice whether you are face there to face here, or face there to *no-face* here. Isn't the set-up asymmetrical, face to 'space', thing to no-thing? This experiment can last from a few minutes to 10 minutes and more. Sometimes people feel self-conscious to begin with, and perhaps a little tense, but if they stay aware of being space or 'capacity' for the other person (and their own feelings) then they tend to go through these feelings to a much calmer state of mind. At the same time, being out of the way themselves, they become much more aware of the other person. It is not uncommon for people to describe the other person's face and self as their own. They might speak of 'being the other person' and of feeling in direct and deep communion with them. This face to no-face perspective can be attended to in any person to person situation.

With larger groups other issues can be explored. The 'Unclassifiable' experiment looks at the process of becoming identified with our appearances and putting ourselves into different groups of people. It involves placing coloured stickers on everyone's foreheads without them knowing the colour, and then asking everyone to go to the appropriate colour-coded corner. How can you know which corner to go to? (You are not allowed to speak, touch or take off your sticker, or look in a mirror.)

The 'No-Head Circle' explores the paradox of being one with others and at the same time being separate from them. Five to 10 people stand round in a circle and look down. Each person can see how their body disappears above their chest into the space of awareness, their true nature. Now, in the circle you can see how everyone else's body also disappears off the field of vision into the same space. Looking down we are all different and separate, but up 'here' at the top of the circle we merge in one awareness. (See Fig. 6.5).

The 'Closed Eye' experiment explores what and who we are without vision. With eyes closed you are asked questions and guided through different areas of experience. For example, going by present evidence alone, how big are you? Where are your boundaries, and what shape are you? How old are you? – not using memory. Listen to a distant sound, a closer sound, and the nearest one. What is closer than this? Silence? Pay attention to thoughts and feelings. Are they any more inside you than sounds? Do they arise out of and disappear back into a 'mind'? Or is there no container? Are they not at large, flowing through the boundless space of awareness? What and who are you without your body, mind, name, family, job, opinions and so on? Verbal answers are not requested during this process. You simply attend to your experience. Afterwards of course there would be plenty of time to talk about your experience and hear what others have found.

Any of these experiments can be developed in many directions, and they can be combined with other techniques. The 'Spinning' experiment is about finding the stillness at the heart of movement, and this dovetails perfectly with Creative Movement and Dance Therapy, as well as t'ai chi. Voice Therapy can be linked with awareness of silence (from which our voices emerge); Art Therapy with 'Creating From Nothing'; Interpersonal Relationship Therapy with 'Face to No-face'; the 'Closed-Eye' experiment with meditation; the 'Storehouse' with creativity in general. They are starting points that lead in to one's true nature, and out into the many different aspects of our lives.

Figure 6.5 The 'No-Head Circle'

Does it work?

Pitfalls

Here are some pitfalls that people come across when seeing who they are.

Seeing is too obvious

Seeing who you are is rooted in seeing the obvious, in seeing one's own facelessness. The difficulty here is that for some people it is too obvious. People glimpse their facelessness but dismiss it as if it is a trick, an optical illusion. I remember one man at the end of a workshop saying that it was too simple for him.

He wanted something more complex, more 'psychological', more cathartic – which can happen with headlessness of course. But the essence is not complex. As Lao Tzu wrote, 'The Sage all the time sees and hears no more than an infant sees and hears.'

Thinking instead of seeing

Even after years of practising seeing people can find that they are *thinking* about who they are rather than *seeing* it, and there is a world of difference between the two. Instead of simply seeing the absence of anything here, a subtle idea of being 'empty', being the Self, being 'headless', creeps into awareness. This is as much a misidentification as thinking I am anything else. In identifying the Self with any qualities at all I misrepresent it and separate myself from the world, even when these are qualities like openness and space (as Lao Tzu says, the 'way' that can be spoken is not the true 'way'). This is like the schizoid defence of the false self. The void is clear like glass, but the idea of being like glass can be misused to form an imaginary barrier cutting us off from others. The remedy to this is to pay attention again rather than trying to think yourself out of it. Experience that there isn't even the thought of your true identity here.

Some years ago a friend of mine introduced me to a Korean Zen master whose teaching was to be aware of and trust 'not knowing', or 'don't know'. My friend told the teacher that I knew about 'don't know'. The teacher's reply was, 'Don't say you know "don't know". I don't know "don't know"!'

Distinguishing seeing from feelings

Often it happens that when people see who they are they feel more open. There can be quite dramatic changes in people's lives. At some point however this changes and to some extent old feelings and behaviour rear their heads again. Sometimes it can seem that things get worse rather than better. The danger here is for people to think they have lost 'it', that they are not seeing who they are any more, or that they are doing it wrong. As a result they may give up on seeing and search for something else that promises good feelings. The truth is that the seeing itself is unchanged. It is the space in which feelings come and go, and is not the same as or dependent on feeling good. It is just as accessible in depression as in elation.

Case study

I am a woman in my 40s, a graduate, married with a son aged 11, and I have had a successful career as a singer and actress before starting to train as a psychotherapist a year ago.

I came across the Headless Perspective about four years ago when I was looking for a new sense of direction in my life. I was increasingly unhappy and frustrated with my performing work, and generally looking for a deeper purpose and sense of self-worth (which I had had a taste of when I was part of a self-help group of mothers in South London). I moved from London to Hertfordshire with my family, and started going to classes in t'ai chi and meditation given by Richard Lang at the local holistic health centre. Richard was using the Headless approach in the meditation group.

First of all I was struck by the simplicity and directness of the approach. Basically it consists of exploring some of the consequences of realizing that we normally see the world and ourselves as separate, and the exercises are in a sense ways of surprising ourselves into awareness, often with laughter. In this way they work like Zen koans or Sufi stories: one is asked merely to experience what it is like, say, to sit face to face with someone, and notice that it is the other person's face we have in our awareness. At times I found myself struggling with scepticism about the idea of being headless, but more often something in me was prepared to take the imaginative leap. I liked the fact that whatever I felt or understood was my own experience, no one was telling me what to think or interpreting what was happening to me. The exercises took place in an atmosphere of curiosity, amusement, acceptance, sometimes awe. They began to bring me more and more to realize my feelings and thoughts as they came and went in the moment, in the same way that sitting meditation does when one is focused solely on one's inner world.

One of the unique features of this approach is that I can use it in any situation, to remind me of who I really am. For example if I am in conflict with someone, can I be headless with her? In other words, can I accept that at this moment her face and her being fills my awareness, and is my reality for now? What this does is help me to disengage from identifying with the difficult emotions and see what they are, as temporary and reflecting back to me an aspect of myself. So it gives a useful, practical sense of perspective on day to day problems. Reminding myself that I am headless has also brought me great joy when contemplating the beauty of nature, and a sense of still centredness and letting go when surrounded by turmoil.

Headlessness can be compared to other therapies used in a group setting like psychodrama or psychosynthesis, but for me it has the added value of an investigative approach to reality: a spiritual perspective without any religious agenda. It introduced me to a way of seeing which has led to my training in transpersonal psychotherapy.

References

Bohm, D. (1980) *Wholeness and the Implicate Order*. London: Routledge & Kegan Paul.
Capra, F. (1975) *Tao of Physics*. London: Wildwood House.
Hay, L. (1991) *The Power is Within You*. London: Eden Grove Editions.
Herrigel, E. (1960) *The Method of Zen*. London: Routledge & Kegan Paul.
James, W. (1961) *The Varieties of Religious Experience*. London: Collier Macmillan.
Lang, R. (1994) *Seeing Who You Really Are*. London: Head Exchange Press.
Suzuki, D. (1970) *Essays in Zen Buddhism, First Series*. London: Rider & Co.
Whitehead, A.N. (1926) *Science and the Modern World*. New York: Macmillan.

A list of books by Douglas Harding

(1974) *The Science of the 1st Person*. Nacton, Ipswich: Shollond Publications. How the science of the first person extends and completes ordinary science, the science of the third person.

(1979) *The Hierarchy of Heaven and Earth: A New Diagram of Man in the Universe*. Gainesville, FL: University of Florida. This book is for those wishing to go deeply into the philosophical side of the Headless Way.

(1986) *On Having No Head: Zen and the Rediscovery of the Obvious*. London: Arkana. This book is a good introduction to the Headless Way. Includes an exploration of its connection to Zen Buddhism.

(1988) *The Little Book of Life and Death*. London: Arkana. Looking at death in the light of the Headless Way.

(1990) *Head Off Stress: Beyond the Bottom Line*. London: Arkana. How being headless relieves you of stress.

(1992) *The Trial of the Man who said he was God*. London: Arkana. This book dramatizes Harding's original techniques for seeing who we are and gauges our myriad ideas about our relationship with the Divine.

7

Focusing

PETER AFFORD

Definition and historical development

Definition

Focusing is a process of creative change arising from an inner awareness that is centred in the body. It is a particular manner of self-reflective experiencing. With a small 'f', focusing refers to a natural human function of searching inside for a bodily sense about something. With a capital 'F', Focusing is a method or technique that helps to develop this function.

The holistic bodily sensing of focusing happens inside and outside of therapy. It is part of becoming fully human; central to art, to scientific invention, to spiritual experience, and to many areas of life as well as to therapy. An appreciation of it helps the therapist to listen more deeply into the client's experience, to respond more empathically and facilitate a spontaneous healing process; and it helps the individual to relate more creatively to their inner life and inner resources.

Historical development

Focusing arises out of research into psychotherapy conducted at the University of Chicago in the 1950s and 60s, when a large number of therapy sessions of different types were taped and studied. From this research Carl Rogers developed many of his ideas on the person centred approach to therapy, looking especially at the qualities and attitudes of good counsellors.

A colleague of Rogers, Eugene Gendlin (1981), looked at the other side of the therapeutic equation – the clients. He noticed differences in behaviour and awareness between those clients who benefited from therapy and those who did not – irrespective of the type of therapy or the experience of the therapist. Put simply, if clients were able to refer and attend to their actual, bodily-felt, experiencing of the life situations they brought to their therapy hour, the therapy was successful, whereas if they were unable to do this, it was not successful.

To his surprise, Gendlin found that clients who lacked this experiential skill at the outset never learnt it – even after years of therapy. Those who did start with it, however, tended to get better at it as the therapy progressed. Furthermore, more clients came to therapy without this skill than with it, roughly twice as many.

Spurred on by the obvious implication that time and money were being wasted in therapy, Gendlin looked very closely at the process of bodily-felt experiencing evident in the tapes of 'successful' sessions. He termed the skill of inner attentiveness 'focusing' because it involves an awareness of a 'something' that at first is unclear to both client and therapist, but that step by step comes into focus, bringing new meanings, feelings and insights, along with a release of tension in the body.

Gendlin started teaching 'focusing' to his own clients, and later to a wider audience through workshops. Focusing skills are pertinent to many areas of the development of the person and of creativity. In particular, they have come to be widely taught as a self-help system, a way to explore one's creative depths and resolve difficulties without the help of a professional therapist.

There is now a loosely-knit Focusing community around the world. It is strongest in the USA, Canada and Germany, but is also found elsewhere, including Britain. It is diverse and quite unstructured. There are therapists who have incorporated Focusing into their work, trainers who teach it in various contexts of self-help and human development, and many people who practise it in their lives, sometimes on their own, often in partnership with other 'focusers', and sometimes in small peer groups.

Founders

The founder of Focusing, Eugene Gendlin, is a professor of psychology at the University of Chicago. He is a philosopher and practising therapist as well as a psychologist, a gifted and humble man who possesses an unusually flexible and fluid mind. In particular, he has applied insights gained from the existential phenomenology of modern philosophy to observations of the experiential process of therapy.

Today, Focusing is a collaborative enterprise involving many people around the world. In Britain a network is growing up to link those who use it and work with it. People who have been closely involved with Focusing in Britain are: David Garlovsky, who was a student of Gendlin's in Chicago; Brenda Rogers, who runs a Focusing programme at the University of Kent; Robert Foxcroft, who teaches in Glasgow; Barbara McGavin, the editor of the network's newsletter who works in Bath; Wendy Webber, who teaches at the Beacon Centre in Devon and at the Karuna Institute; and myself, running workshops in London and now working as a focusing-oriented therapist.

Relationship to other therapies

In the psychotherapy arena, Focusing is most related to the 'person centred' approach. It is a particular aspect of this work, namely, the attentiveness clients give to their inner experiencing. Some person centred therapists have combined Focusing into their skills; Gendlin calls this style 'experiential therapy'. Focusing has been most fully incorporated into person centred therapy in Germany, more so than in the USA.

My own training has shown me that Focusing fits well with psychosynthesis, Gestalt and biodynamic work, and enhances these approaches. Some pioneering methods that emphasize mindfulness and being body centred have made particular efforts to incorporate Gendlin's insights. These include Franklyn and Maura Sills's Core Process Psychotherapy (Chapter 4, this volume) at the Karuna Institute, and the Hakomi method of Ron Kurtz. Focusing is compatible with most therapies including psychoanalysis. Its inward, bodily-felt manner of experiencing is something that is likely to help all clients.

In the area of self-help, Focusing can be practised in a partnership arrangement. Two people take it in turns to be the focuser and the listener. There is equality and reciprocity, and no money changes hands. The focuser learns to guide their own process and journey rather than rely on the listener for guidance and direction. This enables friends to support each other safely and effectively.

Focusing has also been described as a western form of yoga, a daily discipline of cultivating one's inner life, similar to meditation. This practice embraces the banal realities of life, the unwelcome feelings with which everybody contends, and the richness of the creative and spiritual depths and heights that everyone is capable of experiencing. The method has also been applied to other avenues of human development: teaching, creative writing, working with terminally ill patients and decision making in business are just some examples.

Central concepts

Focusing is a mode of awareness that is entirely compatible with whatever psychological or spiritual philosophy of life the person who uses it subscribes to – including the absence of one! What distinguishes Focusing is an appreciation of how we experience our living in a bodily way.

The central concept here is the 'felt sense' or 'body sense'. We can use our bodies as 'sense organs', referring our attention inwards to our felt sense of the matter at hand. This is a holistic and inner sensing, unlike our five outer senses.

Our language leads us to talk of felt senses as 'feelings', yet they are different from the usual sorts of 'feelings'. The felt sense is less intense than an emotion like rage or grief. Nor is it as familiar as a feeling that can be named easily, like 'happy' or 'sad' or 'disappointed'. It is less obvious than a 'gut' feeling like anxiety or sexual attraction. And it is not a mere physical sensation, like a stomach ache or shoulder tension.

All these feelings are experienced in the body. So is the felt sense, particularly in the chest and stomach area, yet this is vaguer, more diffuse, just an odd sort of puzzling sense about something. It is easy to ignore, and it may seem unpromising, yet it leads to valuable therapeutic and creative avenues. Often it is felt underneath or behind or around the edge of the more familiar feelings. Many therapists encourage their clients to 'be in touch with their feelings', yet miss this useful species of feeling – out of which, ironically, the strong emotions they believe need to be expressed will often arise naturally.

With felt senses we are apt to say things like 'something about this doesn't feel quite right . . .', or 'I've got a funny feeling about this'. There is an unclarity, a sense of something 'more' that draws our attention and asks to be explored until it comes into focus. We cannot tell 'it' what it is, but we can listen to it, and allow it to tell us.

It can help someone who is focusing to find the physically felt quality that accompanies a felt sense. It may be an odd sort of discomfort like a 'heaviness' or a 'tightness' or a 'jumpiness', or it may be a pleasant 'warm and fuzzy'. It is the way this part of your life lives in your body just now, sensed as one whole thing, before you split it into the various feelings, thoughts, memories and so forth that are contained in its complexity. It is your core or heart imbued with the quality of this particular part of your life. It is the inside place from where new meanings, insights, emotions and shades of feelings emerge.

Feeling the felt sense implies a relationship with one's inner life. There is a centred awareness of self, the felt sense that niggles inside, and there is space for something new to enter in, whatever lies just over the edge of one's awareness. It is, as it were, sitting on the edge of the conscious mind waiting for something to form from that of which one is almost conscious but not quite.

A simple example of this would be my saying 'hang on a moment, something is bothering me about this'; I pause to focus inwardly, ready to use my mind but not just relying on my thinking capacity; 'maybe it's because such and such', followed by a pause to check that out inside; 'no, that doesn't feel quite right . . .' and another pause; 'oh, I know, it's about this-and-that, yes, that's it!' Some relief is felt in the body at these moments.

The same sort of step-by-step process of inner searching and unfolding happens at key points in therapy when a long-standing problem starts to get resolved, and in the creative process when something is trying to be expressed through words or music or painting. We never know quite what will emerge from the felt sense; the process requires some patience; and when something does come that 'fits' the felt sense, there is about it a quality of freshness and authenticity.

Focusing lets the unconscious reveal itself in therapy. Many people will recognize this, certainly many therapists will. Yet we understand so little about it! For example, therapists often intervene by making intuitive guesses about implicit contents of the unconscious, as if that were a bag of the same sorts of feelings, fantasies, images and so forth that fill the conscious mind, only hidden from awareness. Such interventions do not always work. This is not just because the therapist can be wrong, but also because the unconscious is not really that bag out of which ready-formed things can pop.

In Focusing, the unconscious is seen more as a process whereby what is sensed in the body as an implicit 'something' forms freshly into explicit contents. It contains the individual's real experience and needs. The therapist's intuitive guesses may not help this process as much as an empathic facilitation of the felt sense might. The latter can lead to unexpected and surprising openings. Thus, the client's own inner knowing may know better than even the best therapist's experience and intuition. The contents of that knowing are not waiting to be discovered in the unconscious like an archaeological discovery – they only become what they are by being allowed to form out of unformed murkiness.

The concept of felt sense can be difficult to identify and talk about because it does not equate with any other aspect of experience for which we have a term. It is a composite of feeling and thinking, and it includes intuition and sensing as well. It also has a transcendent function in that it allows completely new thoughts, feelings and intuitions to arise in our consciousness. It is easiest to think of the felt sense as connected, bodily centred experiencing, the widest possible term to describe what is going on for us.

We are capable of sensing this meaningful bodily response in almost anything in our lives, and the capacity to do so is teachable. This response, which forms freshly each time we approach ourselves inwardly and which has a life of its own, is the closest we can come to knowing what is true and real for us in the moment. Of its own accord it moves towards greater levels of integration and wholeness, and it reveals fresh levels of meaning – if we let it. If you can find and attend to your felt sense, you can safely guide your own inner journey.

The cause of suffering

Focusing does not demand any particular theory about the nature or cause of suffering. It is entirely compatible with notions of suffering accepted by the humanistic and transpersonal psychologies. It does, however, offer a path to moving through and beyond suffering in a healthy way.

The absence of a natural ability to take the effects of suffering to one's core and find release and a rebirth of life energy leads to other, more congealed and lasting forms of suffering. If that ability can be restored, through the influence of another person who does have it, then a great healing has taken place. This would be the aim of a therapist working with Focusing.

When we know how to approach inwardly our most vulnerable and sensitive places, to be friendly and accepting towards them, and to be willing to give them space and a listening ear – all of which are intrinsic to Focusing – we are well-prepared to face and pass through our suffering. Then the contrasting fortunes of life can all contribute to the formation of a human self within. We may continue to experience suffering at times, but not a suffering that is destined to weigh us down forever, so much as a suffering that adds to the richness and breadth of our lives.

The change process

Focusing implies a process of change – the movement from an unclear body sense about something to a felt shift that brings relief and clarity. This sort of shift can happen once or many times in a single session. Focusing concerns the subtle but precise specifics of this level of experiential psychological change.

The starting point of focusing is to have a felt sense, an unclear edge in one's awareness that can be explored. Other steps may be needed, however, to get to this starting point. You have to come to a relaxed awareness of one concern that is uppermost in your felt awareness just now. If you are concerned about many things, you may need to name and feel each one to find that which feels right to explore just now. If you are in a state of tension, you will need to unwind a little before you can find a felt sense. If you are in an emotional state, you may need to work through your feelings before you find the quieter feeling levels of focusing.

A felt sense comes when you are in a certain 'right' relationship with the matter at hand. This means being close enough to it so that you can feel something about it – the situation must be present in your body awareness. On the other hand, you need to be far enough away so that you can sense yourself apart from the problem. A felt sense will not come if you are submerged in the problem, overwhelmed by it, or stuck in a pit of bad feeling about yourself.

Much of Focusing concerns getting to this point inside where things can be usefully processed – raising one's energy to the point where things can be felt, or releasing strong feelings so as to gain perspective. Many times just talking over what is happening will lead clients to the edge of their awareness. The therapist can be alert for those moments when the felt sense arises, letting a lot of talk go by as clients orientate themselves, and then pointing to the felt sense when it comes.

The felt sense usually arises as just a preverbal, preconceptual 'something' felt inside. The next step can be to find a 'handle' for it – a word, a phrase, an image or a gesture – that seems to fit. This is then checked back with the felt sense to see if it 'resonates', or whether a different handle would describe it better. At other times, only silent attention and an inner attitude of friendliness and welcome is appropriate when a felt sense comes inside.

The felt sense opens up through not just one step, but many. Each step brings a slight change in the physical feel of the problem, maybe with a sigh, a deeper breath, an easing of tension in the body. Steps that do not bring this physical shift may not come from the felt sense, but from what the person already knows, or from an attempt to invent a solution to the problem. When this happens, people say things like 'this must be because . . .', or 'I suppose this is my issue about such-and-such again'.

The change steps in focusing may come from many angles. Finding how we experience a difficulty in our body, rather than just in our head or emotions, can be a step forward. Allowing a symbol to emerge that reflects the felt sense – the 'handle' mentioned above – can bring a greater consciousness of our underlying experience. The appearance of new feelings or emotions we have not felt before is a powerful step forward, for they lead to new possibilities in our lives. Finally, making connections with actual life details can bring shifts – buried memories that resurface, discovering what it is that has really triggered a certain feeling, and generating ideas about future actions.

Felt shifts tend to be surprising, to the therapist as well as the client! In Focusing, we can try all the different angles to see if a shift will come, but only the felt sense 'knows' how this will happen, or what the next step needs to be. To not know the resolution of a difficulty, but to trust that something inside knows and will reveal itself in time, is a powerful, effective and yet humble stance to take.

The coming of change steps and felt shifts is not the end of the story. It helps to take time to welcome them and really take them in, allowing them to integrate inside so that they stick in some way. Moving forward can be a delicate process; our critical minds and the sheer weight of past experience can come back to negate our progress. The final stage of focusing is to trust what has spontaneously arisen from within, to protect it from whatever self-destructive tendencies to which we are prone and to act upon it.

Focusing has been broken down into certain steps or movements for teaching purposes, the best known being a six step system outlined by Gendlin (1981). These step by step methods are for teaching focusing skills to people. They are techniques for encouraging a natural focusing process. In practice, focusing happens differently for every person each time they focus; by definition it is unique, personal and creative. It always happens freshly, and it is quite impossible to encapsulate it once and for all in a technical formulation.

Therapeutic goals

The first goal with Focusing is for clients to come to focus naturally at points in their therapy hour. Some clients come to therapy with the ability to focus in the company of an empathic listener, but others need to learn this skill.

Therapists who embrace Focusing will actively seek, directly or indirectly, to educate clients in focusing behaviour. They will not just sit hoping that one day clients will attend to their bodily experiencing and then complain, when they don't, that they are 'not expressing their feelings', or that they are 'resisting', 'defending themselves' or 'not surrendering'. Instead, they will work harder to meet clients on their own terms and to listen for the felt sense that lies behind what they are saying. This is not to say that engendering focusing is always a simple matter!

Once clients can focus inwardly when needed during the session, and the therapeutic relationship that encourages this is established, then the therapy can really start. This means that the specific life difficulties that they bring can be addressed and explored, or that areas of potential they wish to develop can be worked with.

The goals of the therapy are set by the client and not by the therapist. The same is true for Focusing practised in a self-help context: the individual does with their focusing time what feels right to them.

In practice, Focusing will tend to lead to many outcomes for which other approaches aim: forming more satisfying and honest relationships with others; choosing freely where one wants to go in life; overcoming fear and anxiety rather than being restrained by them; perhaps most importantly, living creatively with oneself, open to the well-spring of one's unconscious, and rooted firmly in one's own inner soil. Carl Rogers described this as 'becoming a person'; a person is someone who is open to experiencing life as an everchanging process. In Focusing terms, this means someone who can contact and attend to their bodily felt sense of situations.

Relationship

Focusing is often taught individually or in small groups where there is a student–teacher relationship. Such tuition is not therapy, though therapeutic moments inevitably arise. Not all Focusing trainers are therapists, which helps to keep the focusing community broadly based in many walks of life.

Focusing can be taught during therapy. This can be done explicitly or implicitly by therapists modelling focusing themselves. It may require little more than listening empathically and reflecting in a way that encourages focusing. A focusing oriented therapist may prefer to listen carefully and allow a spontaneous process to arise, than to intervene with techniques and directions. They will also act as guides sometimes, using suggestions and questions designed to nudge clients into focusing. Here they act more as experts on the client's process than on its content. Instead of saying 'the reason you feel like this now lies in your past relationship with your father' – a statement about content that the client may find hard to refute if it is wrong (and therapist's interpretations often are!) – they are more likely to say things like 'and I imagine you are sensing this whole thing inside you just now', allowing the client's felt sense to supply the next piece of content.

They do not regard themselves as experts on the client's life, they let the client be the expert. They allow the client's felt sense to guide the course of the session as much as possible. That inside place which is usually ignored, that gets lost in the rush of daily life, and that is apt to go underground in the face of an 'expert' on psychology, that place is the primary reference point in the therapy.

Of course, therapists refer to their own felt senses (as any good therapist does) and talk about content a lot. But they will say many things tentatively, ensuring that clients check them out inside and discard them if they do not stir the felt sense. They can be audacious in their contact with clients, feeling very closely with them, but always giving them a lot of space in which to move around.

However, therapists also need to be real people! Avoiding therapist's power games by giving the power to the client's felt sense does not mean letting them walk all over you, the therapist. Clients need a real live person with whom to interact, so they can learn to allow the therapist into their inner world just as far as they like and to keep him or her out just as far as they like, and find their own individuality in contrast to that of the therapist.

Therapists who use Focusing are passionately respectful of the autonomy of their clients, their freedom to grow as they wish or even not to grow. People who respect their own inner autonomy can help others to do the same for themselves.

Techniques

Not being a therapy in itself, Focusing must be integrated into whatever other techniques the therapist uses. Most therapeutic techniques can be used in a focusing way, with reference to the felt sense – Gestalt and Imagery are two obvious examples. As Gendlin says, 'focusing makes these techniques work better, and they make focusing work better'. Unfortunately, many therapists who know only a little about Focusing consider it as a technique to be used apart from other ways of working. Although Focusing can be learnt as a technique for self-help, in therapy it is not so much a technique as an inner behaviour to encourage in the client.

The technique that most helps a person to focus is a style of listening known as 'experiential listening', a refinement of 'reflective' or 'active' listening. Listening lies at the heart of all approaches to therapy. Other techniques can be left out and therapy will still work; good listening cannot be.

The aim of experiential listening is to hear what the person is saying in the way that they are actually experiencing it. The listener tries to respond to the experience itself rather than to the focuser's mind that is interpreting that experience. In Focusing language, this means responding directly to the felt sense; in counselling terms, we would say the client's inner frame of reference – as opposed to the therapist's frame of reference.

This requires different responses at different times. It might require summarizing a long piece of talking to find the nub, or just reflecting the last thing the person said when they trailed off hesitantly. It could be checking back that you have heard exactly; or repeating just the same emotionally-laden word the person used; or saying something back more slowly and with feeling; or silence. Whatever it is, the listener encourages the focuser to attend to their bodily felt experiencing, to go to the place inside from where their words are coming. It may elicit a pause to focus. Let us take an example:

> *Focuser*: I've got a strong urge to start up this new business, but I'm too scared to do it.

An active listening response might be:

> *Listener*: It's your fear that's stopping you from starting the business.

This is an accurate reflection, yet it tends to leave the focuser stuck with their fear; they might then say 'yes, that's right' and in therapy, wait for the therapist to give them a direction for proceeding.

An experiential response might be:

> *Listener*: You want to start it up, and there's a place inside that feels really scared . . .

Notice the following things about this sort of a response:

1 Whereas the active listening response tended to close the experiential issue around the fear, the experiential response leaves it more open in the hope of triggering a spontaneous process in the focuser. Naturally-arising processes are more attuned to the client's needs than processes led by the therapist's knowledge, intuition and guesses. The experiential response will tend to inhibit a purely intellectual discussion of the problem, or the client being stuck with feeling only the fear.

2 The listener has paraphrased the 'urge' into 'you want', but has repeated the 'scared' without changing it, as 'scared' may be just what the focuser is feeling, or will feel when they turn inside.

3 This response reflects the client's actual experience rather than a rationalized

understanding of it. It does not prevent rational understanding, but it does point towards the experience. It does this by referring to both the 'urge' and the 'scared'. The client's experience is a felt sense, or can be in the next moment; that includes both these opposing forces – one whole thing. By pointing to the whole rather than a part of it, the listener invites a spontaneous movement in the psyche towards resolution of the inner conflict, because it creates space for something new to enter in.

4 The listener is both very supportive and accepting of what the focuser is experiencing, and also subtly confrontative because the response points the focuser right on to the horns of the dilemma.

5 The listener or therapist is not directing how the client should work on the problem, but inviting them to find their own way forwards – of course, they will suggest things if the client gets stuck. The client's next step might go either way, into the 'want' or into the 'scared'. Instead of trying to guess the best way to go, the therapist lets the client find which force is stronger in them just now.

6 The listener both keeps the focuser close company, entering some way into their experience, and at the same time offering them the space to explore the problem in their own way. Focusing is a 'non-directive' approach to therapy, yet the therapist will repeatedly direct the client's attention to their felt sense.

The experiential style of responding is geared towards the natural creative idiosyncrasies of the client rather than the therapist's psychological outlook and directive techniques. The therapist is less likely to direct the client along a fruitless track; more likely to hear what the client is trying to express; less likely to get in the way of the client's own healing and problem solving resources; and less likely to have the client become dependent. Good listening does more to melt so-called 'resistances' and 'defences' than any amount of trying to confront and dismantle them.

There are specific ways of talking that direct a person's attention to their felt sense. Referring to 'a place inside', as in the above example, is one way – that place is the felt sense and one can pay attention to it. It allows for more than just the familiar feeling and encourages the person to explore. Another way is to speak of a 'something' – 'something here feels scared', or 'there's something about this that's uncomfortable'. The 'something' refers to the vaguely sensed edge of the experience, and points the person to search inside for something new to emerge. It opens up the possibility that more can be found than the client has yet become aware.

These responses can also refer to the felt sense as an 'it' or a 'this' or a 'that':

It feels heavy in there.

This doesn't sit easily inside just now.

A tightness, *that's* there for you just now.

We all talk naturally with these words, indicating felt senses inside us. It doesn't help to 'own' such feelings by saying 'I feel heavy', as many therapists like to get their clients to do. That works when the feeling is clear, but not when it is unclear as in a felt sense.

As well as experiential listening, a focusing oriented therapist will use questions and suggestions to encourage the client to explore inwardly. For example, to help the client find the felt sense:

Can you get a broader sense of that anger in your body?

See if you can find how this whole thing feels in your body

Or, having found the felt sense, to try and open it up:

Ask your body, 'what's this anger really all about?', and wait and see what comes.

See if an image or some words come inside that would go with this feeling.

Some of these are standard focusing questions and prompts. At other times, fresh ones must be devised on the spot to fit the circumstances.

In a self-help context, focusers use whatever questions and suggestions they have learnt to guide their process. If there is a listener, that person can respond with experiential listening and offer suggestions if the focuser asks for them. Peer-level focusing works best when focusers guide their own journey by following the felt sense, and listeners stick to listening responses and avoid playing at being 'therapist'.

Behind all focusing technique is the implicit assumption that 'the client is always right' – which means that we trust the felt sense to show the way. If something the therapist offers does not work for the client, he or she withdraws it and tries something else or stays quiet. The therapist wants the client to check whatever is said against their own inner experience, and not just sit there swallowing what they are told.

Pitfalls

A pitfall for the therapist is to become so enamoured of Focusing that he or she forgets that it is only one of many dynamics that are needed in therapy. Focusing that is well placed in a broad therapeutic context is more effective than a therapy that relies too much on focusing procedures and the quiet inner sensing they entail.

There are outward, expressive aspects of therapy as well as inward, introspective ones. Thus clients may need to talk at length before quietly sensing in their inner awareness; they may need to be emotional and pass through a catharsis before returning their awareness inside to see what new steps emerge once the cathartic storm has blown over; and they may need to look at what they are doing or not doing in their lives before they examine their inner experience any further.

In other words, Focusing should be used to carry forward the client's whole life experience, and not to create a cosy inner world into which to retreat. A simple example: you could avoid doing something in your life that you know you need to do, and keep going back inside to process the dissonant feelings that arise from your inaction. Focusing could help you to do this!

In practice, I find that focusing tends to mitigate against excessive introspection. Implicitly, it involves contacting the current of life energy inside you, and that current will push your attention to the outside if your conscious orientation is too much inwards. Focusing is a pleasure to do when one balances one's inner and outer life; it becomes boring if we are all on the inside and ignore our outer lives.

A related pitfall is for the therapist to rely too much on acceptance and empathy, and too little on challenge, confrontation, self-disclosure and the authenticity of his or her own personality. Because high levels of intimacy and empathy are needed to approach the extremely sensitive and delicate states for which focusing is so appropriate, it might be too easy for the therapist to forget his or her own self and needs and individuality. Opposition and conflict can lead to valuable therapeutic openings, as well as confluence between therapist and client. In practice, however, I think that the ability to be confluent in an effective way implies the ability to stand well apart from the client when appropriate – paradoxically.

Another pitfall is for the therapist who believes that Focusing is only a technique to use on the client. Unfortunately, some therapists who say they know about Focusing see it in this light, with the consequence that their work embraces very little of the benefits that a deeper appreciation of it offers. In therapy, Focusing entails the encouragement of a certain aspect of client behaviour more than the use of a technique that stands on its own.

When Focusing is practised in a self-help context, the biggest pitfall arises in a partnership where one person crosses the line from being a friendly listener to acting as 'therapist' for the other. It can be very tempting to do this, yet it leads inevitably to disaster! Much of the value of Focusing in a partnership arrangement lies in the mutual respect and friendly support born of the absolute equality of the relationship. It is an extension of the art of friendship, not an attempt at amateur therapy. The pitfall is avoided by the listener avoiding the temptation to guide, direct, or in any way 'help' the focuser other than by their company, acceptance and listening responses.

Research

Research has been done in the USA into different applications of Focusing. The most important piece, of course, is that which led Gendlin (1981) to formulate Focusing as a certain experiential process in the first place. This shows quite clearly that a high level of focusing ability is required if the client is to benefit from therapy.

No formal research has been undertaken into the outcomes of focusing oriented therapy, or of the practice of Focusing as a self-help method – in both areas it would be hard to obtain useful objective results. Nevertheless, there have been studies (Gendlin 1978) which indicate the following:

- Specific formulations of Focusing have been found to help students of creative writing, trainee teachers who have difficulties with a given subject, and mentally retarded people to arrive at the point where they can enter something more like ordinary therapy.
- People who are taught to focus can pick out bodily expressions of others better than those who do not know focusing.

- Focusing can be taught to hospitalized patients called 'borderline' and 'schizophrenic' with measurable benefits.
- Specific EEG patterns have been found to correlate with moments in focusing when an experiential shift is felt by the focuser (alpha and theta, with a lack of beta).

Finally, Gorney (1968) found that old people with high levels of focusing ability – but who had not been taught Focusing specifically – live longer than those with low levels. So focusing might even promote longevity!

Case study

Some people attend workshops on Focusing without having one-to-one therapy, whilst others are interested in individual work and choose not to learn peer-level Focusing in workshops. The following case study of a person who mixed both approaches shows how they can be combined.

Alex's first encounter with Focusing was on an introductory workshop. Having tried a number of approaches to personal growth and therapy, he was hoping that the bodily route that Focusing takes would help him find his feelings more easily. He was in his early 40s, a journalist disgruntled with his job; he was divorced and unable to settle into another relationship with a woman. He had a daughter whom he saw irregularly and from whom he felt distanced.

Alex found the introductory workshop very valuable. In only his second Focusing session some of the emotional pain he had been 'carrying around for years' welled up unexpectedly, and he was surprised to find this more of a relief than something unpleasant. He was also struck by how much satisfaction he gained when it was his turn to listen for another person in the group. He had not imagined he would be even semi-adequate at this task!

After the workshop, Alex recognized that he needed further individual work on some key areas of his life, and more practice in learning to face his inner world. He was also acutely aware that he had only 'scratched the surface' of the emotional wounds that seemed to be preventing his enjoying the fruits of middle age. So we agreed on some short term therapy, a series of six weekly sessions.

The two topics that were uppermost for Alex were his need to discover why his relationships were always failing and his wish to find some clarity about changing his work in journalism. During the therapy, he off-loaded the dissatisfaction he experienced with the sort of writing his job required of him, and started to take seriously some ideas for writing of his own. He decided to investigate the possibilities of working on an entirely freelance basis. He also reflected more deeply about his failed relationships, starting with his marriage and continuing with a number of other liaisons that had come to a rocky end.

For the first couple of sessions, Alex was largely just telling me his story, whilst in the later sessions there was less conversation and more inner exploring. One session was almost entirely devoted to a significant dream he had had a few weeks before that clearly related to his ability to write in a more creative fashion than his job allowed. In another, he expressed his feelings towards his ex-wife with the help of Gestalt techniques.

In most of the sessions, there were moments of pausing to focus inwardly and find the 'edge', allowing the space and time for the therapeutic process to emerge spontaneously. Some of these moments were short, while others were lengthier searches that required careful listening and reflection before anything much emerged. On one occasion, some startling imagery came to Alex that surprised him not only for its emotional richness, but because he thought he lacked the ability to visualize images.

The outer circumstances of Alex's life did not, of course, change dramatically in the course of this short therapy – although the dream did spur him to do some writing, and he found himself getting on more easily with his daughter. However, his inner world had come alive, and his attitude towards both this and the problems in his life was much more positive. He began to see his tendency to get depressed as a signal that he needed to listen to something inside him rather than just wait for the depression to wear off.

The work Alex did was not a return to childhood in search of some supposed original trauma. Whilst he did make some connections to his early life, in the main we worked on deepening his experience of the present. Nor did the therapy involve protracted catharsis. By seeking the source of his troubled feelings, Alex found he could release them surprisingly quickly and easily. He was not really 'out of touch' with them at all – he just had not known where to look to find them.

Alex emerged from these sessions excited at having found his own natural way to let his inner 'magic' work for him. Wanting to continue this inner dialogue and contact, he arranged to meet someone from his workshop group to exchange focusing and listening turns and form a partnership. He later attended a further workshop to learn more about using Focusing in this way.

Comment on the literature on Focusing

Gendlin (1981) is a very readable presentation of Focusing as self-help, for general consumption.

Gendlin (1986) discusses how to use Focusing in dream work.

Amodeo and Amodeo (1986) is a work by two Californian therapists that takes the reader through the use of Focusing to aid the journey into intimacy.

Campbell and McMahon (1985) are two priests who present Focusing in a spiritual context.

Various articles and an unpublished manuscript entitled *Experiential Psychotherapy* by Gendlin discuss the incorporation of Focusing into therapy. These can be obtained from the Focusing Institute, 29 South Lasalle Street #1195, Chicago, IL 60603, or from me at 2 The Chase, London SW4 OHN.

References

Amodeo, J. and Amodeo, K. (1986) *Being Intimate*. London: Arkana.

Campbell, P. and McMahon, E. (1985) *Bio-spirituality: Focusing as a Way to Grow*. Chicago: Loyola University Press.

Gendlin, E. (1978) *Broader Scientific Implications of Focusing*. Paper presented to the Japanese Psychological Association Convention, Fukuoka, Japan.

Gendlin, E. (1981) *Focusing*. London: Bantam Books.

Gendlin, E. (1986) *Let Your Body Interpret Your Dreams*. Wilmette, IL: Chiron Publications.

Gorney, J. (1968) Experiencing and Age Patterns of Reminiscence among the Elderly. Unpublished Doctoral Dissertation. University of Chicago.

Kurtz, R. (1988) *Hakomi Therapy*. Boulder, CO: Hakomi Institute.

PART III

Emphasis on the body

8

Core Energetics

DAVID CRANMER

Definition and historical development

Definition

Core Energetics is an energy and depth-oriented body psychotherapy. To quote John Pierrakos MD (1987), the founder, it is

> an integrated approach for the growth and evolution of the entire person. The common denominator is the way in which energy and consciousness manifests in the human entity and in the universe. A more specific inquiry relates to the stream of life energy which emanates from the core and flows in health but is blocked in dis-ease thus creating illness or dysfunction . . . a process where disharmony counters the real needs of the organism.

In Core Energetics the process of therapy like the experience of life is viewed as a spiritual journey.

Historical development

The practice of Core Energetics has developed as an outgrowth of the psychiatric career of Dr John Pierrakos along with his studies and observations of the human energy field (the aura). The psychological roots of this work can be traced back to the origins of Freud's psychoanalytic theory; his 'discovery' of the unconscious mind and the emphasis placed on repressed psychic material held within the unconscious.

As a young associate of Freud's, Wilhelm Reich chose to focus his analytic work not only on the mind but also on the body. He believed that the energy of the emotions was not only a mental phenomenon as studied in traditional psycho-analysis but that it had a physical, bodily component as well. If the emotions were not allowed full expression he felt that energetic blockages would be created within the body. These would be particularly evident as areas of chronic muscular tension which he termed 'armour' (see Chapter 9, this volume). From his work with clients he saw that an individual's character is expressed physically and psychologically in identical terms. That is, that psychological defences developed early in childhood are manifest in the physical structure of the body. His idea of 'psychosomatic identity' is the basis for most somatic psychotherapies and Reich was the first scientist to unify the study of body, mind and emotions into a whole system of study.

In the early 1950s, as Reich began more and more to pursue his scientific studies, John Pierrakos and Alexander Lowen, both students and colleagues of Reich broke away to co-found Bioenergetic Therapy. They wanted to develop further the concept of psychosomatic identity, psychoanalytic process, and the basic Reichian principle that all organisms are energetic processes which take in and release energy. Bioenergetics was defined by Lowen as 'the study of the personality in terms of the body'. It introduced a variety of techniques for working with the body to release blocked energy so that the fundamental homoeostatic balance of the individual could be restored. The Institute of Bioenergetic Analysis was founded in New York in 1954.

In the mid-1970s, after years of working with this approach, John Pierrakos came to feel that Bioenergetics lacked a basic philosophy which included the spiritual nature of human beings. At this point he met his late wife, Eva Broch Pierrakos. She was involved with trance channelling a series of lectures given by a spirit entity known only as the Guide (Pierrakos 1990). These teachings came to be known as the Pathwork. They were described by John Pierrakos as presenting 'a cosmic view of psychology, medicine, and religion' and providing 'a conceptual fusion of energy and consciousness'. Together they established a community and in 1972 the first Pathwork centre was established as a non-profit educational foundation.

After Eva died in 1979 Pierrakos continued to unify his body psychotherapeutic methods, his observations of the human aura and the conceptual framework of spiritual practices as put forward in the Pathwork material. The result of this continuing fusion is Core Energetics and in the late 1970s the Institute of Core Energetics was established in New York.

Founders

In Britain, as of this writing, there are no individuals working purely with the Core Energetic model of therapy. Over the past several years the Karuna Institute in Devon has sponsored week long workshops led by Miriam Dror, an American therapist who has trained with Dr Pierrakos in the United States. In addition, each summer the Institute of Core Energetics offers workshops in southern France. These meetings as well as the publication of Pierrakos' book in 1987, have increased interest in this holistic approach and prompted individuals to contact the New York institute to find out about training groups. The Core Energetic work has also been spread by the therapists and counsellors who have come into contact with its concepts and taken them back into their own practices.

Because of the strong tradition of body centred psychotherapies in continental Europe, particularly in Germany, Switzerland and Holland, the first international training in Core Energetics was initiated in November of 1988. This training, led by John Pierrakos and institute staff from New York, was completed in August, 1991 by 19 individuals from six countries. A second four-year training programme began in Berlin in October 1991, with at least one participant from Britain. Currently there are Core Energetic institutes in New York, California, Mexico, Brazil, Germany and Italy, with more planned.

Relationship to other therapies

Core Energetics is similar to the traditional Freudian and Jungian depth-oriented psychotherapies in that it seeks to resolve emotional and psychological problems by focusing on the individual's psychological mechanisms of defence. To this it has incorporated the basic (Reichian) principle, shared by the body-oriented psychotherapies: Bioenergetics, Biodynamics, Biosynthesis, Organismic, Hakomi, Radix or Neo-Reichian, etc., that the mind and body are inseparable, such that one can influence the other.

It shares the premises of 'humanistic' psychology which emphasize psychological health, awareness of the individual's felt experience, choice, creativity and personal growth. The broad range of humanistic therapies includes Gestalt, Rebirthing, Transactional Analysis, Psychodrama, Encounter and some of the somatic therapies mentioned above.

Core Energetics differs from those forms of therapy, traditional, behaviouristic and others which come to an end as soon as emotional blocks and neurotic dysfunction are resolved. It continues therapeutically and practically to develop the 'transpersonal' capacity of the individual – those qualities and states of being which can only be fully actualized and expressed as the individual moves towards a higher consciousness and a sense of cosmic or spiritual unity. In this regard it shares the psychospiritual attitude of Hakomi Therapy and psychosynthesis.

The energetic dimension of Core Energetic therapy is philosophically linked with those forms of holistic health practice which believe in the underlying unity of all things. Specifically, the concept of 'chi', the energetic life force in Chinese medicine and the similar idea of 'prana' from the hatha (physical) yoga system of India are fundamentally the same as Core Energy. All three, within their respective systems, are viewed as having a primary, integrative role in maintaining the physical and psychological health of the individual.

Central concepts

Core Energetics is founded on three fundamental principles. As stated by John Pierrakos they are:

1 the person is a psychosomatic unity;
2 all of existence forms a unity that moves toward creative evolution, both of the whole and of the countless components;
3 the source of healing lies within the self, not with an outside agency, whether a physician, therapist, God, or the power of the cosmos.

The first principle is based on the proposition that the basic substance of the person is energy. This is the same energy which pervades the movement of objects throughout the physical universe. It is witnessed at the astronomical level in the movements of celestial bodies and within the atom as the shifting of subatomic particles. At the organismic level the movement of this energy is the life force, the biological energy which at the cellular level informs the cycles of contraction inward towards the cell nucleus and outwards as the cell wall expands to meet the surrounding environment.

Core Energetics views the human entity as a microcosm of the universe around us, sharing the same rhythmic cycles of energy which are constantly seeking to maintain the balance of the greater, well ordered whole. At the anatomical level we see these streamings and pulsations as the beating of the heart, the peristaltic motion of the intestines and in the continual expansion and contraction of the lungs as we breathe.

In the same way that the body works as a unified system within nature and the cosmos it is accepted in Core Energetic theory that the energies of the mind or psyche function in a self-regulatory fashion. When there is imbalance at the psychological or emotional level this is spontaneously reflected on the physical, bodily level just as a physical trauma may evoke an emotional or psychological response. With this understanding of psychosomatic unity to build on we will next look at the second principle of Core Energetics.

As Pierrakos suggests that the fundamental essence of each person is energy, he also maintains that energy is consciousness. Every entity in nature has a form which is considered to be the crystallization of that entity's unique energetic attributes. These characteristics (shape, mass, density, etc.) are defined by that entity's response to its particular place in the universe. Because this movement of energy has the capacity for direction in relationship to the greater order of the cosmos, it is said to have consciousness.

Consciousness, as energy, informs each unit of matter, animate and inanimate, from the subatomic particle to the totality of creation and because of this Pierrakos proposes that everything is consciousness. As witnessed by science this consciousness is constantly transforming itself, at times appearing chaotic, to create an ever more cohesive unity. Each component, as reflected by the second principle, holds a plan within itself for the full development of its unique potential just as the fully mature tree is held within the potential of the seed.

As more complex orders of organic life have come into being so has the innate capacity for direction (consciousness) increased. What distinguishes humanity from the rest of nature is its ability to know that it knows. This potential for greater self-awareness and self-determination is innate in each person and is integral to the third principle of Core Energetics which states that the source of healing lies within the self.

Just as our physical body can be viewed as the manifestation of the quantitative physical processes occurring within and around us so too can the human mind be viewed as the qualitative aspect of these energetic processes. The mind is defined as having an inner and an outer aspect. The outer or thinking mind with its powers of reason and will is likened to the tip of an iceberg. It is seen as the outer expression of a much deeper and greater undivided consciousness. This inner mind includes all aspects of our conscious and unconscious processes and potentials: physical, mental, emotional and spiritual, and is termed the Core. Within us it is both the source and perceiver of the life force and thus the source of our self-healing.

The material and non-material expressions of the Core differ only in their energetic frequency, not in their essence. The vibrations of thought have a higher frequency than emotional energy which in turn has a higher vibration than the physical energies of the body. The higher frequencies are able to permeate the lower ones but not vice versa. For an examination of Dr Pierrakos' theory of human energetic functioning I would refer the reader to his scientific observations as they are detailed in his book *Core Energetics* (Pierrakos 1987). To summarize, he states that

> The penetration of the higher vibratory frequency explains how non-material events – experiences of the emotions, the mind, and the spirit – can shape our very physiology. The quality of the energy movement in the event makes an imprint on the energy body. If the experience is intense or repeated, the imprint becomes visible in the flesh as well as the aura.

Finally then, the Core is defined by Pierrakos as 'the innermost reality of human beings, the source of positive energy which, if undistorted, serves as the source of harmonious functioning' and whose qualitative characteristics can be summed up as being 'one supreme expression of love', a love which has intelligence, will and power.

The cause of suffering

In Core Energetic terms the root cause of suffering is seen to be the fragmentation of the flow of life force (Core) energy as it moves between our inner reality and our outer environment. It is an interruption of the naturally balanced assertive and receptive cycles of energy movement into and out from our organism. This creates stress and dysfunction at the psychological and emotional levels and is expressed physically in tension and contraction of the muscles.

This imbalance is seen to originate at the psychological level when very early on the child chooses to restrict the full emotional and physical expressions of the Core. The child learns to modify its behaviour when pain and suffering are felt as a result of the parents' punitive responses when its actions are judged to be inappropriate. This is seen as an attempt by the organism to protect the Core from further 'wounding'.

The change process

Level 1: The Core or Higher Self
As has been previously defined, the core has complete unity and represents an individual's whole capacity. We experience it in moments of insight as a deeper knowing or truth which is connected to feelings of spiritual longing and personal fulfilment. (Spirituality is defined by Pierrakos as 'nothing else but all aspects of love'.) It is here that we feel the primal positive emotions of

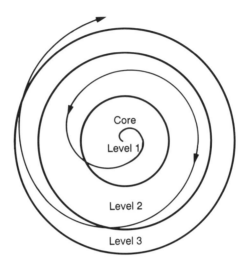

Figure 8.1 Dimensions of Consciousness. The movement of vital energy to and from the Core is not linear but takes a spiral form. The consciousness at each level permeates the physical, emotional and mental aspects of our being such that any one level is not seen as being above or below another.

the Core as it seeks to charge itself by making contact and unifying with our outer environment.

Physically there can be a sense of great pleasure or grace. We may be suffused with joy and feel connected to all of life and all other beings. With its ability to heal, the Higher Self will strive again and again to re-establish the harmony of our inner being in relationship to the outer reality of our lives, the forces at the periphery of level 3.

Level 2: The Lower Self
This layer holds the capacity of the organism to counteract impinging forces moving inward, and to alter Core energy expanding outward. It is the seat of the primal negative emotions, the infantile fear, anger, distrust and envy which is felt initially in early childhood in response to our family environment. These develop into cruel, selfish and destructive actions against the parents in an attempt to protect the Core's innate dignity. Again, it is stressed that these reactions are life saving but can unconsciously be carried into adulthood where they can distort the true perception of reality.

Taken together, the Higher Self and the Lower Self constitute the inner reality or inner self of the individual. The terms 'higher' and 'lower' are used as descriptions of energy frequency rather than any form of moral judgement. The Core has the highest rate of pulsation followed in order by levels 2 and 3. In any entity Pierrakos sees the perimeter layer as having the lowest rate of pulsation because it has the function of 'interceding between the inner self and the enormous range of frequencies in the outside reality'.

Level 3: The ego Mask
This layer also forms an area of defence and mediation of external and internal forces. While the inner self is perceived as energetically fluid and everchanging, this outer self is a relatively static or fixed layer. As stated earlier, the consciousness of the outer self is concerned with volitional thinking and maintaining the image of the individual as being separate from others. It also houses the repressed or forgotten (unconscious) experiences of the past. The aspects of self-awareness, choice, and unconscious influence combine to form the 'ego'. The unique form that this development takes within each of us is our 'personality'.

The ego seeks to regulate the flow of energy and experience into and out of the Core. The child's ego, in learning to control expressiveness, disrupts the pure flow of energy from levels 1 and 2. Over time it becomes compacted into emotional and physical blockages known as 'character armouring'. As the inner energy becomes increasingly trapped in the defensive perimeter the wilful aspects of ego begin to dominate. In so doing, it misappropriates the energies of the Core in an attempt to hide the negativity of the Lower Self and present an idealized self-image or Mask, to the world.

The process of change begins when the individual realizes that their perception of outer reality is distorted, and that the systems of defence developed in childhood no longer serve to protect the individual but in fact have now become the source of the denial of a much fuller life.

Therapeutic goals

The ultimate goal of Core Energetic therapy is to align the isolated, dysfunctional aspects of the ego with the Core in an attempt to mobilize and cultivate the qualities of the Higher or spiritual self. The work proceeds in four stages beginning with the outermost layer of the Mask. Each stage necessarily involves the successively deeper energies of the stage which follows only so far as the client is open to exploring them. The aim is to open the pathway to the heart.

Stage 1: Penetrating the Mask
The main focus here is in working with the mass of energy trapped in the Mask. This is a relatively short stage because the person is driven by the desire to relieve the pain which they feel as a result of their sense of self-alienation and separation from others. The client learns to become conscious of and confront the basic attitudes of their character structure, those distorted aspects of the ego which have become 'frozen' at the physical and emotional level. Work on the Mask turns the individual completely around to gaze inward to affirm life, away from the outward denial of life which is the Mask.

Stage 2: Releasing the Lower Self
This stage works to uncover the cause of the attitudes of denial and negation that have produced the exaggerations of character defences and the hardening of the

Mask. The therapist assists the client in evoking the primal negative emotions. This undistorted energy, uninhibited by the repression of the Mask is then allowed to flow outwards rather than back inwards against the organism. The perceiving self is then guided to explore the content of past experiences and wounds to discover how they are linked to the present. This re-experiencing and acknowledgement of the origins of suffering lead the client to the transitional point in therapy: 'reaching for the Core'.

The acceptance of one's pain, without the tendency to blame and reject others, implies self-responsibility. Consciously, the person can now choose to express negative emotions appropriately while not suppressing the streaming of energy from within. The Core then becomes both the aim of the healing process and its most effective tool. This is the point in therapy when the dysfunctions of the personality have been resolved and a good measure of integral functioning regained.

Stage 3: Centring in the Higher Self

Now, the creative, life affirming aspects of the ego can begin to access directly the potential of the Core. The person senses the opportunity for personal fulfilment and seeks to strengthen and maintain contact with the inner consciousness of the Core. At this stage the fundamental practice of meditation is introduced as a discipline which can take the client beyond the goals of therapy. It assists in reorienting our awareness and intention from negative to positive so that the Core's creativity can be brought into full fruition. This leads to the final stage of therapy.

Stage 4: Uncovering the Life Plan

This stage focuses on expanding the individual's sense of trust. Initially, this is the trust developed with the therapist during therapy but which must now be extended into the person's daily reality. In committing themselves to positive intentionality they begin to pursue the best alternatives of action which their own innate gifts afford them in their present life situation. The client comes to trust their own life process and develops a sense of the interdependence of all things. They begin to ask themselves the question: 'What is my task in being?' Life is then seen as a spiritual journey, a continuing exploration towards ever greater truth, creativity and unity.

Practitioners

Relationship

The holistic orientation of Core Energetics requires that the therapist focus on the innate health of the client and therapy is the process of clearing the way for the Higher Self. Core Energetic philosophy does not accept a hierarchy of roles in the therapeutic relationship. While the practitioner's actions may be supportive it is the sufferer's own vital energy which disperses the 'illness' and allows healing to take place. The trust which the client places in the therapist is received with an attitude of deep responsibility. To uphold this responsibility, to educate the individual in the workings of their inner reality, requires that the therapist remain open to their own Core and to their own willingness to change.

Therapy sessions are about the relationship between the Core and the defences. The therapist does not dwell on 'fixing' or 'correcting' specific distortions as they appear in the individual's character defences and 'neurotic' behaviour because the therapist realizes that this is not enough to generate the fulfilment which the client is seeking. Rather, the therapist as guide and teacher seeks to cast a searchlight into the sufferer's Core to illuminate the innermost truth of the Higher Self. This is the path towards which the therapy works and it is in this sense that Core Energetics can be considered a spiritual psychology.

It is important to remember that whatever method is being employed by the therapist during the course of therapy the primary focus of the relationship is always on a fuller expression of the unique consciousness of that individual.

Techniques

From the onset of therapy the main arena of work is the physical body. The initial, verbalized complaints which have pushed the client into seeking help are listened to while the therapist mentally notes the physical attitude of these expressions: the tone of voice, rhythm of breathing, skin tone, physical posture and movement, etc. A person complaining of depression for example, will be seen as having a depressed level of physical energy which is impairing that person's ability to function fully in their daily world.

This will lead in a later session to a 'body reading', when the client is asked to view themselves in a full-length mirror. Under the therapist's direction the client brings their conscious awareness to those areas which have become 'armoured', where emotional blockages and mental distortions have habitually become 'frozen' in the body. In subsequent meetings the therapist will introduce movement, breathwork and massage techniques in an attempt to loosen and mobilize the energy held in these blockages.

Therapy parallels the development of the human being from infancy through to maturity. In early sessions the client will lie on his or her back and move like an infant. These movements might include holding the legs in the air with the heels flexed upwards until the legs begin to vibrate, or flailing the mattress with hands and arms to encourage the expression of primal negative emotions. These exercises are continued well beyond the ordinary point of fatigue to force the generated energy into the areas of blockage. It is at this point that the therapist might intervene to massage the affected area deeply. The resulting discomfort also serves to call the client's attention to those areas of the body where they have chronically come to hold their energy. More specific 'stress postures' and massage can be used later to open constrictions of the joints, chest, neck and abdomen. All of these movement techniques focus the client's perception on their own experience rather than on the therapist's interpretation. In addition, the individual is encouraged to vocalize whatever feelings that come up so that the voice too can be freed of any characterological distortions.

In succeeding sessions when the client is prepared to move into the stage of youth and adulthood they will intensify the expression of negative emotions in a standing position. The arms strike out, the feet kick and stamp, the voice yells in anger while the eyes glare. The downward discharge of energy through the legs and feet re-establishes the connection with our literal 'ground of being'. This is the felt experience of the body in active balance with the forces of gravity and in contact with the present moment.·We experience the physical aspects of life as being pleasurable and as this takes root psychologically we feel secure in our relationships with others. This important concept of 'grounding' is fundamental to most forms of somatic psychotherapy.

Underpinning the movement techniques, and our very existence, is our ability to charge or energize the body with the breath. The entire body participates in the respiratory process. Breathing in is accompanied by a wave-like movement that begins deep in the pelvis and moves upwards to the mouth. Breathing out reverses this movement. It is accepted that this natural, involuntary rhythm becomes constricted in childhood and that even as adults we hold our breath to suppress feelings during anxious, fearful and painful moments. In therapy various breathwork techniques are used to restimulate those areas between the pelvis and mouth which have become dysfunctional and emotionally deadened over a lifetime of habit.

To assist in this process, as well as in stretching other muscle groups, a 'roller' (a padded drum measuring approximately 14 inches in diameter by 24 inches long), is often used. With knees bent, pelvis lifted and hands behind the head for support, the client lies on the roller keeping the mid and upper back in contact with it while rolling a few inches forward and backwards. This gentle rocking, along with deep or rapid breathing, opens the throat and stretches the back and upper chest, thus re-educating the muscles of the diaphragm to the fullness of the breathing process.

In each session time is also given for discussion of the insights, feelings and memories which may have been brought to light by the body work. By nature we can only absorb into our consciousness those experiences which are relevant to our past knowledge. This analytic part of the therapy focuses on assisting the client to look at the mental distortions and long held beliefs which have maintained the character defences. The central goal of this work then is to develop the client's acceptance of self and strengthen their willingness to change so that a new conceptual grounding can take place in daily life. The practice of meditation supports this intention by emphasizing the person's sense of being present in each moment. Ideally, this allows temporary freedom from the conditioned beliefs of the past self.

The techniques used in groups evolved about 15 years ago after Pierrakos began to observe group auras, particularly lecture audiences where attention was focused on the speaker. He discovered that if the speakers were communicating their ideas well, the auras of individual audience members would vibrate faster. At a certain point, at about 35 pulsations per minute, the individual auras join together and the group aura begins to vibrate up and down in unison. Dr Pierrakos took this 'resonance phenomenon' and began to apply it as a therapeutic tool in his work with groups.

The focus of the work is to increase the energy of the whole group which in turn increases the consciousness of each individual member. Initially group participants work physically with movement and breath techniques to loosen and expand their own energies. The group leader then arranges the group, lying on their backs, into a wheel or mandala. There are three variations of this position: one in which all participants have their feet towards the centre or hub of the circle; a second in which the same configuration is held but men and women alternate position when forming the spokes of the wheel. In the final variation the participant's heads are towards the centre with their feet towards the periphery or rim of the wheel. In each case the therapist initiates a breathing technique followed by movement and vocalization or contact with the person on either side.

The deep breathing which begins each mandala is done in unison and has the effect of creating a powerful cyclotron which energizes the entire group. To the trained or gifted eye, the group energy field (aura) is seen to move around the circle in a counter-clockwise direction. The moods and body placements of individuals create variations in the energy flow so that if the energies of one or two people are particularly blocked the body of the group energy will literally bridge over them to connect with the person on either side. This also gives an indication to the leader as to which people might later need individual work supported by the presence of the group.

In Core Energetic terms, the group is said to constitute a society for each group participant. The emphasis of the group work is on the individual experience of each member which is then extended and shared with the whole. In effect this means being able to take full responsibility for the communication of one's own emotions. The mutual sharing and acceptance of both positive and negative expressions builds a sense of trust. As the group matures, this serves to reintegrate each person, not only within themselves but with their outer world as well.

Does it work?

Pitfalls

Any discussion of the pitfalls of therapy must consider the central role of the relationship between client and therapist. Most forms of psychotherapy recognize the phenomenon of 'transference', when the client responds, positively and negatively, to the therapist as though he or she were a significant figure in the client's past, usually a parent. In Core Energetics the therapist uses the therapeutic relationship to confront energetically and to break gently the client's defences (developed in childhood in response to parental actions and attitudes) such that from the initial meeting the therapist must be extremely aware of the interpersonal dynamics. Specifically, the therapist must maintain an awareness of their own character structure so that any unconscious feelings of 'counter-transference' from the therapist on to the client will be recognized and not prove to be an obstacle to the therapeutic process.

In working with the resistance of the client's defences the therapist requires a thorough knowledge of all character structure 'types'. This insures that appropriate bodywork techniques will be employed which will not break the trust of the client, particularly of the 'wounded child' which is exposed when the defences are down. In this respect, the therapist must intuitively be aware of how much and how fast the client can absorb energetic change so that the physical work does not become purely clinical, thus leaving the client feeling provoked and violated. The therapist must constantly question the issues of power and authority which their role can engender in the therapeutic relationship so that they can work from a position of respect and compassion.

From the client's perspective, a major pitfall in the therapeutic work can be their expectations of the therapy. If they enter therapy with the assumption that Core Energetics or the therapist is offering the great panacea to their problems then they may be disappointed during the course of the work. Core Energetics requires an attitude of self-motivation and commitment so that the individual becomes an active participant in their own healing. Otherwise the therapy will devolve into a mechanical process.

Expectations should be discussed in the initial sessions so that the client and therapist agree on the direction of the therapy. In addition, the client should intuitively have a good feeling about the therapist and decide whether a somatic form of psychotherapy is appropriate for them. As the bodywork aspects of Core Energetic therapy can be physically uncomfortable and evoke deep emotional catharsis the individual must have a willingness to explore those places within themselves that would normally be avoided in everyday life. In this sense, they must have an openness to the process of change and the willingness to trust another person, in this case the therapist.

Research

As with any type of psychotherapy it is difficult to measure the effectiveness of the therapeutic process. The variables involved are too numerous and complex to allow for scientific questioning. It would entail a classification of client problems and personalities, therapists and therapeutic techniques, as well as the circumstances surrounding the therapy. While the client's subjective experience of change can be categorized, it certainly cannot be quantified.

However as Dr Pierrakos has established Core Energetics to be literally an energy-based form of psychotherapy he has been able to examine the impact of increased levels of energy on an individual's character structure and thus, the health or dysfunction of the personality. During the course of therapy he monitors energetic functioning by observing any changes in the vibrational rate of the person's aura. (For accounts of his detailed research into the human aura and energy systems in general, see Pierrakos 1987, specifically, Part 3 Chapter 17 and the analysis of research found in the appendices. In addition, *Energy & Consciousness: The International Journal of Core Energetics* publishes current research, for example, 'The effects of Core Energetics on stress levels and immune functioning of HIV positive individuals'.)

Case study

Richard was a successful 33 year old businessman. He had never been married and was in the process of amicably ending a five-year relationship. He stated that the relationship had held no meaning for him after about the first year. He had been involved with various 'new age' philosophies but had found none of them to be particularly relevant to his daily life. He had chosen to enter therapy because of a general sense of frustration and helplessness. He complained of being dissatisfied with his life and expressed an inability to care about others, including his family and colleagues. He had no friends except for the woman that he had been living with and whom he now felt he had to reject. He described himself as feeling like 'a house made of match sticks'. He thought that he was hiding from something and felt especially vulnerable to criticism from men.

When a degree of trust and rapport had been established after the first few sessions, Richard was asked to view his body in a mirror and relate any associations that came to mind as he observed his overall posture and any specific areas to which his attention was drawn. He expressed both a sense of weakness in his abdomen as well as a sense of numbness in the pelvic region. This was reflected by a 'band' of tense muscles in the area of the upper abdomen and diaphragm as well as extremely tight, almost steel-like thighs and calf muscles. What this indicated was a splitting of the energy flow between his upper and lower body. Energy moving upwards from the earth through the feet could not fully connect with the energy moving downwards from the heavens, the head and heart. Thus the pelvic region, the lower abdomen and genitals remained deadened and undercharged. (Again, the development of muscular armouring is viewed as a response by the organism to protect itself within its environment. At the emotional and psychological levels the Core is attempting to defend those areas of the self which had been insulted or violated during early childhood.) In Richard's case the issues of powerlessness and sexuality would gradually emerge to be the focus of the therapeutic work. In a sense, he had never actually established his own centre of gravity or experienced the true nature and strength of his feelings.

With the introductory sessions and the body reading as a guide the physical aspect of the therapy could begin. Working with grounding exercises brought Richard away from the predominant habit (his Mask), of interpreting experience in a mental/analytical fashion and focused his attention on bodily sensation, including his connection to the earth. Next, exercises were introduced which would energetically 'charge' those areas where he unconsciously held muscular tension: kicking, jumping and squatting movements for his legs and breathing exercises to stretch the muscles of the diaphragm to allow more oxygen into the abdomen. (Just as restricted breathing reduces and numbs the intensity of all feeling so too does muscular rigidity inhibit full movement and the impulse or emotion associated with it.) Richard's increased energy level during these exercises brought forward these deeply repressed emotions and he was asked to give physical and vocal expression to them. During these moments, and in later therapeutic processing at the end of each session, he came to recognize and acknowledge the destructive aspects of his nature (the Lower Self).

As the therapy progressed he was able to relate incidents from childhood when he felt he had been sexually humiliated by his mother. Also, he spoke of being constantly denigrated by his father as not being the man that he (his father) was. Slowly, Richard came to understand from where his great fear of criticism had arisen, as well as the distorted sense of sexual vulnerability which he experienced in his relationships with women. He felt that his drive toward professional achievement was partly in response to a need to be better than his father, and that his successful social position would reinforce his standing in his mother's eyes as being the 'good little boy', not the naughty child with unacceptable sexual feelings.

As Richard gained further insight into the defensive aspects of his character he began to recognize recurring patterns of behaviour which were evident in his present life. He viewed the occasions at work when he would lie to his colleagues as just one example of his inability to truly express his thoughts and feelings. This was also true in a brief relationship he had had with a woman during the one and a half years that the therapy lasted. He understood that his fear of intimate contact and the inability to commit himself in relationships was disempowering him at a more subtle level. The choices he was making in response to other people, while satisfying the false needs of the character mask, were not actually fulfilling his deeper need for trust, warm affection, love and compassion.

At this point the physical work gradually decreased. He was able to sustain more 'belly' feelings such as laughing and crying and increasingly had a sense of being more fully grounded in his sexual identity. The therapy then moved into its final stages. The sessions became periods of opportunity during which Richard could reacquaint himself with his Core, the undefended self. By working with images, inner sensations, and meditation techniques he was able to learn to support that part of himself which wanted to work more consciously for positive change in his life. He ended the therapy when he chose to commit himself more fully to a relationship that he had initiated several months previously.

A comment on the literature

John Pierrakos' (1987) book is the most complete account of Core Energetics.

Barbara Brennan (1988), a former NASA physicist and Core Energetic therapist, presents an in-depth study of the aura and how the human energy field is affected by our relationship to others and by physiological and emotional disturbances. It offers guidelines for working with and healing the aura as well as medically verified case studies.

Pierrakos (1990) is a selection of the Pathwork lectures channelled by Eva Pierrakos. This book outlines a path for personal transformation and spiritual self-realization. It includes an understanding of the sources and consequences of personal negativity and how to transform it.

References

Brennan, B. (1988) *Hands of Light: A Guide to Healing Through the Human Energy Field.* London: Bantam Books.
Pierrakos, E. (1990) *The Pathwork of Self-Transformation.* London: Bantam Books.
Pierrakos, J. (1987) *Core Energetics: Developing the Capacity to Love and Heal.* Mendocino, CA: Life Rhythm Publications.

Post-Reichian Therapy

WILLIAM WEST

Definition and historical development

Definition

Post-Reichian Therapy is a form of body–mind psychotherapy derived from the work of Wilhelm Reich MD who was born in 1897 and died in 1957 (Boadella 1985). It uses breathing, touch, voice and dialogue to bring into awareness stuck, defensive body–mind patterns which Reich (1972) called 'armour'. It encourages clients to get in touch with the childhood experiences that gave rise to these patterns. In letting go of old emotions held in muscle tension and character attitudes, energy is freed for creative action in the present.

Post-Reichian Therapy is especially aware of how our traumas or neuroses are reflected in a low level of life energy and a correspondingly poor flow of this life energy. Reich called it *orgone energy* and the therapy seeks to enhance its flow and vitality within the body and in the field or *aura* that surrounds the body. Poverty of energetic vitality is often expressed in lack of feeling; lack of awareness of feelings in self and others; uncreative thinking and relating – especially emotional and sexual relating; lack of spirit and spirituality; poor breathing; and above all a lack of interest in life around us.

Historical development

Reich was a doctor of medicine who became a pupil of Freud's. He extended Freud's theory of libido, seeing it as an actual body energy which he called *bio-energy* or orgone energy. Reich also developed ways of working with the body, including focusing posture, muscular tension and breathwork. Reich became increasingly interested not just in what people said but in how they said it, what their body did when they spoke and how their body spoke when they remained silent.

Neurosis was seen by Reich as consisting of physical blockages of the flow of orgone energy in the body. Such rigidities in the body were accompanied by rigidities in the mind, reflected in fixed ways of thinking about one's self and one's world, together with other forms of disturbances in thinking.

Reich began his psychotherapeutic work as an innovative psychoanalyst with a deep commitment to improving the life of ordinary people. He focused increasingly on the body and its role in psychological health and illness. This departure from Freud is reflected in the way Reich referred to his work. First he called it psychoanalysis, then character analytic vegetotherapy and finally, emphasizing the body and life energy, Orgone Therapy.

Reich worked first of all in Vienna, later Berlin and Oslo and finally in 1940 in the USA. His moves were initially provoked by the rise of fascism, for Reich was Jewish and involved in anti-fascist work. The controversial nature of his theories of sexuality made him an unwelcome visitor to Scandinavia.

After Reich's death in 1957 several currents or schools arose among those who had worked with him in the USA. Alexander Lowen, a medical doctor, developed Bioenergetics, with the help of John Pierrakos (see Chapter 8, this volume), whilst Charles Kelley, a psychologist, developed Radix Therapy. Fritz Perls, the founder of Gestalt Therapy, was a client of Reich's, and took much from Reich into his own work, as he makes clear in his book *Ego Hunger and Aggression* (Perls 1969). Reich's official successor was Dr Elsworth Baker who continued Reich's work under the label of Orgone Therapy.

These then were the main developments in the USA. In Europe the main person using and developing Reich's work was the Norwegian analyst Ola Raknes. According to David Boadella, editor of the Reich-influenced *Energy & Character* magazine, from Raknes have sprung, directly or indirectly, many of the main Reichian, neo-Reichian and post-Reichian approaches to therapy in Europe, nine in total. In Britain these include both the Boyesen Centre's Biodynamic Psychology and the Post-Reichian Therapy approach of Energy Stream.

Founders

Ola Raknes then was one of the most significant people Reich trained in Europe and he wrote a fascinating book about him (Raknes 1971). In the 1960s there was a tradition that people interested in training in Reichian Psychotherapy approaches would visit and stay in Norway to learn from Ola Raknes. One such person was Peter Jones who on his return to England founded the Orgone Research Group.

One of Peter Jones's main contributions to Reichian Psychotherapy in Europe is in the field of pregnancy, childbirth and child rearing (Jones 1976). This has included work with pregnant women and the use of a form of Reichian Therapy with babies and young children. Peter is also very committed to the home-education movement, and was an early member of Education Otherwise, the UK home schooling organization. Peter educated his daughter out of school. He is currently training to be a midwife.

Peter Jones also developed a new facilitating, unauthoritarian style of teaching Reichian techniques in workshops. Participants are invited to act in turn as 'client' and then 'therapist' with Peter's support and guidance. Hitherto there was not much of a tradition of Reichian group work; and the teaching was often through personal therapy and case study. Peter brought Reichian therapy work out into the open, something that represented a natural, if radical, progression.

I was one of Peter Jones's pupils, and with the help of my early trainees founded Energy Stream/Post-Reichian Therapy Association in 1984. Up to the present Energy Stream has trained over 65 people as Reichian psychotherapists. Along with my colleagues, I have developed Peter Jones's pioneering use of Reichian techniques within a led peer group workshop framework. Besides weekend courses, longer groups over five or seven days, in a residential setting, have been established on a regular basis.

I coined the term 'post-Reichian' to describe our Energy Stream work, to indicate both its origins in Reich's work, but also its openness to new developments in therapy and healing that can be integrated into a Reichian based approach to therapy. It is common now within Energy Stream, the group of post-Reichian therapists, for members to describe themselves as Energy Stream therapists to indicate this moving on from Reich.

In recent years there has been a move within Energy Stream away from direct physical massage work with clients, and a deepening interest in a more verbal approach to psychotherapy and in healing work (West 1984), although there remains a common commitment to Reich's view of the functional identity of 'body' and 'mind' energy patterns.

Relationship to other therapies

Although Reichian Therapy has its roots in Freud's psychoanalysis, and still views the therapy relationship in terms of transference, character analysis and resistance, in many ways it fits best within humanistic psychology. Indeed, many humanistic writers – for instance Jerome Liss (1974) and John Rowan (1987) – credit Reich as being one of the founders of the humanistic approach. Rowan, indeed, regards Reich as a bridge between psychoanalysis and humanistic psychotherapy.

With its emphasis on life energy in the body and in the universe at large it is possible to view Reichian Therapy as being part of alternative or complementary medicine, sitting alongside other approaches that work with life energy, like the Alexander technique, acupuncture and so on.

With the popularity of humanistic approaches to therapy Reichian techniques are gaining a broader acceptance both among therapists and the public at large. For instance, it is noticeable that the United Kingdom Council for Psychotherapy includes at least six member organizations whose students study some aspect of Reich's work as part of their training. These include both the Boyesen Centre and Chiron, both of whom owe much to Raknes's approach. At present Energy Stream has observer status within the United Kingdom Council for Psychotherapy.

Central concepts

Like other forms of humanistic psychotherapy, Reichian Therapy insists that people are basically OK. They have usually been damaged in a process that began in early childhood, often at birth, or even earlier. This damage is reflected in muscular tensions or flaccidity, poor breathing, disturbances in thinking, low levels of feeling, sluggish energy levels, poor relating, poor sexual relating, and uncreative approaches to life and work. Muscular tensions form a holding pattern in the body that protects us from feeling the pain of unbearable suffering. These tensions were called 'armour' by Reich; the corresponding mental attitudes he called character armour. Seeing the body–mind as one, as a unity, we can find examples of character traits that illustrate this unity, e.g. being stiff-necked, which is both a mental attitude and also a physical reality: stiff-necked people do have tense necks. There is a whole vocabulary of unconscious or semiconscious 'give aways' (e.g. tight-arsed, heartbreak, I can't stomach it), that show this body–mind unity and how armouring has both physical and mental components.

Reich saw this armouring as being systematic. For instance if we need to hold back tears we may well tense muscles around our eyes, tighten our throats, hold our chests tense and possibly our diaphragms and bellies. Many men have rigid inflated chests that won't give in to gentler feelings like tears. Women may have been brought up not to inflate their chests, not to feel self-esteem, and personal power, not to be angry. Such armouring leads to disease, with the sites of the tensions being the spots where the disease strikes. Armouring arises then from our not being allowed to be ourselves, not being supported in feeling, in thinking, and in moving. Armouring keeps us from feeling too much in an unfriendly world. It is a way of coping and getting by, a way of surviving as a child.

Reich saw people as having three layers to their character. Buried deep inside us is a core from which our energy springs, a core that is spontaneous, loving, caring, cooperative and, where appropriate, angry. Repression of this core leads to an angry, spiteful, hateful and self-hating response: a secondary layer of 'badness'. This is not allowed, so we coat it over with an outer layer of polite sociability, of 'niceness', a mere echo, and a watered-down version of our true inner core. Reichian Therapy aims to free our true core nature by facing the reality of our secondary layer, by dissolving and dispelling it.

Post-Reichian Therapy seeks to restore our natural capacity for what Reich called 'self-regulation' by encouraging healthy breathing, releasing muscular tensions, challenging rigid thinking patterns, and accepting the emotions that are then often felt and expressed. When this outpouring of emotions happens in the therapy, a sense of peace is often experienced and a feeling of streaming of energy in the body. This flow of energy also occurs with healthy breathing and in sexual excitation. It is seen as an important sign, an underpinning of health.

Human beings, like animals and other living things, are energy systems. Reichian Therapy also works with energy within and around the body, freeing the flow and balancing over and undercharged regions. The therapy also works with people's emotional lives, seeking to bring about an alive but centred way of feeling. Reichian Therapy seems nearly always to alter people's attitudes to, and experiences of, love and sexuality. People often end up wanting deeper and better contact with those to whom they are close.

The ultimate goal of Reichian Therapy is to free the body–mind from armouring so that the client can be in touch with their core, and express themselves from that centre. Such a person could still call on their armouring to defend themselves as necessary, but this defence would be under conscious control. For Reich such a person would be what he termed a genital character, a term which he derived from Freud, and used in contrast to his description of armoured people, for example, oral, anal, or phallic characters, who showed systematic armouring and character patterns of different kinds.

Apart from the obvious aliveness that such a genital character would show, Reich also found a particular breathing pattern, a free form of breathing which he somewhat misleadingly referred to as the 'orgasm reflex'. He had taken from Freud the notion that the energy of neurosis is a sexual energy, so the healthy flow of this energy would need expression within an adult sexual relationship. Without such an outlet mental health was seen to be impossible, and armouring would return, even if it was released in therapy.

Post-Reichian therapists would agree with Reich on the importance of healthy loving and sexual contact for adults, but would question whether it is the only way to health. Reich does not say that promiscuity is the answer, for it is the quality of the loving contact that is crucial. Permissiveness (and indeed pornography) is often the expression of secondary layers of our character and consequently not very satisfying. There is an excellent critique of 1960s permissiveness written from a Reichian viewpoint by George Frankl (1975). Reich also took a negative view of homosexuality, in common with most analysts in the 1920s. Although some Reichian therapists, including Reich's American successor, Dr Baker, still hold this viewpoint, Energy Stream therapists do not share this view, and indeed, we have trained and will continue to train people of any sexual orientation (likewise race or age).

Reichian Therapy is naturally holistic in a very real energy sense, in that through its notion of orgone energy it sees links between people, groups, the planet, galaxies, life as a whole. Reich saw that life energy was not confined to living creatures but was in fact universal. This gives Reichian therapy a unique and cosmic view of things that is both political and spiritual.

One consequence of this universal nature of orgone energy was that Reich was able to construct devices he called orgone accumulators which stored up orgone energy. The use of orgone devices in therapy is not a common part of Energy Stream practice. Further details about orgone devices can be found in Boadella (1985), Totton and Edmondson (1988) and West (1988).

Reichian Therapy trusts the client to find their own answers. Although it has its own world view it does not expect its clients to agree with it. It aims to put people in touch with themselves on a deep level enabling them to act on their own truth in their own unique ways.

Post-Reichian Therapy works very much with the issue of contact. It focuses on the contact between the client and the therapist, knowing that issues that the client has about contact in life will be mirrored in their relationship with their therapist. Changes that occur in the client's capacity for contact in the therapy relationship can then be taken out into the client's life outside therapy.

The cause of suffering

Suffering as such is not seen by Reichian therapists as the main problem. Reichian therapists see some suffering as innate and healthy, e.g. grieving at loss or death of someone we love. We have the natural biological ability to cope with such suffering with the right kind of support. Problems are created when an overload of suffering is imposed on us as children, usually by adults who could know better. The child struggling to cope with this suffering is usually met with further repression by those around her or him: 'Don't cry.' 'She's just having a tantrum.' 'If you don't stop crying I'll give you something to cry about.'

This overload of suffering leads to neurosis, to what Reich termed armouring, in which the child is locked into fixed defensive body–mind patterns. Further overloads reinforce these patterns and gradually a permanent set is established within the person with accompanied posture, musculature, thought, feeling and energy components to it.

Reichian therapists, taking a holistic view, are also aware of the social and political context. The pressures on the family or community can work against the free-flowing life of the newborn child. Education, work, housing, social security (what a misnomer that is!), are not arranged to encourage self-regulation in children and grown-ups, and consequently reinforce the armouring. There are natural links between a Reichian approach and those of natural childbirth supporters and practitioners such as Leboyer (1975) and Odent (1984). Peter Jones's work with pregnancy, childbirth and alternatives to schooling has already been mentioned.

Reich was also a close friend of A.S. Neill, who founded Summerhill. Summerhill is a school run on self-regulation lines by its staff and pupils equally. Reich was Neill's therapist and their relationship and exchange of ideas on children and therapy is described in Placzek (1982).

The change process

As Post-Reichian therapists we work with the health in our clients. We only explore the dis-ease in the client in order to facilitate the healing process. We aim to open up a healthier relationship between our client's thinking and feeling, between body and mind, between self and others, between self and the earth and the universe at large. We seek to reveal at the client's pace what is 'unfeelable' or 'unthinkable', to question what is habitual, especially those thoughts and feelings about our selves that are of a negative, restrictive, self-destructive nature.

We have a deep belief in self-regulation, which occurs when we are healthy, and are able to relate openly and deeply with people and the planet. The therapy aims to liberate this natural biological capacity for balanced self-management and self-healing. In our hearts, in the very core of our being we know what is right and healthy for us. We encourage our clients to contact this knowledge and act from its truth. At this level only the clients themselves know what is true and best. No therapist, counsellor or adviser can replace this inner knowledge, nor should they be tempted to try.

Traditionally Reichian Therapy worked very much with a medical model, with clients described as 'patients' and neuroses being 'cured' in the therapy. Post-Reichian Therapy works with a more humanistic notion of growth. Through the therapy our abilities to self-regulate can be released, enabling our innate potential to flower. Although we don't see the therapy as being endless, we do see that no limit should be set to people's potential for growth; that the part played by the therapy in releasing this potential continues after the therapy sessions are over. The effects of good therapy can last a lifetime.

The therapy is likely to move the client towards being alive, feeling more, having more energy, being more creative. The therapy then, is not a mechanical process, it is alive, it is full of feeling. It is occasionally very uncomfortable and occasionally very joyful.

Post-Reichian Therapy does not promise cures. It offers the chance to explore those things in our lives that we feel unhappy about. Out of that exploration often comes change, but not always the change we wanted or expected. For instance one client after six months of therapy complained, 'I came to you because I wanted a better sex life. I didn't realize I would have to get into all these feelings!' The therapy works with what is often a largely unconscious process of self-realization within the client.

Neither the therapy nor the therapy relationship is plain sailing. Sometimes it can feel like one step forward, two steps back. Clients need great courage and support to face their early, and not so early, traumas. (Reich spoke of three main times in our life for the development of neuroses: early childhood, adolescence and marriage.) Clients will often have to face up to and feel great fear, hurt, anger and rage. The therapy relationship needs to be strong enough to support such exploration. However, the pay-off almost inevitably makes it well worthwhile.

As clients discover more about themselves, more about their feelings, their creative impulses, how they truly want to live, there often comes a time of conflict with their world. Docile clients suddenly become assertive, hard men begin crying and wanting softer, more intimate forms of contact. Their world does not always react positively to their changes. Painful adjustments become necessary. Often there is a tension between client-in-the-therapy-room and client-in-the-world. Some clients quit therapy at this stage. Others often make painful changes in their worlds, sometimes at great cost. However, clients insist they would not put the clock back, and do not regret having come for the therapy. The pay-off in living their lives more connected to their true inner self makes the pain well worthwhile.

Therapeutic goals

Inevitably, given the philosophy of Post-Reichian Therapy, the setting of therapeutic goals is a joint process involving client and therapist with the therapist supporting the client in their exploration. What is apparent is that the real or deeper reason for seeking therapy is often not manifest at the first or subsequent sessions. For instance a client may not have been able to admit to consciousness the fact of their sexual or other abuse as a child. With the build-up of trust within the therapy relationship and the consequent deepening of the self-exploration such personal truths are able to come to consciousness.

Few people come to Reichian Therapy saying 'I want Reichian Therapy, I have read the books and want to become a genital character!' Indeed Post-Reichian therapists regard genitality as an ideal, rather than as something to be achieved. What is possible is clients becoming more alive, more full of feeling, more in touch with themselves and their world, having more energy and creativity and above all being more able to set and achieve their own real goals in life.

Often people come for Reichian Therapy because they are sexually dissatisfied in some way, though they are unlikely to admit it at the first session. People often come due to some life crisis. Others come because they are not getting enough out of life.

Typically the practitioner will make it clear that within a handful of sessions some relief of an immediate crisis may be possible. For instance grief and other feelings relating to a loss may be explored and discharged. However, deep seated exploration and change is unlikely to be possible in a matter of weeks, so if the client seeks that as a therapeutic goal it means months or even years of therapy.

Practitioners

Relationship

The relationship between the Reichian therapist and client is crucial. For the client to realize more of their true self, for them to be able to reclaim and revive parts of themselves locked away, then they need to depend on the health of their therapist and on the health of the relationship established between the two of them.

In many ways the Reichian client/therapist relationship represents the best aspects of the humanistic therapy relationship. The therapist is intended to be alive with the client and responsive to the exploration they need to make. Words like warmth, acceptance and sensitivity spring to mind.

The therapist will also be aware that the relationship sometimes needs to be stormy. She or he will be aware, with the help of supervision, of when the relationship has become too cosy, aware of the transference issues, aware of when contact is being avoided, aware of when to push the client towards a new realization, aware of when to sit back and wait for the client to reach a new sense of themselves.

At times the client will need what amounts to reparenting and will through the therapy regress to childhood or earlier. (Re-experiencing one's birth is a fairly common experience for clients in Post-Reichian Therapy.) In this regressive state the client will relive the memories, emotions and body sensations that led to the neurosis being explored. This requires great skill on the part of the therapist and a very trusting relationship is necessary. It is an extraordinary experience for a

50 year old man to begin crying just like a three month old baby, extraordinary for both client and therapist.

At other times the client will not be regressed and may confront the therapist with their maturity. A very real and honest encounter can then occur between two grown-ups – an encounter in which the therapist may be nearly as vulnerable as the client.

A deep connection between client and therapist has to be made for the therapy to reach its full possibilities for the client. This demands the best of the therapist and draws up the deepest energies from his or her core. Love and contact and safety are necessary, both for the therapist, but also for the client and his or her newly discovered potential. So the therapist has to be real and yet to remain aware that this is the client's therapy, the client's process that is unfolding within the therapy room.

Techniques

To explain fully and to explore the techniques of Post-Reichian Therapy would take more space than I have available here. I will merely touch on the main techniques leaving the interested reader to explore elsewhere (Totton and Edmondson 1988; West 1988). However, these powerful techniques cannot be learnt from a book but by attending an appropriate training course.

Contact is a crucial element in Post-Reichian Therapy. We are interested in what contact the client is able to make with their therapist and with the world at large, what contact they have with their inner self, their bodies, their energy, their feelings. Are they able to remain in touch with themselves and to be in contact with the therapist? This can lead to therapeutic work involving eye contact and other work with the eyes, physical contact, spatial issues in the therapy room and other boundary work, contact with the ground (i.e. grounding), breathwork, etc.

Bodywork, involving the client's body and their awareness of their body as part of the therapy, was a crucial contribution by Reich to modern psychotherapy. This can include awareness held by the therapist, enhancing the client's aware-ness of their body, actually changing posture or using bioenergetic exercises (Lowen and Lowen 1976), Reichian massage by the therapist on the client's body and encouraging the client to use their body in movement, voice work and emotional expression.

Linked to bodywork is breathwork. As part of his bodywork approach Reich drew particular attention to how clients breathe and how disruptions of full healthy breathing contributed to, and were expressions of, neurosis. The therapist will often encourage appropriate vocalization by the clients to free up their breathing and to help release the withheld feelings. The therapist may also do Reichian massage to help the client's breathing. All these approaches are very powerful techniques and they need careful handling.

Over my years of work as a Post-Reichian therapist I have rarely found anyone who could breathe well, easily able to inflate both chest and abdomen. I once found someone who could breathe well, but he turned out to be a heavy smoker! Breathing well gives us more energy and more ability to feel, which is just too painful for the child that we were. We coped by tensing our chest and/or bellies. Typically most people are physically unable to fully inflate either their chest or bellies.

Although helping people to breathe requires great skill, the health consequences of improved breathing are enormous. We don't teach people to breathe, or impose any pattern. This would restrict the aliveness of our clients. The more people are freed from muscular tension and rigidities of thinking the more their natural, healthy, spontaneous, breathing reasserts itself. Often at the end of a powerful Reichian Therapy session one can hear a deep satisfying style of breathing by a client that holds the promise of a healthier, saner life. Of course, the question always arises, will their world accept their new health, their new range of emotions, their new creativity? This itself can lead to a whole new focus for their therapy.

Transference and counter-transference
With its roots in Freudian psychoanalysis, it is inevitable that Reichian and Post-Reichian Therapy work with the transference relationship. However, Post-Reichian therapists tend to be more themselves in the therapy than traditional analysts, and this, coupled with the bodywork, alters the transference. My colleagues Nick Totton and Em Edmondson express this well:

> The therapist's ultimate resource is her [*sic*] capacity to be *honest* – with herself, with her clients, about what is actually going on. This is really the only way to avoid becoming what the client fears yet tries to create – an oppressive authority figure, withholding knowledge as a source of power.
> (Totton and Edmondson 1988: 108)

Resistance
In any therapeutic process there are elements within the client (and therapist also) which seek change and also elements which resist the possibilities of change and movement. Helping the client become aware of, and indeed to celebrate, such resistance is an important part of the therapy. This celebration moves the process on from viewing the client's resistance as a problem to be overcome to seeing it as an accepted and acceptable part of their being. For without such resistance how could they have survived?

Character
Closely linked to working with transference is work with the client's character. Reich's description of classic Freudian character analysis is innovative in its description of physical dimensions to character (see Southgate 1980; Totton and Edmondson 1988).

Totton and Edmondson in particular present a view of character that gets away from seeing it as purely negative and pathological. This is reflected in some therapists' referring to their clients as masochists or hysterics, that is, that the human being has now been reduced to a clinical label.

Totton and Edmondson present six character positions rather than character types. These are boundary, oral, holding, thrusting, crisis and open. They are at pains to present the creative possibilities in each position and maintain that our armouring prevents us from creatively choosing which character position to occupy when.

Reading Reich it is difficult not to view character as negative, as something that needs to be dissolved, to be discarded. Post-Reichian therapists recognize that character, like armouring, is about survival by the child and needs validating before exploring the more creative responses that the present day adult could have. An example of this is where a child has an overbearing father who always squashed any anger, any answering back by the child. Such children grow up unable to be aggressive, indeed unable to assert themselves. Typically they will have a chest that is unable to expand and usually a retracted pelvis and a poor connection with the ground, i.e. unable to stand on their own two feet. Learning to stamp one's feet, bellow with rage, to be empowered, will be very valuable to such a client. The aim is not to produce an overbearing client, but to help them reclaim their ability to be assertive, to stand up for themselves.

Groupwork

Post-Reichian Therapy makes use of groupwork where appropriate to benefit the client. Many clients of Energy Stream attend groups run by their therapists or others. Attending a group can be very empowering for a client. They can benefit from 'spectator therapy', they can see their struggle in the context of other people's struggle, and given the use of pair and group sessions during the group they can help others to grow and be helped in return. It is part of the skill of a Post-Reichian therapist to know when and when not to recommend a group. Naturally the choice remains with the client. Further details about Post-Reichian Therapy groups are discussed in Totton and Edmondson (1988) and West (1984).

Therapist as instrument

Reich (1951) speaks of our ability when healthy to trust our human responses as a guide to what is happening. If we truly know ourselves and have freed ourselves as much as possible from armouring and know where our holding patterns remain, we can then use ourselves and our reactions as a measure of the world. Post-Reichian therapists use their reactions to their clients to guide and inform their work. For instance as a therapist at work we may feel overwhelmed by sadness. This could be a memory of our own sadness at some incident in our past, triggered by our client; it could be our reaction to our client's story; or we could be sharing a feeling coming from our client. I have found that the more a client of mine denies a feeling from his or her consciousness, the more I feel it for him or her.

Only by really knowing myself can I sort out which of the three possibilities are happening to me in the above example. Besides feelings, I can often have bodily sensations in response to my clients, for example, tension in my guts. Also, on occasions I have direct intuition via a symbol or metaphor.

For example, I once saw one client as a beaten dog, a dog that had been ill treated and chained up. It seemed a bit extreme to share it but I did. Out came a tale from his childhood of being beaten without warning by his mother and being locked in a cupboard under the stairs. My image of a beaten dog was an intuitive metaphor for his experience and sharing it had enabled him to share his memory with me.

Does it work?

Pitfalls

The client/therapist relationship is crucial for the success of the therapy. However effective the therapist is in a technical sense, if he or she is not trusted, not respected by the client then the therapy will not work. Likewise the client needs to feel safe and cared for by the therapist. Indeed the client needs to feel that their therapist is interested in them as a human being, not just as an interesting case or a source of income!

At the other end of the spectrum the client/therapist relationship can get too cosy without sufficient challenge, where both parties become overly dependent on their shared therapy sessions. Alternatively the relationship can remain too distant, so that the real therapy work is not done, or not complete, with the client leaving therapy prematurely.

It is important that the therapist does not try too hard, nor push the client too far too quickly. Also, in a therapy which can involve physical contact, the therapist needs to hold clear boundaries, and act always with the client's permission before any physical contact or massage is undertaken.

Research

Recently as part of my MA degree in Counselling Studies 150 ex-clients of Energy Stream therapists were sent a questionnaire. These were ex-clients from 17 Energy Stream therapists, whose therapy had finished over a two year period ending 31 December 1991. Of the 67 (45%) who replied:

31 (46%) were highly satisfied with their therapy.
21 (31%) were satisfied with their therapy.
 8 (13%) were neither satisfied nor dissatisfied.
 6 (10%) were dissatisfied with their therapy.
 – (0%) were highly dissatisfied.
 1   did not reply to this question.

So out of the 45 per cent who replied, 77 per cent were satisfied or highly satisfied with their therapy. Research into the effectiveness of psychotherapy and counselling, whether through interviews or returned questionnaires, usually results in a figure of about 80 per cent of clients saying they are satisfied. It does suggest that Energy Stream practitioners are providing a service that their clients find valuable, at a level of client satisfaction comparable to that of other therapy approaches.

The questionnaire also explored what the ex-clients had found helpful in their therapy. Specifically Reichian techniques such as working with breathing and emotional release were valued and so were more general techniques such as feeling accepted and listened to.

Case study

John was a fresh-faced 22 year old, recently moved to the big city from his university town, where he had gained a good degree. He was sharing a flat with an old school friend, was unemployed, and had no clear idea of what he wanted to do with his life.

He had an overbearing, aggressive, cold, opinionated father and a soft, warmer mother whose side he had learnt to take in the frequent family rows in which she always gave in to his father. His father was often absent from home because of his work.

John had had very little sexual experience to date, mostly unsatisfactory, and mostly under the influence of drink. He was personable and attractive, but a little unsteady on his feet which suggested to me a lack of grounding, probably connected with his inability to express anger and rage. Although he could feel sadness, tears were rarely expressed. His eyes could be very bright and alive, but also dull, as if he was no longer present. He said that he felt safe in his head, but not very present in his body, especially his chest and heart. It was clear that he needed to find his own way in the world, to make his own mistakes. But without the structures of home, school and university – he had lived in a hall of residence – he felt lost.

Initially the therapy focused on the immediate issues in his life – being in a new flat, with few friends, little money and little to do. Gradually as he found his own solutions to these initial problems, underlying issues began to arise, especially about his early childhood and his current relationships with women. There were several turning points in his therapy.

Three or four months into his therapy, John was able to challenge me. He felt that I was being too directive with him. He was right in that I was trying too hard to be helpful. In fact I was identifying with his struggles, which in some ways matched my own 20 years previously. I encouraged John to explore his anger at my apparent authoritarianism and it quickly developed into anger with his overbearing father. He expressed this anger physically, under my guidance, by forcefully attacking a mattress.

After about a year of therapy John began a sexual relationship with a confident and powerful woman called Jennifer. He found he had to face the challenge of standing up to her, something he had never done before with a woman. His relationship with his mother had taught him to be sensitive to women but he had never learnt to hold his own boundaries with either his mother or his father.

Jennifer's forthrightness demanded clear, strong boundaries from him. It took him months of therapy and living to learn to hold his own whilst relating closely to her.

About 18 months into his therapy there was a session in which I felt somehow restricted in how I was working with him. I remember wishing I was leading a group, where I seem to have more flexibility. I recall telling myself to act as if I were in a group. So I stood up and prowled around a bit. We soon found ourselves in a confrontation setting. We seemed like two bull animals fighting for who was to be head of the herd.

Feeling my way into the part I said I was afraid he would humiliate me. (This turned out to be what his father had always done in fights with him.) However, this was not what he wanted. We locked hands and growled at each other, he with more emotion and meaning in it than me. We both found it exhilarating. (There was a clear no violence contract between us.)

This seemed to be a very important session for him. It felt like part of a healthy form of male initiation, an initiation that had not been completed for him. It seemed very much at that moment that his therapy was focusing around boys becoming men, with the help of their fathers and older men. John was reading a lot of men's personal development literature at that time, as was I. His therapy from that point on tended to focus increasingly on the 'here and now' especially on the relationship between him and me.

Comment on the literature on Reich

Energy & Character: The Journal of Biosynthesis is a biannual journal, formally the *Journal of Bio Energy Research*, and is very relevant to Reichian work in the UK and abroad. It is edited by David Boadella and published by Abbotsbury Publications.

Bean (1971) is Reichian Therapy described by the client in a moving, witty and very readable book. Sharaf (1983) was also a client and co-worker of Reich's and his book is an extremely readable account of Reich and his ideas.

Totton and Edmondson (1988) gives a detailed but concise exposition of the Energy Stream approach to therapy. West (1988) gives a brief practical introduction to the Energy Stream approach to Reichian Therapy.

Boadella (1985) is a book about Reich, the man and his therapy by England's leading Reichian psychotherapist and writer. Reich (1972) is somewhat heavy going in places but in the final third of the book he lays out his own body-approach to therapy in a way which is very moving to read.

References

Bean, O. (1971) *Me and the Orgone*. New York: St. Martin's Press.
Boadella, D. (1985) *Wilhelm Reich, The Evolution of His Work*. London: Arkana.
Frankl, G. (1975) *The Failure of the Sexual Revolution*. London: Mentor.
Jones, P. (1976) The use of vegeto-therapy in childbirth. In D. Boadella (ed.) *In the Wake of Reich*. London: Coventure.
Leboyer, F. (1975) *Birth Without Violence*. London: Wildwood House.
Liss, J. (1974) *Free to Feel*. London: Wildwood House.
Lowen, A. and Lowen, L. (1976) *The Bioenergetic Way to Vibrant Health*. New York: Harper Colloquon.
Odent, M. (1984) *Entering the World*. London: Marion Boyars.
Perls, F. (1969) *Ego Hunger and Aggression: The Beginning of Gestalt Therapy*. New York: Random House.
Placzek, B.R. (ed.) (1982) *Record of a Friendship: Letters between A.S. Neill and Wilhelm Reich*. London: Gollancz.
Raknes, O. (1971) *Wilhelm Reich and Orgonomy*. London: Macmillan.
Reich, W. (1951) *Ether, God and the Devil*. New York: Orgone Institute Press.
Reich, W. (1972) *Character Analysis*. New York: Farrar, Straus & Giroux.
Rowan, J. (1987) *A Guide to Humanistic Psychology*. London: Association for Humanistic Psychology.

Sharaf, M. (1983) *Fury on Earth*. London: Andre Deutsch.

Southgate, J. (1980) Physical Dimensions of Character Structure, *Energy & Character*, 11 (1).

Totton, N. and Edmondson, E. (1988) *Reichian Growth Work*. Bridport, Dorset: Prism.

West, W. (1984) *Loving Contact*. Pamphlet available from 1 Hawksworth Grove, Kirkstall, Leeds LS5 3NB.

West, W. (1988) *Melting Armour*. Pamphlet available from 1 Hawksworth Grove, Kirkstall, Leeds LS5 3NB.

PART IV

Emphasis on expression

10

Phenomenological Multi-Media Therapy

DAVID BRAZIER AND CAROLINE BEECH

Definition and historical development

Definition

Phenomenology is the study of perception. Phenomenological Therapy is a matter of attending to the spontaneously arising flow of perceptions, to the natural unfolding of the individual's personal world (eigenwelt), both as it immediately affects the person's feelings, physiology and behaviour and as it can be represented in words, pictures, drama and other media. This is both a receptive and a creative way of working. Therapist and client are both attentive to what arises naturally and 'playful' in their response. This is a way of therapy in which the attitude of the therapist is one of phenomenological inquiry, that is of, as far as may be, suppositionlessness.

Historical development

Phenomenological philosophy derives from the work of Edmund Husserl in Germany. Husserl (1960, 1962) sought to restore respect for subjectivity at a time when the trend in psychology was almost universally toward achieving a 'scientific' objectivity. Husserl envisaged something different, a 'human science'. Husserl's work was developed and modified by Maurice Merleau-Ponty (1962) in France who established phenomenology as the study of *embodied* perception.

Husserl, like his teacher the nineteenth-century German philosopher Frederick Brentano, believed that the life of the psyche is never passive and that all mental acts 'intend' an 'object'. Brentano's ideas had also strongly influenced many other leading thinkers, including Freud and also the existentialists amongst whom Jacob Moreno, the inventor of psychodrama is notable (see Brazier 1991). Moreno placed the idea of *spontaneity* at the centre of his work and gave an important place both to *dramatization* and to *catharsis* in the practice of therapy.

Husserl's phenomenological method involves the inquirer in *bracketing*, or temporarily putting to one side presuppositions, conventions and assumptions.

This suppositionless stance is called *epoche*. Phenomenology is an attempt to approach subjective phenomena on their own terms and, as such, it stands in contrast to approaches which classify or diagnose mental states and processes.

The development of phenomenological method has also been influenced by the growth of understanding in the west of the eastern traditions of Taoism, Hinduism and especially Buddhism (Tarthang 1977; Akong 1987). Buddhist phenomenology begins with the Abhidhamma literature which was being committed to writing around 400 BCE onward and the yogacara and madhyamika schools, amongst others, went on to develop these principles over the next thousand years. Eastern traditions provide a wealth of introspective and meditative methods for inquiring into and working with subjective phenomena.

In the 1950s, 60s and 70s phenomenological ideas were taken up and developed in the USA by humanistic psychologists, especially Carl Rogers (1961, 1980) and Abraham Maslow (1971) who introduced the idea of an actualizing tendency inherent in life, and in Britain by existentialists such as Ronnie Laing (1960). Husserl's bracketing, Moreno's spontaneity, Rogers's unconditionality and Laing's compassion have all contributed to the emergence of a facilitative, phenomenological approach to therapy.

Founders

Phenomenological Therapy is more an emerging mood than an organized movement. Many therapists are, in varying degrees, involved in trying to apply phenomenological principles to work in expressive media, as developed by Natalie Rogers (Merrill and Anderson 1993), introspective experiencing, as developed by Eugene Gendlin (see Chapter 7, this volume) and such European workers as Mia Leijssen and in the framework of the conversational approach, Emmy van Deurzen-Smith (1988, 1990) and Ernesto Spinelli (1989). Others have drawn inspiration from the eastern teaching methods of lamas like Sogyal (1992) in London or Zen master Nhat Hanh (1990, 1991) in France who have been particularly influential in bringing Buddhist methods to the attention of western therapists.

In Newcastle upon Tyne, the Eigenwelt Centre was established in 1982, and work there, in which the authors of this chapter play a central part, is concerned with inquiring into the root principles of phenomenology and developing an integrated approach to their application in verbal, expressive and introspective media. It is primarily the Eigenwelt approach to phenomenological therapy which is described in this chapter.

Relationship to other therapies

Phenomenological Therapy, like the person centred approach, trusts the process of the client and assigns a facilitative role to the therapist without restricting itself to a reflective verbal style of response. Like Existential Therapy it gives central attention to the client's search for meaning, but achieves this through experiencing rather than through cognitive analysis. It makes use of the dramatic and expressive media employed in Art Therapy, Drama Therapy and Psychodrama, but without giving the therapist a diagnostic, directive or interpretive role. Like focusing and the meditative spiritual traditions it encourages awareness and introspection and integrates them with expressive work. Like psychoanalysis it is concerned with the wisdom of dreams and the unacknowledged dramas of everyday life but without recourse to a fixed model of psychic functioning, seeing all such models as valuable metaphors rather than objective truths. Like cognitive behavioural approaches, it assumes that perception of the world is uniquely affected by deep beliefs and learnings from life, but proceeds by appreciation rather than persuasion. Like hypnosis, it recognizes different states of consciousness and frames of reference, but seeks to explore rather than manipulate them.

Phenomenological Therapy enriches perception through varied means, 'flowing' from one medium to another. The idea of a single medium therapy is, from this perspective, unnecessarily limited. Our world becomes real to us as we 'walk around' phenomena. Representing them in different ways facilitates 'walking around' and enables a sense of wholeness to emerge naturally and directly. Phenomenological Therapy is thus most markedly different from any approach to therapy which seeks to understand the person by analogy to a mechanism. It is distinguished not so much by possession of a particular set of techniques and methods as by a radically subjectivist view of 'reality'.

Central concepts

This section introduces some of the central concepts and technical terms (italicized) of Phenomenological Therapy.

Therapy as a spatial experience

In phenomenology *perception* or *experiencing* is seen as the leader of the human dance. Experience is immediate, i.e. direct and holistic, not something cognitively built up from its parts. Words and rationality follow experience rather than vice versa. Therapy is enrichment of experiencing.

Consciousness is always consciousness of something, says Husserl (1985: 13). The *object* which the client has in mind exists within a *perceptual field* or *ground*, standing out as a *Gestalt*. Consciousness is thus spatially organized. The perceptual field has an open *horizon* and is simply one aspect of the client's *life-world* or *Lebenswelt*. The objects perceived, which make up the *material* of therapy constitute a *Mitwelt*, a subjective environment. The client's 'inner' experiencing state, or *Eigenwelt*, arises in dependence upon the Mitwelt. Phenomenological Therapy involves the use of a variety of media to represent what appears in the client's Mitwelt. It is important to realize, however, that the objects (e.g. mother) which appear in the Mitwelt are products of the client's *intentionality*, that rather than objective entities they are *constructions* (e.g. the mother as the client sees her is not mother as others see her, nor as she sees herself).

Meaningfulness depends upon this spatial *organization of consciousness*. *Felt meanings* change as we view from different perspectives and against different backgrounds (*frames*). The therapist acutely notices how material is spontaneously placed by the client. More than a metaphor, the sense of closeness and distance in relationships is a manifestation of embodied perception. All phenomena appear within a space of some kind.

Viewing from a number of *angles* may be necessary before a phenomenon is experienced as 'real'. The therapist can help the client to consolidate a spatial relationship by *amplification*, or through *projective* or *embodying* techniques or can facilitate the client moving around the material exploring new *horizons* or can help *shift* the spatial fixity of the material.

Transitions between media also effect perceptual *shifts*. Moving from, for example, a body sense to a painted projection reveals different qualities. Awareness of space permits the observer to walk *around* the phenomenon as represented and thus achieve the perceptual shifts which make life *multidimensional*.

There is thus also a *distance* between *role* (object) and person (perceiver). Any attempt to turn one's own person into a direct object of perception implies a 'new' perceiver. A person cannot, therefore, be ultimately grasped as 'object'. An intrinsic *parity*, beyond roles, exists between therapist and client. If therapist and client initially project notions of each other these too are simply images – more material. The parity or common *humanity* may come to be experienced however when the *epoche* is complete and all normal criteria of judgement have been *bracketed*.

The key operation in phenomenology is that of suspending belief and disbelief while remaining warmly involved. This is called *epoche*. Epoche is a *suppositionless* frame of mind within which the therapist is able to move freely into the perspective of the client (*empathy*) and into any other real or *surreal* frame of reference which will throw a new and more innocent light on the phenomenon in hand.

Catharsis is a function of achieving *optimum distance* from the material (Scheff 1979; Leijssen 1993). Thus when the client says 'My mother hates me' the therapist does not decide that this is or is not so. He or she does not confirm and does not argue but appreciates the fullness of feeling in the client's perception. The epoche requires the therapist to stay open to all possibilities. The epoche is not an abandonment of all knowledge and experience, but, rather, a free-floating relationship to it.

A river which finds its own way

Client and therapist are both engaged in similar paths. The practice of therapy is as healing as the receipt of it. Enrichment of experiencing comes about most directly when there is a mutual recognition between therapist and client of each other as persons facing the same basic existential dilemmas – identity, sexuality, death and so forth. It is the human condition which is the 'raw' material and, in this, therapist and client stand side by side.

The material has its own flow, like a river. The therapist will initially attempt to enter the flow alongside the client, so that they swim side by side into deeper water. With growing confidence, they begin to play together. They then have less need to remain so close. At times the therapist may stay in the river, at others she or he may stand on the bank, taking in a wider view of the river's course, and the client may join her or him. Occasionally, the therapist may stand against the current, interrupting the flow, seeing how it will redirect itself, but she or he will never dig a new channel for it. The river will find its own course. Thus in spatial terms the therapist, for the most part adopts a 'side by side' position in relation to the client, only occasionally moving into a confrontational 'face to face' stance.

Flow implies an innate ability in each person to find and follow his or her own way, which will emerge in many settings, of which the therapy session is just one. Other settings also offer new angles on material which might not emerge in the therapy sessions. Thus the client is encouraged to see the therapeutic process as a broad path, encompassing not only the work done in the consulting room.

Some therapies describe distressed people as lacking boundaries. Phenomenological theory is more likely to see them as suffering from a surfeit of boundaries. The *fully functioning person* is fluid, not fixed. Phenomena are not determined by their boundaries because boundaries change with *perspective*. Real life always has an open horizon. It can always be seen differently. Phenomenological work leads us to appreciate the multiform possibilities of life rather than to solidify it into a 'known' structure.

Therapy works on several levels of meaning simultaneously. Even apparently straightforward interactions contain *metaphoric significances* which illuminate in the therapeutic process. The therapist may respond in ways that embody several layers of the therapeutic metaphor simultaneously. An important concept here is the notion of *resonance*. When empathy is holistic, the therapist will *resonate* and so will find arising within himself or herself feelings, images and intuitions which when disclosed prove meaningful to the client.

Phenomenology is the capacity to enter other worlds than one's own. *Narcissism* is the inability to let go of one's self-centred view. Narcissism and phenomenology are thus mutually exclusive. The therapist, as phenomenologist, seeks to appreciate the world as it must appear from the client's viewpoint and is equally willing to entertain other possibilities. The client, through phenomenological work, learns by experience to appreciate new perspectives. *Compassion*, in this sense, is both about experiencing with the other and about opening new doors together.

The cause of suffering

In essence, the phenomenological perspective assumes that suffering flows from rigidities of perception which impoverish experience. In Buddhist phenomenology this rigidity is referred to as attachment. Jacob Moreno, the inventor of psychodrama (see Appendix B), calls it an insufficiency of spontaneity. Rogers reasoned that these rigidities arise from the operation of 'conditions of worth', i.e. that the child learns to limit his or her experience to fit in with the terms upon which love is offered. In the Eigenwelt approach it is conjectured that the fundamental factor may be an inherent need to love, that is, to reach out positively toward the world, rather than to be loved and that the struggle of life may be the struggle to maintain a positive intention toward others in the face of discouragement (Brazier 1993). Either way, the happy child retains an active curiosity about all that life holds, which is to say, the fully functioning person is one who is continually exploring new angles, new possibilities, new perspectives.

It is this playfulness which lends life its vibrancy, whereas the child who is rebuffed by life must use every effort to hold fixedly to its hope and so imposes upon life what it would like to see rather than engaging with what is there to be found.

The change process

An illustration

Phenomenology is a matter of working with perception. When we represent, in words, on paper or in drama, what we perceive, our relationship to it shifts. A series of such shifts can allow a person to arrive, by one step flowing from another, at a completely new perception of life and, perhaps more important, to the realization that there does not have to be just one fixed perception.

An example may illustrate this process best. The following was written recently by a person who had engaged in this process:

> Things happen when you least expect them. There I was in Newcastle watching someone else's psychodrama. When it finished, Caroline suggested getting out the paints and paper. It was as if she had pushed a button in me. I immediately thought, I am going to paint my birth.
>
> The actual painting process is now a bit hazy. I just remember the feelings. I was completely engrossed in what I was doing. Afterwards a member of the group said they had watched me stroke the wet paint of the baby.
>
> My birth was a planned Caesarean, the picture not a pretty one. A torso, jaggedly cut, and gaping open, showing the baby inside attached by the umbilical cord. I must have gone and got a pair of scissors and cut round the jagged bits without detaching it from the torso. What is still with me are the feelings. At the time I Was That Baby. I was no longer the adult me, I was still in my mother's womb, and about to be removed. Yet my adult mind was working separately. I became very afraid and needing to be back in my 'adult body'. I took another piece of paper, painted my hands blue, and put my prints on the paper, which somehow gave me back my adult identity. I don't remember being aware of other people in the room, though there were eight others. I then lay back on the cushions and gazed out of the window at miracles.
>
> It was as if I had had scales removed from my eyes and could see properly for the first time in my life. Every single leaf, flower, sunbeam, was perfect, and I just lay there, soaking up all this beauty. Afterwards, I realized that I had been lying with my arms bent at the elbows, palms up, fingers curled, the way babies do. For days afterward I would find myself lost in just looking, fascinated by an object, a colour or a face. Or just listening to sounds. That striking newness of sight and sound has now passed, but things still look and sound different, brighter, clearer.
>
> But that was only the beginning! Over the next couple of weeks I used pastel crayons to draw my birth over and over again, each picture a different colour, a different moment. Again I lost myself in the process but now I

wasn't afraid. Anger and fury erupted from these pictures. I wasn't ready to be born, how dare 'they' remove me from my heaven. But they did, and the pictures were then of me born and on my own. Still the anger and fury, but soon changing to grief and desolation. In one picture I'm drowning in my own tears. Then came pictures of my mother, who I don't remember since she died when I was three. These are of a sad, depressed, overwhelmed looking woman.

Next time I was in Newcastle, Caroline strung the sitting room door like a loom, and I wove my 'baby' up near the top, umbilical cord still attached. A couple of weeks later, while walking in Jesmond Dene, I found two small feathers and gave my baby wings. During much of this time I had been working with John, my counsellor, on my childhood, and with his help, discovered it wasn't 'them' I was angry at, but my mother.

At home I then created my baby in clay. A small clay figure full of angry energy. This felt better. This anger felt productive.

Then I was back in Newcastle for another weekend workshop. As soon as I saw my baby on the loom, I knew the time had come to cut the umbilical cord. It wasn't until lunchtime the next day that I actually got around to doing it. I then made a small ritual in the garden on my own, saying goodbye to my mother, and burying the cord under a lavender bush. As I sat there, I realized it was summer solstice, the day between my oldest and youngest children's birthdays. The title of the workshop I was taking part in was 'Letting Go: Endings in Counselling, Psychotherapy and Life'!

But that wasn't quite the end. For the next few days I had an incredibly itchy belly button. I thought I must have got an insect bite and even dabbed cream on each night. It took until Wednesday evening for it to dawn on me!

I felt a bit mean for not sharing the letting go experience in the workshop that day, but I needed to keep it for myself for a bit. This way I'm able to share the experience from the beginning.

What this description illustrates is the loop of perception, representation, shift, flow, new perception, representation and so on and the way in which the shifts from one form of representation to another, drama to pictures, pictures to dialogue, dialogue to inward reflection, inward reflection to weaving or sculpting, each provides an extra pulse of vitality to the process, allows it to be experienced in full rather than unidimensionally.

Therapeutic goals

The goal of phenomenological work is to find new visions of life, to come alive, to experience in richer ways. Phenomenological Therapy assumes that the 'actualizing tendency' in sentient beings is not an instinct but is the product of accumulating 'apodicity'. This loosely means that when you have experienced something as true or real, you can never go back to the state you were in before that experience. A kind of 'ratchet effect' is in operation. Our instincts tend to pull us backward but perceptual enrichment carries us forward. In the well known vase–face picture used by Gestalt psychologists, once one has 'seen' the second

Gestalt, one cannot thereafter be unable to see it. Of course, this does not mean that one continues to see the new Gestalt all the time. It simply means that one's perception in relation to the picture now has two possibilities and can never go back to only having one.

If we cannot go back, we must go forward. If a person's repertoire of perceptions leaves them in pain, we cannot take any of them away. But we can add to the stock and open up additional possibilities so that they need dwell on the painful ones less. The goal, therefore, is to overcome perceptual rigidity. Forgetting is achieved by adding to perception, not by subtracting from it.

The commonest perceptual rigidity is a self-centred view of the world. By direct implication, therefore, a goal is to help a person find views other than the purely self-centred one. Empathy and compassion for others are signs of perceptual flexibility and permit a more lively engagement with the world. Paradoxically, the self-actualized person is one who is very little concerned with self, being too busy living to be overly concerned with self-defence. In this respect the Zen axiom that to study the self is to forget the self applies.

The goal is therefore, essentially creative and future oriented. It is not a matter of repairing something but of growing beyond the present state. It is not a matter of recovering something from the past but of learning the art of weaving past and present into ever new fabrics. It is not about problem solving but about growth. It is not about finding the right street but about gaining the freedom of the city.

Practitioners

Relationship

The essence of Phenomenological Therapy is in the attitude of the therapist rather than the technique. The attitude which turns therapy into phenomenology is one of appreciative wonderment.

Paradoxically, the therapist does not try to change the client. As the process of perceptual enrichment leads to life being experienced as 'real', the client will know what, if anything, needs to be done. The therapist maintains an open curiosity about the encounter, its meaning, what it may hold, and what it can teach the participants. The therapist is there to learn, just as is the client.

The basic attitude required in phenomenology is called the *epoche*. This means that as therapist one holds whatever knowledge and life experience one brings lightly, assuming a naive stance in which whatever the client puts into the encounter is experienced freshly. One tries to receive everything the client offers and accept it in a radically non-judgemental way, assuming that everything is meaningful and important. The *epoche* means suspending judgement about what is trivial or significant, desirable or unhealthy.

Since everything is important, the therapist is appreciative. The therapy relationship is one in which the client will entrust to their common work material which the therapist will regard as the most precious gifts and the two of them will examine and re-examine these from many different angles until each facet has been imbued with careful attention and become fertile with new possibilities.

This does not mean, however, that the therapist only follows. The therapist may suggest 'experiments' such as 'How about painting that?' or 'So how would that look from the other side?' These suggestions are not designed to manipulate the client into a 'better' perspective on the problem but rather rely upon the experience that with a variety of perspectives a new depth of experiencing of the material commonly emerges.

Shifts of media or perspective are not, however, random, but are based upon signs of spontaneous shift within the client ('act hunger') which suggest that a particular move may be appropriate. Therapists are alert to such cues which are usually subtle. These shifts should never be mechanical, however, but are ideally part of an easy give and take between therapist and client in which each trusts the other's intention.

Techniques

In this approach the ideal would be to be able to turn any circumstance to therapeutic account. Therapy is not, therefore, something which only occurs in the consulting room. The limits of technique are set by the limits of imagination and the degree to which the epoche can really be achieved. It is the therapist's inability to let go entirely of the rigidities of her or his own perceptions which limits the therapy, i.e. it is the therapist's ego that gets in the way.

Every piece of therapy, therefore, is also a therapy for the therapist, challenging her or him to go beyond the already known. Going beyond self, therapist and client are plunged into new territory together where spontaneity becomes a necessity for both.

The therapist's engagement with the client may be conceptualized as going through four degrees of epoche analogous to the four jhanas of Buddhist meditation practice, each involving a greater degree of 'letting go'. This is induced in the client by its happening first in the therapist. We may say that it is 'the client's world' which becomes the object of meditation. For simplicity, in the description which follows we will assume a female therapist and a male client though the same approach applies whatever the genders may be.

First epoche
The first therapeutic epoche establishes the therapeutic space as different from ordinary conversation. The therapist lets go of her own preoccupations and responds immediately to the client in a way which implicitly yet effectively establishes that this interaction is different. An explicit statement will rarely achieve this. It has to come, rather, from the unconditionality of the therapist's manner. The therapist should be centred before the encounter begins. This initial stage of establishing the therapeutic epoche marks off the therapeutic time from the rest of the client's life and allows the client and therapist to access a slightly altered state of consciousness in which normal boundary walls will be lowered.

Second epoche
In the second epoche the therapist is getting into resonance with the material. This involves letting go of 'being a therapist', of theorizing *about* the client, and attending with precision. Reflective responses may help warm the therapist up to

the client's world. The therapist imagines her way into the material, allowing herself to be inwardly moved.

The therapist is now happy to have the client's world in view and is getting into the spirit of it. This is a stage of exploration, elaboration and resonance. The primary operation of phenomenological method is non-evaluative description whether by enactment, visual representation with art materials or simply verbal description. The therapist develops a strong sense of the spatial significance of locations within the therapy room as elements of the client's world become invested in them. The 'world' set up in this way may have several distressing or shameful areas. The therapist is, however, in a free floating state of mind in which judgements are not taken on as fact and in which the full panorama of therapeutic material can be taken in rather than just the narrow area which might be defined as the client's problem. Initial presentations may soon change.

Third epoche

The third epoche can begin when a mutability begins to appear in the material. This is commonly a shift into metaphor. The client has been describing a concrete situation and then says, 'It is as though I'm in a prison' or 'I spent so long building things up and now they are crumbling'. This invites the therapist to let go of literalism and to go with the client into building relevant yet imaginary worlds. We move from the fixed into the possible. This is creative. Now neither client nor therapist is leading. Rather there is cooperative experimentation with symbols, roles, spaces and experience. New perspectives emerge in the form of images, painted or imagined, metaphors, stories, described or enacted, inter-pretations or comparisons with history, mythology and so on. The therapist's knowledge of literature, art, history and psychological theory may contribute. The essential point is not to look for one 'right' interpretation but to get as all-round a view as possible. In this playful stage, what Freud or Mother Theresa or Woody Allen or Mae West might have said about the matter might be equally useful.

Shifts from one medium to another provide contrasting perceptual experiences. By painting, the person puts the material outside of himself and can then move the painting about and have a relationship to it. By drama he experiences it multi-dimensionally from the inside. By bodywork, he can experience the material viscerally and feel not just the responses of the eye and the ear, but those of the heart, guts and musculature. It is not that one of these media holds the key to the matter but rather that a person comes most alive when the relationship they have to their world is kaleidoscopic.

Amplification and containment

An important factor in maintaining the epoche is the achievement of an 'optimum distance' from the material (Scheff 1979), close enough to experience it at a feeling level, and sufficiently distant not to be overwhelmed. Different media allow the client to experience the material as closer or more distant. For the client who is too distant from the material, amplification is necessary. Such a client may be encouraged to surround himself with material, perhaps psychodramatically, or bring it within himself using a body focused technique. For the client who is too close, containment or projection may be necessary by, for example, painting. The phenomenological therapist, therefore, needs mobility. She needs to be able to enter the client's world(s), but also to step out of it, to move to different vantage points, beside, opposite, close or distant, and to check her own inner responses. Often different positions are monitored concurrently as work touches a number of layers of metaphor simultaneously.

Fourth epoche
Finally, the fourth epoche is reached when there is a kind of peacefulness. There comes a time to let go of creativity too. At this point, client and therapist are together, have worked together, have shared in the creativity, and now feel at peace with one another. The process of the work will have demonstrated to each of them that both are human: each is unique yet, in another sense, both are on the same path. The sense of shared humanity is tangible. This is a state of acceptant awareness. At best it is what the Zen master Shunryu Suzuki (1970) used to call 'big mind', a space in which smaller problems have not disappeared but seem no longer so significant. In this big mind it does not really matter whether anything is said or not and a calm may seem to settle upon the room. This is the most complete epoche, since it is the condition in which there has been a bracketing even of concern for therapy, progress, satisfaction or dejection. Roles and technique have now dropped away and peace of mind is no longer dependent upon circumstance. Such a meditative state is, of course, not always reached, but it is the natural conclusion of the phenomenological process.

Does it work?

Case study

Ann at 35 is childless. Her husband died tragically shortly after their marriage 10 years ago. She was born in Newcastle, where she still lives. She has a fairly successful career in the NHS. She entered therapy reporting depressed feelings and worry about her failure to form any new sexual relationship. Three months of therapy has involved working with grief feelings and with memories of a troubled upbringing. The following is an extract from her thirteenth session.

Ann sits in silence, eyes unfocused, wrapped in thought. Her body, slightly slumped in the chair, looks tired and heavy. Abruptly, there is a change. Although she hardly moves, Ann's body is now more alert. She looks to the left. Her hand gestures in the same direction. 'It's like, my mother always had to control me . . .' she says angrily. Then, flashing a glance to the right, she adds, '. . . and my father did nothing . . .' Then looking towards the therapist opposite her, she sighs and holds her head. She looks frail now.
  The therapist has registered where the client has placed mother and father in the room and Ann's sentiments toward each of them, and also the appeal contained in the final look in her own direction. In quick succession the client has passed through four different felt sense states, each with corresponding perceptual objects. A sense of the client's life world builds up out of the clues

provided by involuntary changes in posture, voice tone, gaze and semi-articulate utterances.

> *Therapist*:   It seemed for a moment as though each of your parents were here for you, and then you looked at me and I felt you were kind of reaching out.
>
> *Client*:   I wish she would just leave me alone.

The client has settled for now upon the image of mother and switched to the present tense.

> *Therapist*:   Can you see her there now? What she is wearing? How is she standing?

Ann describes her mother giving her an almost tangible presence in the room. It looks as though the work will move into dramatic dialogue between the client and mother. However, the therapist now notices a change in the client's face and asks 'What is happening now?'

> *Client*:   I've gone back . . . I don't know what it is. I can never remember.
>
> *Therapist*:   No clear image, but . . . something.
>
> *Client*:   It's all grey.
>
> *Therapist*:   It's grey.
>
> *Client*:   Yes, just grey.
>
> *Therapist*:   Could you paint that?

The client mixes some colours. However, the picture is not just grey. There are red streaks also. The therapist holds up the painting for Ann to view it. 'Red is the pain,' Ann says.

> *Therapist*:   Red pain . . . And grey.
>
> *Client*:   The grey stops me seeing behind.
>
> *Therapist*:   If you just use your intuition, can you go behind the grey?

Ann works intently. Soon she has a series of pictures, each representing another layer of perception. The last shows a pattern of circles divided by a red line. Ann does not know what they mean. Soon however, she says the different coloured circles may represent members of her family. She has, in effect, drawn a map of her life-space.

The therapist suggests they can lay it out, using cushions. Ann chooses carefully cushions of particular colour and size for each family member. Now that her 'world' has been set up, she and the therapist move within it, experiencing the shifting felt-sense as Ann tries one angle after another. She is also able to sit on some of the cushions, role reversing with her significant others and seeing her world from their perspective.

The red line is now represented by a piece of wool. When the therapist draws her attention to it, Ann says 'It's a wound.'

> *Therapist*:   A wound . . .
>
> *Client*:   It's still open.

Therapist: An open wound . . .

Client: Yes, all bloody, it cuts right into me.

Therapist: It cuts into you . . . Here it cuts through the family, and it also cuts into you.

Client: Yes, I always have it.

Therapist: And your father is on one side of the wound and your mother is on the other.

Client: They tore me in two.

Therapist: And it looks as though, when you focus on this open, bleeding wound . . .

Client: It is so painful. It is right here. [She points to her chest.]

The session encompasses different representational media, visual, dramatic, imaginary and descriptive, as the client explores her life-world. The phenomenological process is an inquiry into the things which evoke the subjective life. As each layer is explored, the client experiences a series of felt shifts. The therapist is mindful of these and focuses attention upon the objects which trigger them.

Ann continued in weekly therapy a further 12 sessions and progressed to more infrequent attendance coupled with participation in therapy groups. She reached a partial reconciliation with her father and was pleased to announce, one day, her involvement in a new love affair. She has also discovered an expressive side to her personality which she continues to enjoy.

Pitfalls

A main pitfall is simply the fact that this is not an easy approach to therapy to master. This is both because achieving the degrees of epoche necessary requires the therapist to be able to set aside his or her own narcissism to a great degree and also because the therapist needs to be freed up enough to feel at ease with a wide range of media and forms of expression. When one considers that there are full length training courses available for therapists who propose to work only in one medium, say Drama Therapy or Art Therapy, and one then considers that the multi-media therapist must not only be fluent in each medium but also be able to judge and use sensitively the vital moments of transition between them, one might at first think the task insuperable. The key is to be found primarily in the therapist's own personal development being such as to make it possible to exercise the epoche effectively.

Training is thus a difficult issue. Much contemporary personal development work does not serve to make people better therapists because it increases preoccupation with self rather than freeing the person from it. Much professional training does not serve our purpose either because it narrows rather than broadens the trainee's perspective. Escaping from dogmatism is essential if one is to be able to hold the free floating state of mind in which all material is held as provisional, which is essential to this method.

A serious pitfall is illustrated by the fact that one does encounter people who have learned an approach which is phenomenological in theory but in such a way that they have turned phenomenological principles themselves into a set of dogmas. Thus one may find psychodramatists for whom the form of psychodrama has itself become a cultural conserve and person centred therapists who hold to the Rogerian core conditions as if they were articles of an intolerant faith. This kind of 'spiritual materialism' in which the work is corrupted from within, as it were, is the most serious pitfall.

A less serious but equally common pitfall is a lack of rigour. It is an inevitable pitfall of any method which advocates a multifaceted approach that some will let it degenerate into an undisciplined eclecticism. Phenomenological Therapy is not the random application of all and every method. It is a matter of paying precise and sensitively disciplined attention to the spontaneously emerging process of the client. This requires great concentration and a highly trained willingness to set personal whims aside.

Research

The only strand of Phenomenological Therapy which has been extensively submitted to outcome research is the person centred approach. This research has tended to support the notion that empathy especially is a valuable element in the therapeutic process and that the therapist's genuineness as perceived by the client as well as his or her warmth and positivity also contribute to good outcomes.

Three important points can be made in this respect. The first is that research generally does not show major differences in effectiveness between different schools of therapy. All come out, overall, as of roughly similar effectiveness. The second is that even where outcome research has come close to demonstrating an association between a factor such as empathy and good outcomes we are still left to puzzle over what this connection might actually be. In this example, for instance, is it that the client benefits directly from the empathy of the therapist or is it that the client learns to become empathic themselves from the therapist's example, or is it that the empathy is itself simply one instance of the achievement of a perceptual shift, or what?

Third, phenomenology includes, indeed in many respects may be said to be, a critique of the validity of the positivistic approach to science of which outcome research is a typical example. Phenomenological (or constructivist) approaches to research are not concerned to demonstrate what is replicable and what could therefore be reduced to a routine or mechanical approach. Rather they are concerned to bring out the meaningfulness to the participants of whatever does occur in a given sequence of events even if it is unique, as human events generally are. Phenomenological Therapy does not aim to achieve something with one client which could be replicated with another one. It aims to open up possibilities for this client which are uniquely meaningful to this client. In this respect, every piece of Phenomenological Therapy is actually a piece of constructivist inquiry it its own right and the measure of the outcome can only ultimately be formulated by the participants themselves. Along these lines, some very interesting research has been done by David Rennie and others (Rennie 1990) using video to help therapy participants to recall their inner process as therapy unfolded. This produces excellent and fine tuned descriptive material which allows one a fascinating glimpse into the inner process. It does not, of its nature, yield quantifiable results however.

A comment on the literature

Ernesto Spinelli (1989) is an excellent introduction to the basic principles of western phenomenology in very readable form with a good résumé of the development of the approach from the work of Husserl through to that of Rogers and of Laing, each of whose works are also worth attention.

Tarthang (1977) challenges us to dig beneath or get outside of even our most fundamental assumptions about how things are, and opens up a vista of infinite possibilities. It represents the eastern approach to phenomenology in modern language. A more practical manual along the same lines is Akong (1987). Another eminently readable selection of essays designed to help us shift out of fixity of perception is a book edited by Hofstadter and Dennett (1982).

Guide to Psychodrama (Brazier 1991) provides an easy introduction to this dramatic method and *Beyond Carl Rogers* (Brazier 1993) shows how the person centred approach is now developing along more broadly based phenomenological lines. These and a range of other shorter relevant works can be obtained from the Eigenwelt Centre, 53 Grosvenor Place, Newcastle upon Tyne NE2 2RD.

For those who want to look deeper into phenomenology the works of Edmund Husserl (1960, 1962) and Merleau-Ponty (1962) should be consulted.

References

Akong (1987) *Taming the Tiger*. Eskdalemuir, Dumfriesshire: Dzalendara, Kargyu Samye Ling.

Brazier, D. (1991) *A Guide to Psychodrama*. London: Association for Humanistic Psychology.

Brazier, D. (1993) The necessary condition is love: going beyond self in the person-centred approach. In D. Brazier (ed.) *Beyond Carl Rogers*. London: Constable.

Hanh, N. (1990) *Transformation and Healing*. Berkeley, CA: Parallax Press.

Hanh, N. (1991) *The Miracle of Mindfulness*. London: Rider.

Hofstadter, D. and Dennett, D. (1982) *The Mind's I: Fantasies and Reflections on Self and Soul*. Harmondsworth: Penguin.

Husserl, E. (1960) *Cartesian Meditations*. The Hague: Nijhoff.

Husserl, E. (1962) *Ideas*. New York: Collier.

Husserl, E. (1985) *The Paris Lectures*. The Hague: Nijhoff.

Laing, R. (1960) *The Divided Self*. London: Tavistock.

Leijssen, M. (1993) Creating a workable distance to overwhelming images. In D. Brazier (ed.) *Beyond Carl Rogers*. London: Constable.

Maslow, A. (1971) *The Farthest Reaches of Human Nature*. Harmondsworth: Penguin.

Merleau-Ponty, M. (1962) *Phenomenology of Perception* (trans. C. Smith). London: Routledge.

Merrill, C. and Anderson, S. (1993) Person-centred expressive therapy: An outcome study. In D. Brazier (ed.) *Beyond Carl Rogers*. London: Constable.

Rennie, D.L. (1990) Toward a representation of the client's experience of the therapeutic hour. In G. Lietaer, J. Rombauts and R. Van Balen (eds) *Client-centered and Experiential Psychotherapy in the Nineties*. Leuven, Belgium: Leuven University Press.

Rogers, C. (1961) *On Becoming a Person*. London: Constable.
Rogers, C. (1980) *A Way of Being*. Boston, CA: Houghton Mifflin.
Scheff, T.J. (1979) *Catharsis and Healing, Ritual and Drama*. Berkeley, CA: University of California Press.
Sogyal (1992) *The Tibetan Book of Living and Dying*. London: Rider.
Spinelli, E. (1989) *The Interpreted World: An Introduction to Phenomenological Psychology*. London: Sage.
Suzuki, S. (1970) *Zen Mind Beginner's Mind*. New York: Weatherhill.
Tarthang (1977) *Time, Space and Knowledge*. Berkeley, CA: Dharma Publishing.
van Deurzen-Smith, E. (1988) *Existential Counselling in Practice*. London: Sage.
van Deurzen-Smith, E. (1990) Existential Therapy. In W. Dryden (ed.) *Individual Therapy: A Handbook*. Milton Keynes: Open University Press.

11

Dance Movement Therapy

HELEN PAYNE

Definition and historical roots

Definition

At its simplest Dance Movement Therapy (DMT) is the focused use of expressive movement and posture within a therapeutic alliance and with the aim of enabling a stronger definition of self.

It is amongst the many forms of non-verbal intervention but is unique in that a) expressive movement is a function of our innate biological rhythms and is closer to natural human expression than other art forms and b) dance alone engages the total physical being and in so doing makes an art object of the self. One cannot distinguish the dancer from the dance, there is a recreation of the self, as self and as object, in the integration of body and mind.

Historical development

In the UK DMT began in the 1940s with occupational therapists, nurses and psychologists experimenting with the use of movement in psychiatric hospitals. It developed into work within special education in the 1970s and since then the emphasis has mainly been in these settings. However, more recently a few practitioners are offering DMT in the community and in private practice.

The professional association, Association for Dance Movement Therapy (ADMT), formed in 1982, grew out of a collaborative group of pioneers who met regularly for peer supervision and training in the 1970s. The first executive council comprised Lynn Crane, Catalina Garvey and myself. By 1984 an American training had been imported to the UK and a certificate course began at Roehampton Institute. In 1987 the first training nationally validated by the Council for National Academic Awards at post-graduate level was developed at Hertfordshire College of Art and Design, St Albans (now the University of Hertfordshire).

Founders

In the 1970s Audrey Wethered (1993) and Marion North (1972) evolved the use of Laban-based movement and dance within therapeutic settings. Rudolf von Laban (1949) himself shows he was also interested in this application as far back as the 1940s. Veronica Sherbourne, also trained by Laban, explored movement within the Withymead Therapeutic Community (run on Jungian lines) in the 1950s. She later applied her findings to children with severe learning disabilities. Kedzie Penfield, an American trained in Laban Movement Analysis, initiated DMT practice in a therapeutic community in Scotland in the mid-1970s. I trained in Laban Dance in England in the early 1970s and developed the work in hospitals and special schools. In 1991 I published *Creative Movement and Dance in Groupwork* and in 1992 edited *Dance Movement Therapy* which is the first book to document UK DMT practitioners' work (Payne 1991, 1992).

From these roots DMT practice has grown into work with a wide range of populations from those with special needs and mental health problems to the elderly, addictive groups and those 'functioning' members of society who require personal development. Aspects from DMT are now being used to train managers and assess personal and team effectiveness in corporate business and the workplace.

Relationship with other therapies

DMT is one of the four recognized arts therapies (art, drama and music being the other three). Like them it has its own professional association with criteria for full membership, standards and ethics, quarterly newsletter and university validated, post-graduate training. There is an Institute for the Arts in Psychotherapy which offers short courses, publications, training consultations, assessment, apprenticeships in DMT and clinical services for a range of people, including those with special needs.

There is no evidence that DMT has anything in common with Cognitive Therapy or Transactional Analysis, or these models of understanding personal process. It is also differentiated from hypnosis.

Central concepts

Dance has been part of all cultures since ancient times, with shamanism using dance as healing. It has been an integrative force in societies throughout our world. The dance in worship and other ceremonies can be said to serve the purpose of manifesting the mental and spiritual health of those societies.

In our society where words are at the top of the ladder there is little recognition of the individual whose trauma lies below the level of words, whether because of a psychological, emotional or physical impairment. The expression of emotions is rooted in the body, and normally accompanied by an intellectual recognition, yet some people cannot experience them and remain blocked at a feeling level.

In the field of non-verbal communication early studies such as those of Darwin (1965) document the importance of gesture and posture in communication. Later research points to the way physical contact and movement are crucial in primary relationships such as the preverbal experiences of infant–mother interaction.

DMT could be said to be on the fringes of the complementary therapies in that it advocates an holistic approach to promoting well-being and, with its emphasis on the body/mind/spirit/intellect relationship, can appeal to those interested in alternative routes to healing and health. Psychosomatic symptoms may be more easily worked with where there is an experiential avenue to the exploration through the body itself. There are strong links between DMT and Reichian Therapy (see Chapter 9, this volume) and Biodynamic Therapy in, for example, the emphasis it places on the breath, touch and spontaneous movement (and vocal) expression.

Since DMT is an experiential approach it shares something with 'action' psychotherapy and verbal psychotherapy as well as many aspects also found in Neurolinguistic Programming (NLP), for example, Gestalt Therapy with its use of the 'here and now', posture and imagery. Group psychotherapy approaches such as group analytic work shares the use of metaphor and group process, free association and interpretation; and the collective and archetypal phenomena are often evident in movement material which connects to Jungian approaches and the use of active imagination, dreams and myths. DMT can be seen to use directive approaches such as those found in the behavioural systems of relaxation and assertiveness training or NLP as well as non-directive/unstructured client centred and psychodynamic ways of working. Inevitably it will depend on the client population, the setting, the aims and objectives and world-view and training of each dance movement therapist which orientation is adopted. A more recent approach is to be found in Integrative Movement Psychotherapy which is designed specifically for in-depth, long term work for individual adults wanting a psychotherapeutic relationship with movement and words as the media.

Cause of suffering

This refers to the idea that people may have damaged or hidden aspects to themselves which can be restored or discovered through therapy. If left undealt with people may under or over function, have symptoms labelled as depression, addictions, low self-esteem, poor interpersonal skills, and so on. The dance movement therapist may believe the cause of suffering to be concerned with a lack of integration between feelings and the body, a blocking in the expression and therefore in the integration of aspects of the self on a bodily level. By working with both the feelings and the body a more direct relief may emerge than when working with words alone which may be used to resist change and defend against transformation. Similarly if only the body or movement is emphasized the process will be superficial and in time the patient may revert back to old familiar patterns which would be manifested in the bodily movement.

On a more transpersonal level there may be therapists who believe suffering is what we are here to experience; that the most that can be done is to change misery into ordinary sadness. To believe there is a cause is itself a rather strong assumption. My own belief is that we are part of our world and there is no cause and effect *per se* but a complexity of patterns which we live out and change if we can, only to be confronted by another one even more challenging.

The change process

No understanding of the process in DMT can be complete without the client's view. A group participant comments:

> I would describe what happened to me in the DMT group as like an archaeological dig with my body; it was my psyche I was digging into through my movement experiences and it was unearthing, recovering parts of myself . . . just becoming more whole.

Contact arises naturally out of movement and is used intentionally in the process of DMT. The idea of body language is not unfamiliar to most of us; it is this which often reveals our authenticity to each other. This phenomenon is the basis of DMT and techniques are designed to tap the unconscious wisdom we 'know' in our bodies.

Posture, gesture and movement are media in which hidden, forgotten or buried emotion can be acknowledged and communicated, expressing a more whole self. This idea is not new, humans have always used movement and dance to release the natural, primitive being.

The communication offered is a special language through which patient and therapist speak and understand. It is dance movement in so far as the entire motility is used with a belief in its symbolic function and the recognition that all emotions can be experienced, expressed and perceived in the body's posture, gesture and movement.

A greater range of feeling and expression is facilitated by the unblocking of resistance to growth as held in frozen musculature. It is claimed in DMT literature that emotional, social or behavioural disturbances are invariably reflected in the limited movement range due to tension patterns of patients as well as in the limitations in choices of responses in thinking and abstracting.

The idea that the body and mind are one unit is far from new. We are our bodies and express our unconscious and personhood through them in a most direct and powerful way. The idea that feeling and motion are intertwined is an ancient one too; as the *I Ching*, which claims to be the oldest book written, says: 'Every mood of the heart influences us to movement'. Bodily movement which is assumed to relate to emotion can be worked through to give an immediate response at a feeling level. This provides for an opportunity for preverbal feelings to become integrated through the symbolism of expressive movement.

In this way DMT can provide for change, awareness and exploration as well as being diagnostic. The emphasis is on the personal or group movement statement or 'dance'. The integration results from the feelings and physical presence being worked with together. The therapist creates a holding environment in which feelings can be safely expressed, acknowledged and communicated. The therapeutic relationship is part of the process in that transference is interpreted where appropriate.

There has been more literature written in the USA than in the UK and, interestingly, it now reflects a greater influence of Laban's ideas such as in assessment and diagnosis. In the USA the terms Movement Therapy and Dance Therapy are interchangeable and it is often written Dance/Movement Therapy or Dance–Movement Therapy. In the UK where it became recognized later we use the term 'Dance Movement Therapy' which is seen to illustrate the nature of the work most accurately.

Therapeutic goals

In relation to therapeutic goals the therapist and client may identify them together, or the therapist may need to liaise with the treatment team in an institution to identify goals. Many clients in my practice are able to clarify their own goals from mutually arrived at ideas. For example, for one client there was a therapeutic goal agreed at our first session which was concerned with her 'knowledge' that she had been abused by her father (see the later case study in this chapter). There was only an intangible feeling that this had happened however, no real memory or evidence from other sources. Although this was in my mind it was not aimed at directly through any interpretations or suggested structures. It was both aimed at and not aimed at and in that way it was worked with.

Assessment procedures are crucial in clarifying goals and some therapists make very detailed movement assessments and/or psychological tests/personality tests prior to treatment. I tend to take a detailed case history and suggest perhaps what might be useful to have in mind in our work together. In addition, based on my understanding of the nature of the difficulties I may recommend one, two or three sessions per week and/or a group. The important thing to remember however is that the goal is in the process rather than in the outcome. By focusing on the goal we may miss the process and vice versa.

Practitioners

Relationship

The role the therapist adopts is dependent on the type of client. For example, whether the therapist joins with the client or group in their movement expression or not may depend on factors such as the ego-strength of the client. For some clients such as those with autism, learning difficulties and some with severe mental health problems it may be necessary to engage in movement interaction and/or physical contact. For other populations this 'joining' may not be the most helpful approach. However, the material emerging out of the therapeutic relationship will become visible whatever level of physical involvement the therapist has with clients. Indeed it is often illustrated by the type of involvement.

For the client there is always a degree of power attributed to the therapist, manifested in, for example, the client's comments about the therapist's ability to move or their understanding of the significance of movement or as having the solutions to the client's perceived problem.

Techniques

There are a number of techniques applied in DMT. Space does not permit a full documentation. Some are designed to heighten awareness of movement patterns, such as exaggeration where the movement is made bigger, smaller, faster, slower, stronger or lighter, more free or more controlled. Suggestions to explore the opposite movement can also aid awareness of what may be an avoidance of a particular feeling. In group DMT the group is normally held together in a group movement improvisation with the therapist reflecting individual movement themes as they arise; sometimes participants are able to speak about 'moving like . . .' during the movement experience itself. The therapist may speak about a particular pattern as it relates to the group process either during the movement or in the verbal processing afterwards.

Therapists use their own movement to echo or mirror movement patterns, creating a positive feeling of 'being with' the client. Verbalization and vocalization are present during movement interaction and where an individual is exploring his or her inner worlds. The therapist may describe the movement pattern as the client moves or simply draw their attention to aspects which seem important. Some clients are encouraged to work with eyes closed or half closed to become more sensitized to their inner feelings and the movement sensation. With others this is not advisable, particularly with psychotics.

Transference and counter-transference is normally acknowledged and utilized, particularly in ongoing DMT. Therapists working in institutions are often required to run short term groups and individual or ongoing groupwork is normally less prolific than in say private practice, where the work may be termed Movement Psychotherapy. Therapists' listening skills are crucial both in terms of the verbal outpouring and the movement expression.

Does it work?

Pitfalls

The moving therapist's own movement needs witnessing by themselves since it may be counter-transferential whilst in the process of moving with the client. Only on reflection afterwards may the therapist realize that they were moving in that way as a result of their interpretation of the movement relationship which was stimulating their own material.

One obvious limitation for a participatory therapist in movement is their own bodily vulnerabilities, such as back problems, a broken leg and so on.

For the client pitfalls may be concerned with their assumptions about the nature of the approach. For example, if they believe they have to be able to dance to participate, learn specific steps, enjoy their body, move and not talk and so on. They may feel a frustration when not directed by the therapist how to move: 'Come on tell us what to do, show us how to do it . . . the dance – teach us the dance then', is a quotation from a group of severely disturbed adolescent girls in care. Others may demand the therapist dances for them, entertains them. These comments are significant material to be worked with and need to be used as a further manifestation of the client's inner world. Fears concerning entering the movement space, the shame of being seen as a body and not being 'good enough' at moving are common in the early stages of therapy. Labelling sessions 'dance' may not always enable clients to engage in the therapy; finding the right language for each population is crucial in successfully engendering participation in the first place.

Not least the issue of sexuality is often a powerful phenomenon in DMT. Is this a pitfall, I ask myself? Well, for the therapist who is unsure about their own sexuality it may be. The movement process can become sensual and any physical contact may be confusing for clients who have experienced physical or sexual abuse. Therapists are often female and, for example, with an all-male hetero-sexual group of adolescents sexuality will almost always emerge as a major theme. It could be scary for a client to engage in a movement experience with a therapist they love in the transference. For these reasons a ground rule concerning the client–therapist relationship and use of movement and touch as being non-violent and non-sexual introduced at the beginning of therapy is important.

Research

Research is extremely limited in this field. Cases documented in the USA how-ever, are profuse. They describe individual practitioner's views on their work. Systematic, rigorous inquiry is badly needed to develop knowledge and a fuller understanding of practice application. There is very little evaluative work and virtually nothing about client's views on the process for them. There have been two UK studies to date, both of which go some way to using a non-traditional inquiry paradigm to explore DMT questions within a clinical framework.

What is appropriate to measure in the DMT process? In my experience measurement has meant finding out about things which entirely misses the point: the event of DMT – its unique essence. It seems to me it is not something we can be 'scientific' about, in the traditional meaning of the word. Yet credibility needs to be established in order for DMT to be truly accepted in the mainstream of society. Since art, including dance movement, is about meaning and the quality of people, no research approach which avoids an understanding of this will be appropriate for inquiry into DMT. Questions concerning the epistemology of the Dance Movement Therapy experience are exciting; it is to areas such as this that DMT research needs to be addressed.

One way to inquire as to the value of the Dance Movement Therapy experience for clients is to ask for their evaluations. One such research study did elicit client's views about the process of DMT (Payne 1987, 1988). Participants had several interesting ideas to put forward. For example, that sessions were primarily concerned with moving and talking, getting more relaxed, finding out about feelings and understanding their relating to each other and the therapist. Another client exclaimed recently that 'No one could ever understand what went on in DMT, it was so emotional, so powerful; not like intellectual knowing at all'.

Case study

In her initial telephone conversation with me the client referred to a feeling that she thought she may have been sexually abused by her father as a child. She also felt she needed something deeper than the therapy she had previously tried; 'was my approach a kind of shamanistic dance?' she asked. She then told me that she had read about my approach and thought it might be suitable.

She began to move without knowing what it was she was moving about. We had no identified theme today, only a sense of being stuck and a preference to explore in movement for the session. After 10 minutes of moving with eyes closed, a movement pattern emerged which seemed to be concerned with familiar movements, ones she said she felt safe with. I suggested she imagine she was stuck with these movements and see what emerged from the further exploration. Her head was rolling, shoulders shrugging, arms and hands pushing away, body weight rocking slowly from side to side. After about five minutes or so she began to grasp with her hands as though pulling something towards her from in front of her. She walked slowly forwards as she grasped an imaginary object which seemed somewhat diffused. This pattern continued around the space for some time until she met a wall. She exclaimed aloud it was a barrier, stopping her. I noticed the tension in her fingers increase. 'What do your hands need to do now?' I said. They immediately began to open and close angrily. 'Scratch' she said. Her jaw began to tighten and I drew her attention to this. She then roared, kicked and scratched. It reminded me of a tiger (her power animal); sounds and movement were as one. This lasted for about 10 minutes. Then her hands came into contact with her thighs. As I suggested she pay attention to this self-contact she began stroking her legs and her pelvic area. She sank to the floor sobbing. During the verbal processing afterwards she revealed that the movement experience was to do with a fragment of a memory. She believed she was a young child about 4 or 5 years of age who felt she was not allowed to make any angry noise but felt the rage. She was aware of herself wiping off 'a sort of liquid' from around her legs and pelvis. 'It was all to do with my father', she said 'sexual abuse . . . it happened, I can believe it truly now' – a forgotten memory. She had been consciously trying to uncover this memory for many years.

A comment on the literature

Chodorow (1991) is an excellent book about the client/therapist in private practice. Personally written throughout with an interesting theoretical section on Jungian concepts as applied to DMT, she gives the reader a real sense of what it is like to be a therapist or client.

Levy (1988) *Dance Movement Therapy: A Healing Art* is published by the American Association for PE, Dance, Health and Recreation. It is an excellent book giving an important overview of the American field from the east to the west coast. It covers theoretical perspectives from all major pioneers framed in historical research. A second volume is shortly to be published.

Payne (1991) is an introductory text of a very practical nature offering 180 ideas for sessions and resources for finding out more about DMT. Brief historical, developmental movement and theoretical sections introduce DMT.

Payne (1992) is the first book to document DMT practice in the UK. It provides an easy to read overview of practice in a range of settings, including private practice, special education, arts therapies centres, therapeutic communities, day centres, family centres, and psychiatric hospitals and day hospitals. Essential reading.

Siegal (1984) was written by an analyst with a ballet background. This book is a theoretical overview of Siegal's approach.

References

Chodorow, J. (1991) *Dance Therapy and Depth Psychology: The Moving Imagination*. London: Routledge.

Darwin, E. (1965) *The Expression of Emotions in Man and Animals*. Chicago Press.

Laban, R. von (1949) *Some Notes on Movement Therapy, Revised Version: Movement and Dance*.

Levy, P. (1988) *Dance Movement Therapy: a Healing Art*. Virginia: American Association for PE, Dance, Health and Recreation.

North, M. (1972) *Personality Assessment through Movement*. London: MacDonald and Evans.

Payne, H. (1987) 'The perceptions of male adolescents towards a programme of dance movement therapy', MPhil Thesis. Manchester University.

Payne, H. (1988) DMT with Troubled Youth. In C. Schaefer (ed.) *Innovative Interventions in Child and Adolescent Therapy*. New York: Wiley Interscience.

Payne, H. (1991) *Creative Movement and Dance in Groupwork*. Bicester: Winslow Press.

Payne, H. (ed.) (1992) *Dance Movement Therapy: Theory and Practice*. London: Tavistock/ Routledge.

Siegal, E. (1984) *Mirror of Ourselves: Psychoanalytical Dance Movement Therapy*. New York: Human Sciences Press.

Wethered, A. (1993) *Drama and Movement in Therapy*, 2nd edn. London: Northcote House.

12

Voicework

MELINDA MOORE MEIGS

Definition and historical development

Definition

Voicework is about using the medium of your voice to find and develop aspects of yourself which may be new to you and to understand what these aspects mean for you. It is a term used to cover singing, overtone chanting, improvisation, breathing techniques, bodywork, visualization and ear training when they are used to expand the expressive range of your voice and, through this, to explore your Self. This involves a search for emotional understanding and integration. Voicework is a vehicle for self-development although the work may benefit the development of a career. Green (1987) and Linklater (1976) describe voicework from a practical point of view.

Historical development

Recently there has been a renewed emphasis on voicework as therapy, although it was well established as an ancient form of therapeutic and creative endeavour. Perhaps its earliest use comes from ancient Greece. The alternation of text and song in Greek tragedy brings together conflicting experiences and holds them together in a way that allows for a new integration and harmony. Music gave access to the seemingly unfathomable reality underlying the world of phenomena. Music could speak to the dark and irrational underside of human nature.

The Greeks seemed to suffer greatly under the tension between desperate emotional vulnerability and great intellectual prowess. For coping with this tension and for protecting themselves against being destroyed by it, they evolved a form of art in which music is merged with structured language. There is movement from inarticulate sound to poetic language. Aristotle defined Greek tragedy (to paraphrase *Poetics*, chapter 6) as the imitation of serious and purposeful action of sufficient magnitude, which achieves through pity and terror the purgation of passions of that kind. This is achieved partly with poetry and partly with music, in language rendered pleasing by its metre and its versification. The music drama of the Athenians was a catharsis, a therapeutic invention which could allow an audience to release powerful emotions and to remain safe in the twilight between ritual and reason, sacrament and reality.

The Greeks may have been the first to be aware of using the voice in a conscious way for therapeutic aims, but vocal sound is the basic human instrument for communication and 'primitive' societies cope with physical and mental ills through the use of vocal sound as an integral means of dealing with pain. An example would be the Healing Song as used by some American Indian groups (Densmore 1948). Here, the musician gives expression to his or her own healing energies by trusting the depths within the self to give forth melodies that will enable the client to be transformed both physically and mentally. This is what is often going on when a therapist and client are improvising.

Another source is the use of ritual throughout the major religions (Stewart 1987). Here vocal music is used in specialized ways to enhance and broaden the spiritual consciousness of adherents. By expanding their awareness through vocal sound, individuals could understand and perceive their lives, problems, illnesses and their relationships with the world in new harmony. Radical changes can be experienced within the personality after the repetition of mantras – the chanting of sacred sounds – from the Hindu, Sufi, Buddhist and Christian traditions. These spiritual sound techniques can reach some very deep levels and make it possible for a person to contact his or her own healing powers which were previously hidden.

Founders in Britain

There are several initiators of voicework in Britain, each using the term to mean different things.

Groups such as the Sound Research Group in Sussex and individuals such as Jill Purce and Chloe Goodchild have been influenced by vocal rituals of world religions and use techniques from them, such as Tibetan overtone chanting and the Indian scale, in their workshops.

Patsy Rodenburg (who studied with voiceworker suprema of the Royal Shakespeare Company, Cicely Berry) and members of the British Voice Association stress the importance of the body in their work but, while acknowledging that voicework can touch deep vulnerabilities and long buried memories, particularly of a physical nature (injuries, incest etc.), argue for a strict separation between vocal training and emotional counselling. This may be a valid point as many voiceworkers are not trained in counselling.

There are some members of the British Society for Music Therapy such as Peter Wright who use 'toning' (a term created by Laurel Elizabeth Keyes, 1973) as a vocal means of therapeutic healing. Here one allows the voice to groan freely through an open mouth without controlling the sound that issues forth. How the sound develops depends on the aspect you hold in mind, whether the body as a whole or a particular emotion that feels threatening.

Much voicework has been founded in connection with preparation for a life in the theatre and in the world of music. The late Iris Warren of Lamda, the many drama and music schools and the Centre for Performance Research (Wales) have contributed greatly to this field. I myself trained both as a professional singer and as a therapist in humanistic psychology and psychoanalytic counselling. I believe it is possible to combine the exploration and expansion of vocal expression with an understanding of physical and psychological dynamics.

Relationship with other therapies

Voicework links with both humanistic psychology and with psychoanalysis in the shared belief in the therapeutic value and benefit of contacting and understanding deeply felt and often conflicting emotions. Voicework involves the body and encompasses the potential for both touch and catharsis. In this respect it differs from psychoanalytical theory and practice and from the Object Relations school – Klein, Winnicott, Bion, Balint, etc. (Cashdan 1988). However, it is possible to use these theoretical approaches to understand and think about what is going on in voicework, which enriches the experience greatly.

Voicework can necessitate bodywork of one sort or another. This may be through the humanistic psychology therapies such as biodynamic massage, or other therapies such as the Alexander technique, yoga, t'ai chi and so forth, contacting integrated movements which are unique to you. This strand of work links to that of Reich, Boyesen, Pierrakos, Rosenberg, Lowen, Laban and Lamb (see chapters 8 and 9, this volume).

Giving voice to different aspects of our inner life, originally stemming from the Greeks' notion of 'catharsis', connects voicework with Gestalt, Dramatherapy, the Roy Hart Theatre and the work of Alfred Wolfsohn (Newham 1992). Wolfsohn believed that the voice 'is the muscle of the soul' and developed exercises to expand the vocal range to several octaves. Where there were blocks to this development, there usually emerged forgotten memories, obscured by tightly held muscles. Once the memory and concomitant emotion were worked through, the muscles could afford to relax into the minimum amount of tension necessary to produce free tones.

There are also strong links with psychoanalysis. The idea of a forgotten and muscle bound memory connects voicework to Breuer's and Freud's early work on hysterical conversion symptoms. Freud treated singers who could no longer perform (Case of Fraulein Rosalia H, in Breuer and Freud 1988). In most cases, the paralysis or other physical manifestations were due to the sexual nature of the repressed memory. Because the voice is supported from the lower part of the body and requires a flexible pelvic area for this support, breathing exercises to unlock this part of the body often bring up sexual trauma, which needs careful working through.

Central concepts

The cause of suffering

The voice shows the stresses of inner and public life. What causes differences in vocal tone is the amount of tension in muscle habits. How we acquire these physical habits leads to the areas of physical, mental and emotional suffering which diminishes the spirit and energy available for vocal expression. Voicework is not based on one single model of human development so there is an eclectic understanding about how suffering develops.

There are different levels of this suffering. For example on the physical level, you may have broken a leg skiing on a holiday a few years ago. Although it has healed perfectly well enough for everyday use, you may have created new physical habits to compensate for any weakness in that leg. Then as you do some of the voicework breathing exercises that involve changing these habits, you reawaken the emotional and physical pain of that skiing accident. You might feel the shock and helplessness of not being able to move, the gratitude and love towards others who helped you to safety and recovery, or the terror of lying there alone. You may need to cry and shake and get angry and feel tenderness before the muscles can move in a new way which frees your voice.

Or you have a cold or respiratory illness but insist on using your voice. You manage to get through the performance whether on stage, in the classroom, or the boardroom. It is not unusual to recover from the illness, then lose your voice. You are being forced to stop and rest, to listen to your body's needs and perhaps to the voices of others. You need to rest and resume using your voice very gently and carefully. The body will need time to build up its stamina to support the voice.

On the emotional level, you may have suffered the loss of a loved one early in your life and you perceived that it was not safe to grieve. You could not cry, nor get angry at the person for abandoning you. You could not really let go of that person internally so that they might occupy a different place in your psyche and thus allow new growth and development in your life. If you then decide to undertake voicework, you are likely to get in touch with this pain through the physical breathing exercises.

Sometimes the pain is caused by words from those perceived to be in positions of authority. 'You can't sing; you're tone-deaf'; 'children should be seen and not heard'; 'if you can't say anything nice, don't say anything at all'. These 'authorities' must be right, mustn't they, so we take the words to heart and believe in their power. We then close down the physical movements which would allow us to sing and speak freely. When these movements are rediscovered, so are the verbal messages that led to loss of self-esteem. While many of these messages are absorbed early in life, some are taken in later when we try to adopt roles, postures and attitudes 'suitable' for our chosen line of work. These messages include the sort of dress deemed appropriate (which might be restrictive to the voice), as well as the vowel sounds which will command attention.

Expansion and contraction

I see the most fundamental cause of suffering as the lack of 'fit', both in physical and emotional terms, between mother and child. Patterns of growing and shrinking movements derive from the rhythm of breathing and have to do with feelings of comfort or discomfort, attraction or repulsion in interacting with the environment. Inhaling diminishes the distance between the mother holding the child and the held infant's body, while exhaling promotes some distancing of the bodies. Expanding and contracting correspond to the basic elements of approach and distancing patterns on all levels – purely biological, psycho-biological, and psychological. These patterns, which vary greatly individually, underlie the idea of 'optimal distance' between mother and baby. This optimal distance, which Judith Kestenberg (1975) has studied, is very important for the sense of feeling held. Feelings of safety merge with those of comfort, and caution with those of discomfort. An infant held securely feels safe and comfortable, while inadequate support brings on anxiety, caution and discomfort.

When a child's movements are inadequately held, the child has the feeling of falling forever, of annihilation, psychic death. There is a blankness, something missing, an area that Michael Balint (1968) describes as a 'basic fault' where there is a lack of a structure of a conflict or instinct. Balint traces this back to a considerable discrepancy in early care between the needs of the infant and what was offered. This deficiency has a wide influence

> probably over the whole psychobiological structure of the individual, involving in varying degrees both his [*sic*] mind and his body . . . This creates a state of deficiency whose consequences and after-effects appear to be only partly reversible.

The change process

Technical knowledge about how the voice works is an important part of the change process. Clients need to be able to feel this knowledge in their bodies so that they can sense when something is physically interfering with clear vocal production, and know how to put it right. They need to 'own' this knowledge.

As there is no 'gospel' of voicework theory, the work can be approached from many different angles. Primarily the voice involves the body in a direct and powerful way. The sounds are the result of muscle habits built up over a lifetime. Changing these involve confronting layers of defences – physical, emotional and mental.

Change comes about by being deeply in touch with the muscles, feeling the movements from the inside of the body. This sounds a lot easier than it is – at least at first. You need to pay attention to the way you hold your body and act as a physical presence in the world. You need to still the chattering mind in order to be totally concentrated on the moment, so that the finest of movements can be registered and understood.

Many of the movements stem from earliest childhood, before language has developed to help make sense of emotions and environmental atmosphere. By changing your habitual movements, you then experience the feelings and forgotten memories underlying them. These are often physically painful and emotionally traumatic. These feelings and sensations may need sustained work both in terms of catharsis and intellectual interpretation in order to be worked through. Then new mental habits can transmit new messages to the muscles that it is safe to move in new ways. It is possible to make new movements in a flexible and reliable sequence.

Different methods for reaching these new movements work for different people, but ultimately you come into dialogue with the breath. Is it held? Is it released too forcefully? Is it taken in in snatched and gasped moments? Do the sounds flow on the breath, or do they and the breath go their separate ways? What does it mean for you to speak while stopping the breath? What does it feel like? What is the experience of going with the flow?

Working with breath often evokes profound experiences – of birth, death, new life, transformation, release, power, pain, joy. After uncovering the hurt child and acknowledging its needs, it is possible to discover the playful child within, the childlike part which is naturally curious, adventurous, open to new experiences, and which allows physical flexibility and freedom.

Voicework involves moving the boundaries of muscle wall and this can be a stimulus for changing the shape of the internal self. This internal perception of change can be both exciting and terrifying. The first time one of my students felt inside the full space for singing, a look of wondrous terror came over her face and she said, 'It is like giving birth.'

The process involves coming to terms with your experiences and fantasies about aggression, both damaging and constructive. It is about being able to transform one into the other. Often this confronts you with feelings of shame and inadequacy because it takes considerable effort and concentration to change habits of any sort, physical, mental or emotional. So you not only remember the damaging experience, for example, a teacher who hits you if you make a mistake while simultaneously saying 'You can't sing', you are now being asked to make something new of this information and give your new creation to the world via sound. This is a huge task which can feel overwhelming at times, but each time you do achieve even a bit of this, your self-perception changes, you have a different place in the world, you are empowered.

Confronting your experience of external and internal aggression can mean that you face looking at and accepting the reality of death. Whether you have actually lost an important person through physical illness or emotional abandonment, each time you asked for something, through crying as a baby or intelligible sentences later on and you were denied, either through wilfulness or inadequacy on the part of the other, that experience creates a cluster of emotions in you to do with the issues of death, annihilation, shame and inadequacy.

As you change and stretch the physical and emotional ties through voicework, these issues are likely to emerge and need sensitive reconciliation in order for you to make new kinds of emotional bridges to others and to express these through unblocked vocal sound. You may need to embrace a new sense of life which is heard through the power and clarity of your voice.

Therapeutic goals

The primary aim of voicework is to unlock unnecessary tensions in order to enable you to use your voice to express the experienced gamut of emotion and subtlety of thought. The process of unblocking opens the range of possible choices of vocal tone and expression. The results of this process include improved sincere communication, concentration, the development of self-esteem, confidence, identity and the sense of being in touch with the inner world while being able to discriminate between the world of feeling and sensation and the world of outer reality.

People come to voicework with different motivations. These influence the goals desired. Some want to improve the quality of their voice in order to persuade and manipulate others. Some find voicework a term more acceptable than psychotherapy; they wish to do work on themselves while trying to avoid the idea that something is wrong. Others are aware that something is amiss and voicework could be a way of tackling that with the by-products of increased vocal range, variety, clarity, power and volume. Whatever the motivation, voicework aims to free your voice so that it reflects a wide range of feelings, variety of thoughts, beauty of content, clarity of imagination, and the appropriate power and volume needed to communicate.

Because voicework is very physical, as you change the muscle habits, you may find the need for catharsis. There needs to be room for this within the psychophysical re-education and perhaps, more didactic modes of vocal teaching. However, catharsis *per se* is not the goal of voicework, nor by itself is it enough to change physical, emotional or mental habits. You need intellectual understanding about the process as well. The integration of these different aspects allows for greater refinement and efficiency of thought and physical movement. You are then likely to become more sensitive to your inner world and to creating sounds which reflect it. You may become more sensitive to the effect and meaning of your own and others' spoken and sung words.

The goal of the voiceworker is to become redundant, having passed on a set of skills and a way of working which gives the client tools for life.

Practitioners

Relationship

Voicework practitioners, or voiceworkers, first need to find out what problem or group of problems have led the client to explore this way of working at this particular time. They need to hear and see what happens when a client takes a breath and speaks or sings; to listen both to the quality of sound and the meaning expressed in it. They need to have great patience and to create a safe environment. The client needs to be free to play and experiment, which is only possible when there is a reduction in the amount of fear and anxiety, due to an absence of intimidation or forced compliance.

The voiceworker regards the client as a whole person, not just a voice or a set of physical problems. The physical symptoms can be signposts to possible areas of significant growth, but the voiceworker needs to listen and respond to the client's sounds in a unique manner, which differs from the purely didactic and mechanistic approach.

The voiceworker is just another human being who has had problems which have been overcome and who is still open to working with new difficulties as they arise. It is not enough just to be an authority and specialist, though these attributes are important – particularly in assessing whether a client will benefit from voicework at all; to what extent and depth of intensity the work can be done and where the work might lead. Because voicework is subtle and powerful, it is possible to tap into serious psychopathology very quickly. Both practitioner and client need to approach the work thoughtfully.

The work is about finding new experiences and overcoming debilitating habits, but as most of us have considerable investment in our old ways, change can meet with forceful resistance. The voiceworker needs to have determination and care in confronting the client's desire to avoid the feeling of new sensations and thoughts which would allow the voice to soar.

Several exercises are found in Linklater (1976), Ristad (1982) and Green (1987). They are very effective, but it takes a great deal of discipline and determination to learn new habits. It takes far more to do the work on your own, even if you use a tape recorder.

So it is more efficient to work with a skilled voiceworker, but this means that you are confronted with issues such as trust, power, fear, vulnerability, and past relationships which affect the use, sound and freedom of your voice. Working with someone else adds another dimension to the challenge of creating new vocal habits as early anxieties surface.

Techniques

Because the voice is produced by a large number of clusters of muscles and is influenced by experience and emotions, any technique which helps to bring any of this into awareness is useful in voicework. Taken out of context a list of techniques is misleading as it only has meaning in the context of the client's work. The dialogue with the breath mentioned earlier (p. 179) is crucial. Moving the body or holding a position whilst making various sounds is important.

Techniques of voicework can best be understood with reference to what is presented by clients. Both Lee and Helga wanted to sing.

Lee

Lee came to me for voice lessons. She wanted to sing in clubs but felt too nervous to do so. She sang as if she were a little girl even though she is a woman of about 39. Her voice was very breathy, that is, it allowed a lot of air to escape without projecting sound over much distance. She found it almost impossible to open her mouth; her jaw and cheek muscles were quite rigid. She often complained of neck and shoulder pains, headaches and great physical tension in the upper part of her body. She said she had little physical feeling in the muscles of her legs and abdomen but, in spite of these problems she said she had and continues to have a fulfilling sexual relationship with her partner. When the work enabled her to relax her jaw a bit, so that she could open her mouth more, she felt nauseated. The creation of inner physical space seemed a daunting prospect for her. It was especially difficult for her to yawn and allow the breath to fill the lower part of the lungs. This involves letting the lower ribs spring down and out to create more room for the lungs to fill. In doing so, the diaphragm (a large slab of muscle which attaches to the ribs and separates the upper and lower part of the body) flattens and moves the organs of digestion downwards.

The internal organs are massaged by this movement. For Lee, this was quite traumatic.

After one episode of nausea, she remembered being strangled at the age of 15 by her father, and being forced to be quiet any time she did not agree with him. She was both terrified and angry. She was physically abused for most of her childhood, predominantly by her mother, but also by her father at her mother's instigation.

It was not until we began work to free the upper part of her body through physical relaxation, visualization techniques and using the breath to strengthen her connection with the lower part that earlier information began to emerge. In singing, the lower part of the body, feet to waist and in particular the pelvic floor, buttocks and abdominal muscles become very strong in order to support the upper part of the body so that it is left free to sing. The singing voice is anchored on the pelvic floor.

What emerged for Lee was her confusion between physical and sexual abuse, both of which threatened her right to exist. This is what Joyce McDougall (1989) terms 'archaic hysteria', where there is a lack of verbal links for psychic pain and where there is more concern with protecting the right to exist than with guarding the right to the normal satisfactions of adulthood. In contrast, classical neurotic hysteria which Freud wrote about is mostly dependent upon language and seeks to deal with anxiety concerning the adult right to sexual and narcissistic gratification.

For Lee, yawning produced the most anxiety. There seemed to be a link between the anxiety stirred up by this physical movement, the upheaval in her workplace and her need to contain the concomitant anxiety of others there and the loosening of previously constipated bowels. She was more concerned about taking care of her colleagues than herself, which had been her function at home. She had tried to contain the anxiety through her body, which rebelled. There was far too much anxiety to be able to sing, an activity at other times felt to be healing.

Lee often spoke of her mother's overwhelming anxiety and her mother's need for her to be 'clean', starting potty training at six months. Lee also had had great difficulty in sleeping as a baby, needing to be held and rocked all night for many months. Her difficulties seem to illustrate McDougall's thesis.

> Provided the mother's unconscious fears and wishes or the pressures of external circumstances do not render her incapable of modifying her infant's physical and psychological suffering, she will enable her baby to maintain, in times of physical or mental pain, the illusion of being one with her. When the infant is impeded in its attempt slowly to create an internal representation of a caring and soothing maternal environment and to identify with this 'internal' mother, the lack of an internal protective figure persists into adult life. (The psychosomatic disturbance that gives rise to life-threatening infant insomnia is one manifestation of this lack in babyhood . . .)
>
> (McDougall 1989: 54)

By exploring her material, connecting the emotional content with the physical sensations and re-evaluating the meaning of those connections, Lee is now able to write her own songs and perform in concert in a way she previously never thought possible. She enjoys singing, her voice is freer, more open and able to carry over space and time. Her freedom in song has been won through hard work on many levels, including the discovery of both her destructive and creative aggression.

She is now more able to do her own work independently of me. As she was singing one of her songs, there was a point which became vocally difficult and instead of glossing over this or avoiding it, Lee stopped and worked at it as if she were with me. She broke the difficulty down into small parts by saying to herself, as I have in the past, 'Where is the pivot of the problem? Where is my tongue? What is going on? What do I feel?' After a while she had solved the problem for herself.

Helga

Helga came to me not knowing quite what she wanted. She thought she wanted to sing but first she wanted to talk. Helga was here in Britain for about a year. She had accompanied her husband from their home in Finland in order for him to further his career. She was at home with a baby and very depressed. She felt that if she could 'find her voice' she would feel better.

She came from a family of four children. Her mother seemed a rather shadowy figure, preoccupied with the younger children, but not really there for Helga. Her father seemed like a dominating patriarch whom Helga had taken in as extremely damaging. She felt totally undermined by him, particularly in the areas of being able to think for herself and making a successful life on her own terms. She had complied with his wishes for a successful life for a woman – to find a rich husband and to be a dependent wife and mother. She both hated herself for this and found it almost impossible to fight for another way of being.

This conflict took the form in Helga of feeling nurtured in the sessions and then having the thoughts, feelings and physical memories disappear soon afterwards. Then she felt depressed and could not, soon would not, try to practise. She would threaten not to come to sessions, but always showed up. The work felt stuck for a long time.

As long as I would agree that there is a dimension to music which is larger than an individual and not easily understandable except in terms of spirit, we could work together. Gradually Helga began to use the space to improvise, to create her own sounds. Often they were almost unbearably sad for me, as if I were hearing the grief of centuries. Helga herself felt nothing of this. She felt pleasant physical sensations. The emotional content had been poured into me. I held these and waited until Helga could feel the physical sensations of producing open vowels more strongly before talking about the feelings conveyed. When I spoke of feeling as if I were at the Wailing Wall in Jerusalem, Helga began to cry and then rage and create vocalizations to express these feelings.

Helga had the potential for a really beautiful, rich, operatic voice. At this point, she had no intention of becoming a professional singer, but she had the instrument, albeit needing work, to do so. By the time she was to leave she was looking for ways in which to further her studies to become a singer. As Helga and I worked to create an even vocal instrument, one that had both power and colour from top to bottom, her own life changed. She was not as relentlessly depressed and when she practised at home she 'had the feeling of being filled up inside'. She also stopped smoking.

One of the tasks Helga had to do before returning to Finland was to take part in a performance for her religious group. Every member was to do something and Helga offered to sing an improvisation. This meant going inside herself, getting in tune with her inner world and then expressing this in sound. When Helga sang for her group and invited outside friends, everyone was in tears. What they said to her and she to me was, they were not only moved by the beauty and freedom of her voice; they were also moved by its inner tone.

We both felt sad at having to stop the work. But Helga felt that she had a completely new experience of herself and her vocal potential which she could keep alive even when far away from me. She felt mentally and physically freed.

Pitfalls

As voicework can open you to deep vulnerabilities, both client and practitioner need to be sensitive to the appropriateness of this type of work. It is necessary for the practitioner to bear in mind why the client has come. Is the client physically well? It is important to know this as damage can be done to the vocal mechanism by pushing or refusing to rest during illness. Did the client specifically want to work therapeutically, or not? Is she or he open to this possibility? Is the client in crisis? And if so, would he or she not be better off with straightforward counselling? It is possible, I believe, to work on many levels of the self through exploring the voice, but it is important to think about what may be involved, to be careful and to work gently.

Another consideration for both client and practitioner is to do with the motivation behind the work. Voiceworkers who are not trained and licensed as counsellors may not be conscious of their need for power. They would probably not have individual therapy and supervision which might tackle this point. They might not be aware of the influence and damage possible.

One 'hot potato' is the issue of touch. There is a tradition in voice training which uses touch to make it easier for the client to understand how a muscle needs to work in order to create a certain sound. In this case, the client would feel the muscle movement of the practitioner. It can also help the practitioner understand how a client's muscle is inhibited if she or he can feel the actual tension.

But instructive touch raises a number of issues which both clients and teachers of voice may not have considered. One issue is that the client must grant permission to the teacher or practitioner before any physical contact can be made. Both practitioner and client need to think about what touch means and what feelings might be attached to this action. It is not enough for a practitioner just to ask the client for permission. In accordance with the power issue above, a client may agree in order to please the practitioner, or to comply, but then be angry and upset afterwards. A practitioner must be able to find words and other ways of making muscle movements comprehensible to a client without needing to resort to touch.

The practitioner needs to be well versed and sensitive to the many issues to do with touch. Some practitioners hold that touch is always inappropriate. Freud's rule of abstinence demands that an analyst maintain frustration of the patient's libidinal wishes so that there is no discharge other than through verbal expression. Patrick Casement makes a moving statement about discovering the importance of maintaining this rule while looking at the possibility of touch made available to a client reliving an early trauma and who put considerable pressure on him to do so. He quotes Bion's (1962) 'A theory of thinking', where the child takes in a nameless dread instead of a fear of dying made tolerable, and used this to understand a similar process at a later developmental stage.

> I consider that it was my readiness to preserve the restored psychoanalytical holding, in the face of considerable pressures upon me to relinquish it, which eventually enabled my patient to receive her own frightened personality back again in a form that she could tolerate. Had I resorted to the physical holding that she demanded the central trauma would have remained frozen, and could have been regarded as perhaps forever unmanageable. The patient would then have reintrojected, not a fear of dying made tolerable, but instead a nameless dread.
>
> (Casement 1986)

Confronting this nameless dread is particularly poignant and powerful when working with survivors of sexual abuse, as there often seems to be a core of non-existence or despair. This despair can put pressure on both client and worker to use touch to avoid facing the lack of contact that exists. Singing and voicework can be intensely pleasurable on many levels but is therefore open to abuse as a defence against facing the despair of early trauma.

Research

All the individuals and groups mentioned in this chapter would say that they do 'research'. Through its new journal, *Voice*, the British Voice Association publishes research papers in this area. They intend to include objective research on the efficacy of therapeutic voicework.

In addition, in February 1991 David Garfield-Davies, consultant laryngologist and Director of the Voice Clinic at the Middlesex Hospital, London, made a video stroboscopy recording of the working larynx of Paul Newham exercising extended phonation according to the principles established by Wolfsohn. This investigation found no physiological abnormalities or damage and helps verify that pitch and tonal range can be extended without visible damage to the laryngeal apparatus. Garfield-Davies and Newham have suggested that such work be denoted by the term 'psychophonics' (Newham 1992).

There has also been scientific research done on the effect of low frequency sound and music on muscle tone and circulation carried out by Anthony Wigram and Lynn Weekes (1990). They are Head of Music Therapy, and a physiotherapist respectively at Harperbury Hospital. They looked at certain physical disorders and disabilities and found that specific frequencies are felt in specific areas of the body: 30/40 hz in ankles and calves, 40/50 hz in the knees, thighs and lower abdomen, 50/60 hz in the lumbar and thoracic areas and 60/75 hz in the neck and head. By combining the use of a low-frequency sound with harmonically compatible music, they were able to make significant changes in the range of use of muscles previously disabled through spasm. The combination of the two elements were far more effective than either one in isolation. The low sound treated the body and the music treated the soul and the intellectual and emotional needs.

Case study

Lee and Helga who were discussed above wanted to sing. Stan used voicework as part of his therapy. He was referred to me through his personnel office. He is a senior manager suffering from stress. Symptoms included disturbed sleep patterns, an increase in alcohol consumption and absenteeism. Although his company made the referral, he himself made the appointment with me.

Stan is in his mid-40s, divorced for five years, father of a son and daughter whom he sees every other weekend. He has considerable financial commitments – mortgage, school fees, maintenance etc. He has watched many of his colleagues be made redundant or forced to resign as his automotive company 'down-sizes' to survive. He has always worked hard, but now the hours are considerably longer and the rewards more meagre. He feels trapped and isolated. He perceives his way of working – caring about employees' morale, creating effective teams through encouraging employees' strengths, empowering employees to succeed – at loggerheads with what is being demanded of him by his boss. Although his sales are the highest in the company, his boss often says in front of other managers that 'he is too soft'. Stan is now being given the 'choice' of further reducing his workforce and taking on even more duties, or leaving.

Stan's company has recently been taken over and his boss has been given notice that results must improve quickly or he, too, will face the sack. Stan's boss, Henry, is desperate and keeps changing policies and procedures. Stan feels that he has no sooner understood and begun to implement the new strategy than something else is demanded. Structures and goals become increasingly complex, so that employees are often confused and demoralized. Nothing is as it seems – pay cuts are denied and covered up by complicated figures so that Stan and others cannot tell what they will in fact earn.

When Stan arrived for his first appointment with me, he was in 'top salesman gear' – shaking my hand on the way in, presenting an agenda, talking non-stop at me, ignoring any interpretations. I felt as if I faced a combination of a steamroller and a cardboard cut-out figure. It took several sessions before Stan could tolerate silence and let a 'real' person emerge. Here was a man who was very frightened, depressed, lonely and, at a deep level, unsure of his essential existence. As our work progressed there emerged a terrible gap, an early experience of death at birth; Stan had been unable to take in nourishment from his mother, but had taken in her depression and rage. He had not really been able to have his own life.

Stan discovered that the stress he felt at work was not dissimilar to that experienced as a child at home. There was constant denial of feelings and reality. Stan believed his parents' demands that everything was 'nice' when he knew at another level that his parents were miserable and angry. But he was afraid to think about this. He felt that no one actually cared or wanted to hear what he thought and he was most afraid to make himself heard. He often held his breath. It was difficult for Stan to confront his own rage, hatred and envy.

As we grappled with the dynamics of his inner relationships, however, Stan was able to learn to trust. Once that could be established, we could explore what it felt like to breathe differently. Breathing exercises led to greater awareness and to new movements, both physically and psychically and to a different way of speaking. Stan became more able to stand his ground – to be heard by Henry and respected by him and other managers for doing so. While he still had difficult decisions to make, Stan was now able to think more creatively, find words to say that which was impossible before and to have less physical and mental strain. The original symptoms of stress disappeared as the deeper issues were confronted.

Some practical literature in voicework

According to Linklater (1976)

> To free the voice is to free the person, and each person is indivisibly mind and body . . . the natural voice is most perceptibly blocked and distorted by physical tension, but it also suffers from emotional blocks, intellectual blocks, aural blocks, spiritual blocks. All such obstacles are psycho–physical in nature, and once they are removed the voice is able to communicate the full range of human emotion and all the nuances of thought.

This book provides exercises to do so.

Ristad (1982) gives many examples and exercises of 'upside-down experiences that lead to new right-side-up insights'. It provides a discussion of nervous energy from a physiological understanding of human behaviour under stress – whether in musical performance or in daily living.

Green (1987) uses some principles developed by Tim Gallwey for sports learning. It provides exercises to nurture and enhance natural skills and to reduce mental interference that inhibits the full expression of human potential. It is a practical guide for improving the quality of music experience so that learning and performing can be full of enjoyment, competence and fearlessness.

Stewart (1987) analyses the deeper meaning of music as a means of altering consciousness for spiritual development. It discusses the power of chanting, vowel sounds, and correspondences between musical patterns, life forms and the body. The book offers a practical system of musical symbolism for inner metaphysical and psychological development.

Rodenburg (1992) is very physiologically oriented and stresses the separation between voice training and psychotherapeutic work. This excellent book nevertheless gives many exercises to engage and energize different parts of the whole vocal mechanism. This gifted teacher and Head of Voice at the Royal National Theatre makes a forceful argument that 'your voice belongs to you, it is your responsibility and right to use it fully'.

Newham (1993) sets voicework in context, including its role for change in society and politics. He builds bridges with other therapeutic ways of working and, through research and case studies, looks at the complex meanings – held, symbolized, sounded and silent – of the voice.

References

Balint, M. (1968) *The Basic Fault.* London: Tavistock Publications.

Bion, W.R. (1962) A theory of thinking. In W.R. Bion (1967) *Second Thoughts.* London: Heinemann.

Breuer, J. and Freud, S. (1988) *Studies on Hysteria.* Pelican Freud Library, Vol. 3. London: Penguin Books, pp. 241–5.

Casement, P. (1986) Some pressures on the analyst for physical contact during the re-living of an early trauma. In *The British School of Psychoanalysis: The Independent Tradition.* G. Kohon (ed.) London: Free Association Books.

Cashdan, S. (1988) *Object Relations Therapy.* London: Norton.

Densmore, F. (1948) The use of music in the treatment of the sick by American Indians. In D.M. Schullian and M. Schoen (eds) *Music and Medicine.* New York: Henry Schuman, pp. 25–46.

Green, B. (1987) *The Inner Game of Music.* London: Pan Books.

Kestenberg, J. (1975) *Children and Parents: Psychoanalytic Studies in Development.* New York: Jason Aronson.

Keyes, L. (1973) *Toning: the creative power of the voice.* Marina del Rey, CA: DeVorss & Co.

Linklater, K. (1976) *Freeing the Natural Voice.* New York: Drama Book Publishers.

McDougall, J. (1989) *Theatres of the Body: A Psychoanalytic Approach to Psychosomatic Illness.* London: Free Association Books.

Newham, P. (1992) Jung and Alfred Wolfsohn, *Journal of Analytical Psychology,* 37, 323–36.

Newham, P. (1993) *The Singing Cure.* London: Random Century.

Ristad, E. (1982) *A Soprano in Her Head.* Moab, UT: Real People Press.

Rodenburg, P. (1992) *The Right to Speak.* London: Methuen.

Stewart, R. (1987) *Music and the Elemental Psyche.* Wellingborough Aquarian Press.

Wigram, A. and Weekes, L. (1990) Treatment and research into the physiological effect of low frequency sound and music on muscle tone and circulation, *International Society for Music Education Conference Proceedings,* Tallin, Estonia, 1–4 August 1990.

PART V

Emphasis on ancient systems

13

Men's therapy and patriarchy

ANDREW FORRESTER

Definition and historical development

Definition

Men's therapy forms part of a growing men's movement in Britain which has followed on from the women's movement and in many ways has grown out of the feminist critique of 'patriarchal' society. It is not – at present at least – a distinct method or school of psychotherapy, rather it describes a dimension of consciousness that informs a growing number of male therapists and practitioners in their work. Though younger and smaller than the women's movement, the men's movement shares the central basic assumption that gender is socially, culturally and historically constructed rather than being a biological given. Further, within patriarchal societies, men/the male/the masculine is seen as superior to women/the female/the feminine.

The emergence of men's therapy is based on the assumption that men suffer from a profound alienation under patriarchy. What distinguishes 'men's therapy' from 'therapy for men' is the understanding of the problematic nature of 'being a man' under patriarchy. Needless to say, the common human experiences of loss, abuse, illness and so forth are not disregarded but are seen in the context of a sex–class hierarchy.

Historical development

It is premature to speak of a single distinctive approach of men's therapy in Britain. This chapter would probably not have been commissioned if it were not for the effect of the book *Iron John* written by the American poet, Robert Bly (1990), on public awareness of men's issues. It was first published in the USA, where it sold half a million copies, and then in Great Britain. It has brought the issues of masculinity to a much wider readership.

The men's movement is about 20 years old; the first anti-patriarchal men's group in Britain started in 1972, the first Men Against Sexism Conference a

year later and the first edition of *Achilles Heel* magazine in 1978. John Rowan,
a psychotherapist and prolific writer has been one of the leading lights of the
movement in Britain. He describes in *The Horned God* (Rowan 1987) the mixture
of 'consciousness' and 'unconsciousness-raising' groups in the 1970s, the former
drawing upon feminism and socialism, the latter on humanistic therapies like
Gestalt, Bioenergetics, and Co-counselling. Throughout the men's movement,
there is a fruitful tension between social action and personal growth. Men's
therapy makes personal growth the foreground without divorcing personal issues
from the wider consequences of patriarchy such as discrimination, the under-
valuing of child care and the despoiling of the environment.

At present, it is impossible to say how widespread men's therapy is in Britain
as there is no registering or training body in this approach. Aside from the (largely
invisible) activity of private psychotherapists, a range of initiatives under the wide
umbrella of men's therapy has taken place including:

- 'Wildman weekends' and ongoing groups,
- Counselling projects for men who are abusive to women (e.g. Bolton MOVE
  and the Men's Centre, London),
- Treatment programmes for sex offenders (e.g. Gracewell Clinic, Birmingham),
- Groups for fathers (e.g. Parent Network, Exploring Parenthood),
- Anti-sexist education groups for young people in Youth and Community
  Work.

In later sections, I will, of necessity be selective and focus on the area of practice
I know best and the conceptual framework that informs it.

Founders

It is hard to single out founders of an approach that is both diverse and in the
process of formation. What strikes me as significant is that the sources of inspiration come largely from the underclasses (or male shadow):

- Women: through the statements and actions of feminists;
- Gays: through their reflection on what it is to be a man;
- Tribal cultures: through their relation to the natural world and the importance
  they attach to initiation rituals.

Robert Bly, and the Jungian tradition that underpins his analysis, has also
promoted the wisdom found in fairy stories, which latterly had been relegated to
children's stories.

Where does men's therapy fit in with other approaches?

Clearly, men's therapy owes a lot to feminist thinking and practice. It also
recognizes that men need to find their own answers, their own mentors, otherwise
they will perpetuate their traditional emotional dependence on women.

Jungian psychology is the other main influence on men's therapy. It provides
a vocabulary (of archetypal and other images) for exploring different energies

inside an individual man, both female and male. What it lacks is an explicit understanding of power relations in a given society and how certain gods, e.g. the Heavenly Father, the Earth Mother, may be selected to reinforce the dominant ideology.

The mythological/spiritual dimension and the interest in tribal cultures in Bly and others' writings have come together in the shamanistic strand in men's therapy. Many Native American beliefs demonstrate a respect for women, a respect for nature which can help to heal the patriarchal split between sexuality and spirituality, between mankind and nature. Through their difference, these belief systems offer a hope that things can be different for western man. In the long run, though, we must 'grow our own' rituals and not rely on importing them from exotic locations.

In practice, I and other men's therapists will draw upon a range of techniques and ways of understanding. Particularly helpful for men are approaches like bodywork and Gestalt that help to restore a man's connectedness to his body and his feelings.

Central concepts

If I were to identify a common denominator in the suffering of men today it would be a sense of alienation – a feeling of being walled off in a bubble, behind a transparent screen – cut off from their own feelings, detached controllers of their bodies, struggling for words to emotionally touch other men and prone to see women as distant and dangerous. The factors that come together in creating this experience include the following concepts.

The idea of gender difference

In a society in which power and privileges are vested in one group of people (those with a penis) at the expense of another group (those without a penis), the dominant group have a vested interest in emphasizing their difference. Physiologically and psychologically 'we are, clearly, a multi-sexed species which has its sexuality spread along a vast continuum where the elements called male and female are not discrete' (Dworkin 1974).

Patriarchy thus dictates that males are both distinct from and superior to females. The consequences to women have been well spelt out by women writers.

The consequences to men are that men learn to numb areas of body sensation and feeling that are considered female, e.g. receptivity, tenderness, communion. They also channel awareness and activity into male areas, e.g. the mind, feeling dissatisfied in their capacity for intimacy as they are more in contact with their ideas of who they should be and what a woman should be than in touch with their inner 'moist' selves.

The absent father

Many men in therapy uncover a tremendous amount of grief for the lack of fathering in their childhood. The father may be physically absent through death or divorce. He is usually peripheral in terms of child care. The boy may be sent away to boarding school. All these experiences have telling effects: the boy lacks a substantial model of being a man; he has little reality to set against the media stereotypes and the similar lack of information from his peers; he may ascribe all manner of powers (good and bad) to the absent father; he may learn to dissociate power (absent father) and responsibility (close mother); and perpetuate the social devaluation of women's work.

The father, whether he is physically absent or not, has grown up in a society where men learn to cut off their feelings and so will often be emotionally absent for his children. The boy will learn the value of self-containment and self-control, and will often have a limited emotional vocabulary consisting of varying degrees of anger and nothing else.

Hatred and fear of mother

John Rowan (1987) cites a view that

> the common root of sexism and militarism is fear of the 'Other' and originally fear of the mother . . . the immediate power over the infant was female. We cannot help but live in fear, in dread, for any power on which we are so deeply dependent.

If this ambivalence is not recognized in adult life, it fuels the patriarchal dogma, namely that women are either exalted as the Virgin Mary or degraded (and exploited) as Eve. Either way, women are distanced and objectified. Once they are seen as objects, no longer as subjects, men can subscribe to the patriarchal presumption of ownership of women.

Denial of responsibility

When we numb our awareness of unmanly feelings, we diminish our response-ability. When we deny our ambivalent feelings towards women and project our hatred on to feminist 'ball-crushers' we deny our responsibility. When we abuse women and say 'She made me do it' or 'I couldn't help myself, I just saw red', we deny our responsibility. As Adam Jukes (1990) puts it in relation to men who are violent to women 'The most common justification is that "She deserves it", the most common excuse is "I lost control" '. His argument is that 'physical violence is part of a continuum of controls which men use to get our own way with women and maintain power over them'. In similar vein, John Rowan quotes 'Rape is the end logic of masculine sexuality'.

The male therapist needs to work hard to face his own capacity for violence towards women so as to avoid the trap of seeing themselves as 'normal' and those men who act out their violence as 'abnormal'.

The change process

Therapeutic goals

A precondition for therapy is that the man or someone who has power over him sees that there is a problem. Many feminists would say that the so-called well-adjusted masculinity is a problem (similarly black activists insist that white racism is the white person's problem). Because of the widespread denial of responsibility in men, voluntary take up of health and social services targeted at men is notoriously low. Bly speaks of two typical male responses to their emotional wounds – the grandiose path, to rise above them, and the depressed path, to sink into them, for example to drown themselves in drink. They are both dependent personalities – Peter Pan on the one hand and the addict taking refuge in the spurious dependency on a substance.

Once a man steps (or is pushed) into therapy, the first stage of the work is to reclaim the feminine within and honour and respect the female without. Bly skips over this step taking it as read that the 'soft male' – the man in touch with his feminine – has superseded the macho models exemplified by John Wayne or Humphrey Bogart. I believe he is choosing to ignore the host of evidence which suggests that the 'male chauvinist pig' is still wreaking havoc – domestic violence, rape, the aggressive individualism of the 'free market', the exploitation of human and natural resources – there are few signs of these practices evaporating.

This first step in therapy will involve disentangling his mixed feelings towards his mother in particular, and to women in general; learning to recognize his body sensations and feelings, learning to trust intuition as well as rationality; learning to let go of his need for control of self and others; to see women as fellow human beings not appendages to his desires.

The next step, to contact his deep masculinity, needs to be taken only when a respectful relationship to the feminine principle is established. Bly has been criticized rightly for down-playing (in his recent work) the mother–son relationship in an effort, perhaps, to fill the silence on the father–son relationship. The 'Wild Man' as Bly calls the particular archetype embodying fierceness who plays the role of guide and initiator in the story of Iron John, can be seen by macho men as an invitation to continue channelling their dulled emotions into anger and hostility.

John Rowan puts the dilemma graphically: when men start to acknowledge their contributions to maintaining patriarchy, they experience their powerful, penetrative penis as bad; they then develop a non-threatening nicey-nicey limp penis. On a long-term basis, this is not a viable solution for the human race! Rowan sees the development of a good penis as not a compromise between bad and nicey-nicey, but a transformation into a powerful being that has power with women rather than power over women.

The role of men's groups is important in this context. It has become fashionable à la Wildman Weekends to see the men's group as a way of initiating men into manhood in the image of a tribal society. At their best, men's groups break down a lot of the alienation between men – the sense of threat, competition and greater or lesser homophobia. They can also provide the containment for men to rage and grieve for the fathering they did not get. At worst, they can perpetuate male clubbiness and a sense of complacency that leaves their relationship with women undisturbed. They can also idealize the nature and quality of life and relationships in tribal culture and lead to a kind of backwoodsy retreatism.

Since men's therapy uses an explanatory framework that goes beyond the psychological, it is important to say something about the change process beyond the maturational goals described above. Here, there is evidence of considerable divergence. The socialist feminist wing would see the personal and political as wedded; in other words, inaction is equivalent to tacit support for the patriarchal status quo. As I see it this does not mean taking up campaign politics – it means taking my personal growth into my marriage and into how I father my children.

On the other wing, Bly, Rowan and the Jungians see the change process as informed by a spiritual mythological dimension. Jungians see the individual psyche as participating in having as bedrock a collective psyche. Bly locates the Wild Man as one of seven masculine 'souls' in the depths of the male psyche:

> If a therapist doesn't dive down to meet the Wild Man or Wild Women, he or she will try to heal with words. The healing energy stored in waterfalls, trees, clay, horses, dogs, porcupines, llamas, otters belong to the domain of the Wild People.

I think Bly is saying two things here. First, that the therapist needs to ally himself or herself with the collective psyche and the healing energies of nature. Second, that the therapist demonstrates through the use of words that poetry (and creative expression) enlarges experience where an exclusively rational, scientific approach to therapy may reduce experience ('the territory') to a set of linguistic signifiers ('the map').

Practitioners

The therapeutic relationship

The role of a men's therapist varies from setting to setting according to the nature of the therapeutic contract. Adam Jukes at the Men's Centre redefines his task with violent men as 'psychoeducational'. His contract with the men includes the explicit understanding that he is in touch with and will represent the battered woman's interests first and foremost. Treatment programmes for convicted sex offenders are often part of a probation order where again the therapist is explicitly serving the interests of past (or future potential) survivors of sexual abuse.

By contrast, Robert Bly, James Hillman, Michael Meade and others have addressed men's gatherings in Britain taking the role of Wise Man, story teller, keeper of the legends – sowing the seeds for some men to join self-led men's groups or go into individual therapy.

The role I am drawn to in my own practice as an individual psychotherapist is one articulated by Gary Corneau (1991): 'The role of therapy is to give meaning to men's suffering as a kind of initiation experience'. This presupposes that my own therapy has initiated me into this realm of human suffering and that I can encourage the man to be with, to sit alongside his woundedness. I will also let him know that I am similarly conditioned as a man and invite his wiser self to challenge me if we start playing the games men play, for example theorizing, sparring, defensive camaraderie, etc.

I am not there to fill the gap left by the absent real father – or only transitionally; rather, I am there to support the man through his anger and grief for what he didn't have and witness the emergence of his capacity to father himself.

Men's therapy in practice

I will illustrate men's therapy first from my own practice as an individual psychotherapist and second from a residential workshop I was involved in a year ago.

Individual therapy

I work in an integrative way, drawing upon my training as a Gestalt therapist and knowledge of other humanistic approaches whilst being mindful of the transferential elements of my relationship with clients. I have organized the illustrative material developmentally, broadly mapping the main stages of a therapy.

Beginnings

With a client who is beginning (and especially if they are new to therapy), I see my role as educational and modelling – dipping a toe in the water first to encourage the man to try it. A client (A) came to see me worried about his violence which he felt was getting out of control. We talked about driving and I told him how furious I sometimes get if a driver pulled out in front of me, but that if I reflected on it, I was scared first and rapidly got angry on top of that. My client recognized that in himself and he agreed to start an anger log to increase his awareness of what was happening inside him and around him when he got angry.

With another client (B) who had been in therapy for over 18 months, he felt that we had reached a plateau and he was ready to move into the unexplored area of his sexuality. The following week, a friend wrote from abroad mentioning he had got drunk and slept with a black teenage prostitute. My client asked me for my reactions which I gave him – a mixture of curiosity, prurient interest and disapproval – which helped him to put into words his own reactions and fear of seeming weird.

Contacting feelings and sensations

After a few months of therapy in which a man (C) had talked of his upbringing – cold mother, distant naval father, boarding school – I invited him to revisit in fantasy the family home, visiting each of the rooms, seeing the scenes from family life, recognizing how he fitted into the family system. The following week, he commented on a shift in his view of his past, a greater awareness of his part in it and a more forgiving feeling towards his parents.

If a client comes in feeling stuck, stale or blank, I often invite them to take a fantasy trip into their body or to a specific sensation in their body. One man (D) went into the right side of his abdomen, where he felt the stuckness: he got a sense of old resigned anger and recalled his last day at school. This led into a fantasy

of meeting Gollum (an old nickname of my client) in the river, by the school –
Gollum had lost his fire and was waiting for it to return. The following session
he talked of 'not having had a real father'. As he talked to an empty chair
representing his father, his hand went to his stomach – here resided the 'real me'
which he would not let his father see. My client could see the connection to
Gollum and how he had let the 'fire in his belly' die.

Talking about

At times I slip into talking with my male clients in a comfortable old boy's club
kind of way. The subject matter may be personal but there is a safety-first quality.
If this continues for a long time, I will comment on it. A man (E) came to see me
saying he had worked through his anger with his previous therapist. He now
wanted to concentrate on his fear. After five or six varied and interesting sessions
(a dream here, a family tree there), my client said he was angry with himself
for not getting down to real issues and asked me for my comments. What came
to mind, I said, was he had talked about wanting to work on his fear with me,
but I had not experienced him bringing his fear into the room. We then moved
down a level and worked directly on how he makes himself small (nicey-nicey
penis), when he feels afraid.

Transference issues

The two illustrations I give of this issue reflect on the themes of distance/closeness
and directiveness/receptiveness.

Early in B's therapy, mentioned above, the question of my silences came up.
He, by and large, is eloquent and likes to fill the silence. He realized when
challenged that he experiences my silences to mean 'I've done something wrong
but I don't know what'. This connected strongly to the message he feels he gets
from his dad.

A few sessions later, he referred to a suggestion I had made early on in the
therapy – to express non-verbally (using cushions) what he felt towards his father.
At the time I felt I had made a mistake, as the evident anger he felt got locked
up and turned back on himself (he said he felt disappointed in himself, cowardly).
He talked of it as the soldier mentality – give him an order and he'll enjoy over-
riding the pain. Following this conversation, it was easier for him to say 'No' to
any suggestions of mine he did not feel comfortable with. It was an important
lesson for me that when I make a suggestion, this will have parental overtones
that need to be addressed.

Empowerment

Men's therapy work is incomplete if there is not a new empowerment following
the work with his woundedness. An older man (F) came to see me because he felt
Gestalt might help him improve the quality of his contact with others. He had
done a lot of therapy on himself and worked part time as a bodywork therapist.
At times in the therapy he would contact powerful healing energies in himself but
he would invite me (Good Daddy) to give him a kick to take these healing qualities
into the world. What he faced was a choice – to hang on to blaming his dad for
undermining him or to take responsibility for fathering himself. We identified

that he was stuck at the point where awareness needs to be transformed into action that expresses and so affirms identity and so decided to work towards ending therapy.

Endings

Often it helps to crystallize the work of therapy around some symbol or guiding vision. F, above, had some experience of shamanistic work and had contacted several spirit guides (for healing subpersonalities) during and before our therapy. As we came towards ending, he recontacted the Zulu warrior in him, an image that countered the sterilizing upper-crust Englishness of his background and affirmed the powerfully physical energy and understanding in my client.

For another client (C), the figure that he took away was a wise man, an inner resource he had not tapped into before. He was facing the feelings of isolation – reawakening his memories of boarding school – as he said goodbye to me, and possibly to his marriage. The wise man embodied self-acceptance and a dependability that he offered to others but rarely to himself.

Groupwork

This extended illustration exemplifies the power of an initiation ritual which evolved out of the therapeutic process rather than one that was imported or superimposed. Since I was the protagonist, it has special significance for me.

I attended a five day residential workshop on Sexual Identity run by Malcolm Parlett and Dolores Bate, two acclaimed Gestalt Therapy trainers. It began with the group of 24 men and women creating a huge collage of images of men and women taken from magazines or personal photos. Some of the workshop time was spent in gender groups, some in mixed groups. On the morning of Day 3, we were told that in the evening there would be a party/gathering. We were invited to choose an identity from the wealth of images on the collage and come to the party as that self. I made an almost instant decision – to come as a primitive, an aboriginal (an advert for Obsession perfume sparked this idea). My next decision was I will have to be naked and that will mean shaving my beard off.

I went to the men's group that followed shaking with fear and excitement about my decision. As I reflected with my fellow men on the significance of shaving my beard off, I recalled that I had grown it at the end of my Gestalt training, eight years prior, and that it had been a semi-conscious bow in the direction of my trainer/mentor (who had a big white beard!) It felt fitting that at a Gestalt training event, I should shed the novice mantle and be seen for who I was.

Talking about it surfaced some feelings – many of them scary. I asked the men to be there while I shaved. We didn't think 'How are you meant to conduct a rite of passage?' – there seemed an inner sense of appropriateness in the way it happened. I felt incredibly moved by the experience of being seen and 'held' by a group of men as I shaved – I felt I was letting go of my mentor/trainer and felt very vulnerable and naked. Afterwards, I was reluctant to leave the haven of the men and re-enter the world (outside the men's dormitory where the ritual had taken place).

There is a lot more to the story but the purpose of my account is to substantiate the importance and impact of initiation rituals in marking the passage from youth to manhood.

Does it work?

Pitfalls

There are a number of pitfalls for the therapist in this area:

1 We need to explore our motivation for working in this area as it can be fuelled by macho (it is a real challenge) or 'mummy's boy' (pleasing the strong feminist woman in your life) motives.
2 If we take the Wildman approach unleavened by the feminist critique, we may be avoiding our despair about effecting real social change and foster a retreat into a 'Golden Age' or myth of the Noble Savage glow. This is not true of all Jungians in the field. Gary Corneau (1991), who compares the therapeutic task with that of the initiating father, appears more grounded: 'The task of the initiating father is to ease his son's entry into life by sharing his imperfect humanity'.

For the client, there are a number of pitfalls, some of which I have touched upon:

1 Like the therapist, a man may come into therapy or into a group with the covert agenda to please his feminist friends.
2 If a man comes to a Wildman Weekend without recognizing his capacity for abusiveness, he may have it reinforced rather than challenged.
3 Any workshop formula gives rise to 'highs' which can falsely be seen as a short cut to therapy. Initiation, shamanistic and Wildman Workshops emphasize action and enactment and may leave out inner work and digestion.
4 Paralysis with guilt; apologizing for being a man is a common phase in therapy when the abusive nature of your actions and attitudes is first confronted (bad penis). If your therapist doesn't feel good about his penis, you may get stuck there.

Research

There is a dearth, as far as I am aware, of research studies on the effectiveness of men's therapy. Work in the USA and the UK (*Bolton Move* – a counselling service for men concerned about their own violence – for instance) with men who are violent to women has been researched and has substantially reduced the abuse rate. The very existence of such centres and the fact that men are using them (MOVE receives several hundred enquiries from men a year), has brought the size of the problem into wider consciousness. (Police are now more likely to intervene in domestic violence whereas previously there was 'an Englishman's home is his castle' mentality.) Of course, much of the increased awareness is due to the efforts of the women's movement.

Work at the Gracewell Clinic has reduced reoffending rates with the sex offenders they have treated, but they are being pressured to dilute their programme to increase throughput. Research shows that prison on its own does not reduce reoffending rates (except whilst offenders are in prison) and may compound them as they are frequently abused and humiliated by fellow prisoners.

Research is needed on the effectiveness of men's therapy with so-called normal neurotic (normally abusive?) men of the kind I have described from my practice in terms of outcomes such as their sexuality, self-image, fathering, capacity for intimacy with men and women and attitudes to the planet and its resources.

Case study

The subject of this study, A, referred to in a previous section, has seen me for ten sessions at the time of writing. During our work, I have used techniques and concepts drawn from my training background. What I will focus on here is how my awareness of men's issues has influenced my approach with a man, uninitiated in therapy and embodying many of the experiences and qualities of mainsteam culture.

A is a businessman in his 40s who came to see me as he, and his cohabitee, were worried about his violence. In our first session he said he had been fighting all his life: with a disciplinarian father, with school bullies, in the Forces and as a 'bullish' businessman – and was beginning to tire of this. Frightened by the most recent violent outburst, and the risk of losing his cohabitee, he decided to give therapy a go.

From the outset, I sensed a sadness, an emptiness beneath the genial exterior and the fighting talk (the place of 'ashes' in the *Iron John* story). When I reflected back that what I saw and what I felt were at odds, he recalled adopting a 'mask' as a child to cover up the 'unhappy frown' he used to carry as a result of the beatings and the coldness of his father. He added that he feels most real when he is angry. Anger, then, was seen as not something to be eliminated – A's initial objective – but as a blunt emotional instrument which had helped him to survive in a cold emotional climate.

This emerged in a daydream he reported recently of wanting to leave the futility of Earth and travelling to 'The Red Planet', Mars, which, in Edgar Rice Burroughs' story, embodies the traditional martial arts of hand to hand combat.

As well as validating the healthy aspect of A's anger (the Warrior), I have focused on his relationship to his female side and to women. In order to do this, I have confronted a number of 'images' that he has put forward – jet setter, tropical island recluse, working in a wildlife rescue park – as escapes from ordinariness. He traced this to his school days where he would make up stories 'to look big' to cover up his low self-opinion. At the beginning of therapy, it was as though he challenged me to see through him. Now, he is more genuinely interested in having insight himself using awareness practice and paying attention to his dreams and fantasies. He is becoming more able to sit with his woundedness – his unhappiness and his shame – instead of rising above it through chasing glamour or sinking into it with drink. It is still a struggle for him to come to therapy – the exposure of therapy seems to go 'against his nature'. When he expresses 'weakness' he feels like a 'deserter' to the family ethic of prowess, strength and fortitude. He still has violent fantasies. What seems clear to me though, is that he now recognizes the sources of pain and fear that bred the fighter in him; he has more ability when angry to 'let it go'; he has a growing respect and compassion for all the sides of his personality, including the dull and the unhappy, not just the aggressively successful. He has respect for the woman in his life and a growing compassion for the more vulnerable aspects of himself.

In conclusion, this piece of work illustrates some of the typical masks or images that men in our culture are invited to adopt or aspire to. Having a men's therapy consciousness helps me to understand and confront them and therapy enables men to meet themselves and others with more passion and humanity.

A comment on the literature on men's therapy

Bly (1990), a Jungian poet, analyses the Grimm fairy tale, 'Iron Hans'. It is about a wild, hairy man who lives at the bottom of a pond in the forest. Bly takes this as a symbol for the Wildman inside every man. He intersperses poetry with detailed commentary on the fairy tale to unfold his thesis that modern western man needs to look to fairy tales, legends and myths for models of ourselves and our world. Bly's talks, workshops and book have caught a tide of interest and have dramatically increased public awareness of men's issues.

Stoltenberg (1990) is a series of essays by an American radical feminist writer. He writes very directly, almost shockingly: Rapist Ethics, Sexual Objectification, Male Supremacy and The Forbidden Language of Sex (about pornography). He argues that men in western cultures are socialized into confusing sexuality with violence and domination and that our sexuality reflects and perpetuates the oppression of women and the alienation of men.

John Rowan is a British psychotherapist in the humanistic psychology field. He describes (Rowan 1987) 'three channels of healing' interspersing personal history with analysis. The first two he describes as men's consciousness and men's unconsciousness raising groups. The third is the spiritual dimension and male sexuality – the Horned God – which needs to be harnessed in service to the powerful feminine principle – the Great Goddess.

Gary Corneau is a Canadian Jungian analyst who identifies 'the father's silence' (Corneau 1991) as the keystone for the search for masculine identity. Like Bly, he draws parallels between therapy and initiation but the book is much more directly applicable to the practice of men's therapy as it is well stocked with case material. He draws upon the wealth of material in Jungian psychology on male and female psychology (e.g. James Hillman, Robert Johnson).

John Lee (1989) is an American therapist who describes his own therapeutic journey very vividly. The title is a reference to Robert Bly's epithet used to describe men who avoid commitments, responsibilities, intimacy and their own bodies. Flying boys often grow up in dysfunctional families – Lee's father was an alcoholic. Lee advocates treating such families as a whole since all members may be involved in reinforcing destructive patterns of communication.

References

Bly, R. (1990) *Iron John*. London: Element Books.
Corneau, G. (1991) *Absent Fathers, Lost Sons*. London: Shambhala.
Dworkin, A. (1974) *Woman Hating*. New York: Dutton.
Jukes, A. (1990) Working with men who are violent to women, *Counselling*, 1, November.
Lee, J. (1989) *The Flying Boy*. Deerfield Beach, FL: Health Communications Inc.
Rowan, J. (1987) *The Horned God*. London: Routledge.
Stoltenberg, J. (1990) *Refusing to be a Man*. Glasgow: Fontana Books.

14

Astrological counselling

CHRISTINE VALENTINE

Definition and historical development

Definition

Astrological counselling is a form of therapy in which the practitioner uses the symbols of the horoscope as a means of reflecting, exploring, deepening and containing the client's experience. The horoscope, or map of the heavens drawn for the individual's time and place of birth, provides a picture of the client's internal situation, a means of understanding their psychic patterning and of charting the movements of the psyche, its cycles of growth and change. Counselling techniques of listening at different levels, mirroring, accepting and empathizing are also used to establish a therapeutic alliance and provide a supportive, nurturing framework.

Historical development

Astrology's value as a counselling tool is becoming increasingly recognized. This no doubt reflects current humanistic and psychological values in which the quality of the relationship between client and therapist and the process of self-discovery are now perceived to be crucial to healing. Thus, in addition to the astrological consultation or chart reading which offers clarification and guidance, more and more astrologers work with the horoscope in an ongoing, open-ended and exploratory way.

Astrology itself is a very ancient study and was originally synonymous with astronomy. Astronomical data provided the basis for astrological interpretations, the movements of the celestial bodies being important only in so far as they revealed something of the nature and purpose of earthly living. Indeed astrology seems to have been one of our earliest attempts to understand and regulate our lives by referring human activity to the regular cyclic motions of the planets. It was bound up with religion and medicine as well as affairs of state, and used by priests and rulers for timing religious ceremonies, wars, agricultural and other activities upon which the community depended.

The individual horoscope did not appear until Renaissance times and the emphasis was still placed upon outer events rather than self-knowledge. In a fatalistic world one's only hope was for some advanced warning, though some astrologers felt that fate was negotiable and the alchemists, who used astrology to time their experiments, believed that we have a hand in our fate, that psyche and matter are somehow interrelated.

In the seventeenth century, after the invention of the telescope, astronomy separated itself from astrology to explore the workings of the universe for its own sake. A heliocentric universe replaced the geocentric world view so that human beings were forced to re-evaluate their place in the scheme of things. This led to the idealism of the Reformation with its belief in the power of the human mind to develop scientific principles to master and control the environment. Thus astrology fell into disrepute since it was not an exact science. Indeed it became sensation-seeking and commercial, cashing in on people's insecurity in times of change, until the end of the nineteenth century when it once more became a subject for serious study. Its potential as a means of understanding something of the nature of our relationship to our world was rediscovered. Its value as a map of the psyche and its processes has now brought this ancient study into modern relevance.

Founders

It was Alan Leo (1860–1917) who began the process of rediscovering astrology's value and potential and restoring its status as a body of ancient wisdom. He emphasized the correlation between our internal and external worlds, that our psychic patterning as revealed by the horoscope helps to shape our lives. He joined the Theosophical Society where he became a friend of Annie Besant, and founded the astrological branch called the Lodge which was set up in London in 1915. His work was continued by one of his students, Charles Carter who did much to clarify and deepen the understanding of astrological symbolism. He became the first President of the Faculty of Astrological Studies founded in 1948 by Lorenz von Sommaruga and Edmund Caselli to promote the serious study of astrology. The Faculty is still the major astrological teaching body offering a professional training in astrological consultancy and a qualification which is internationally recognized. It has recently extended its training to include a 'Counselling in Astrology' course to meet the needs of those who wish to work in a more ongoing, therapeutic way. The Centre for Psychological Astrology is another teaching body which emphasizes the horosope's psychodynamic perspective.

Relationship with other therapies

Astrological counselling has strong affinities with Jungian, transpersonal and humanistic perspectives in that it emphasizes human potential at both individual and collective levels and includes a spiritual perspective. The horoscope reveals both our potential wholeness as well as the gaps and splits in the psyche. Thus, like the Jungian approach it is concerned with healing the splits through the containment of opposites. Like the alchemical model which Jung did much to revive, astrology views growth as arising out of conflict, as long as frustrations and anxieties can be contained. This is facilitated by the planetary symbols as images of psychic processes, similar to Jung's theory of archetypes and his belief that many of our problems stem from a loss of connection to our imaginal life and archetypal roots.

Like the Jungian perspective the horoscope portrays the psyche as polytheistic and animistic, a mythic drama rather like the loves and quarrels of the gods of Olympus. This gives rise to 'complexes' which astrology calls 'aspects' or split-off parts of us which take on a life of their own. In the language of psychosynthesis (see Chapter 5, this volume) the horoscope can be seen as a map of our sub-personalities, or, in psychoanalytic terms of our unconscious fantasy life and internal objects. In addition it offers a means of timing life cycles and under-standing process, something which is relevant to all types of therapy.

Astrology is also an energetic system based on the 'Four Elements'. These can be seen as both indicators of temperament, like Jung's Psychological Types and homeopathy's humours, and of energy flow and blockage, as in the zone therapies such as acupuncture, shiatsu and polarity therapy, and the humanistic therapies such as Bioenergetics, Gestalt and Core Process (see Chapter 4, this volume). Indeed astrology is a valuable diagnostic tool which can usefully inform all therapeutic disciplines.

Central concepts

Cause of suffering

An astrological perspective views suffering as an integral part of our human condition, an inevitable part of the experience of growing and becoming who we potentially are. Yet it also believes that it can be made more bearable and manageable if some kind of meaning or pattern to our existence can be found. This involves understanding one's life as part of a larger whole, that our personal lives are a reflection of a universal order or archetypal dimension which is in some way purposeful. In other words there is some underlying intelligence which is guiding and unfolding our development which we can learn more about by means of the horoscope's symbols. The more we develop a symbolic awareness the less attached we become to a literal, egocentric view of life, more able to see behind appearances and to ask 'What does life want of me?' as well as 'What can I get out of life?' This allows us to begin to reflect on and cooperate with our own process and feel more connected to our archetypal roots, more at home in our world. Then we can gain some perspective on and acceptance of our suffering rather than becoming overwhelmed by it.

The concept of universal mind

The horoscope embodies a sort of psychic blueprint or pre-existent pattern, an evolutionary plan which exists outside time but unfolds in time. This is similar to the concept of the 'Word of God' or 'God's Providence' which is an image of life as meaningful and purposeful. Like Plato's 'archetypes' from whom Jung borrowed the term, an idea exists before the manifest form, an original intention or seed of the fruit to come. In other words thought precedes action, mind precedes matter, something we experience each time we plan a project or seek to embody some image or idea that we have conceived. This takes us into a realm which is beyond space and time and therefore allows us to step out of the immediate, practical business of living and explore new possibilities. The horoscope is a tool which enables us to study ourselves in this way, to discover something of our own intentions, the kind of seed we are.

The birth or seed moment

The horoscope is a snapshot of a moment in time based on the notion that whatever is born in that moment embodies the quality of that moment. This is like Jung's notion of 'synchronicity', that events occurring at the same time, though qualitatively different, embody the same archetypal significance. It is based on the image of an interconnected universe in which the same idea can be seen to be reflected at different levels. Thus the planetary level reflects the human level just as the seasonal changes in nature reflect our changing psychic states. When we are in touch with such correspondences and connections then one has a sense of the time being right, that things occur in their own time, that 'to every thing there is a season, and a time to every purpose under the heaven'. One glimpses a realm of meaningful coincidence where our normal space–time boundaries no longer exist. Psychic and physical reality combine to give a sense of the numinous, that something has arranged it. For example we may decide to pursue a course of action and at the same time have a dream which somehow embodies our decision, as well as running into someone who encourages it in some way. Then if we look at our horoscope at this time we will discover a planetary correspondence which forms yet another coincidence, as well as providing a means of understanding the archetypal significance of what is happening. Thus the horoscope offers a means of exploring the archetypal significance of one's birth moment, the various life themes and issues with which one has come into the world, and those which are relevant to particular life stages.

Life cycles

Astrology is a means of understanding our lives as cyclic or the unfolding of something from its seed potential through a series of phases to its fullest expression and then back to its seed again, rather like the waxing and waning of the moon. Thus if we are to attempt to understand the wholeness of something we need to consider it in all its phases, not simply as it is at any one given time. Our lives now are intimately connected with who we have been in the past and what we are now is already conditioning what we will be in the future. The horoscope can help us to understand something of what we are bringing to birth at any given time, as well as link past and present in a meaningful way. And it embodies not only our personal but our collective life cycles, those periods of growth and change we all meet at roughly the same age. For example, the Saturn Return occurs around the age of 29, a time of greater realism, and the Uranus Opposition at mid-life, when neglected parts of us start demanding attention.

Symbolic correspondences

Astrology provides us with a set of symbols by means of which we can think about the nature of the psyche. These are based upon the planets as images of psychic processes, each planet embodying a particular impulse or internal object. For example, the moon is our lunar impulse to give and receive nurture, the needy, dependent, security seeking, oral part of us, as well as the motherly, protective, sustaining part, the mother/child archetype. Then the zodiac of signs forms a sort of backcloth to the planets which gives our impulses an individual colouring. Though we are all driven by similar needs and desires we express and channel them in different ways. Thus my style of nurturing and getting my needs met, my Moon, will be different from yours, so that if my Moon were in Taurus, an earth sign, I would tend to take care of myself and others in a very physical, sensual way such as cooking a nice meal, giving or receiving a massage, tending a garden. If however my Moon were in Libra, an air sign, then I might nurture myself by reading a good book, having a serious discussion, sharing a candle-lit dinner, activities which feed my intellect and need for companionship.

It may be, however, that such lunar needs become denied because they are still bound up with unresolved painful experiences of infancy. Thus, other parts of us may dominate, something which the 'aspects' can help us to determine, the angular relationships between the planets which embody the stresses and strains in the psyche as well as the strengths and resources, the helping and hindering figures of our internal world which are also projected out there. This takes us into the realm of the 'Houses' or the experiences we encounter by means of which our internal reality becomes shaped and modified. And in turn external reality becomes shaped and modified by our fantasies so that there is a constant inter-action between the two. Thus if my Taurus Moon is in the Ninth House then as well as needing a physical and material sense of well-being, my feelings of safety and containment will also depend on involving myself in experiences which widen my horizons and give me a sense of meaning like studying, travelling or teaching.

The change process

Therapeutic goals

Astrology offers us a means of understanding how we see and meet the world through our unconscious fantasy life or by projecting our internal reality on to the outside. In other words our relationship to external reality depends upon our fantasies which are in turn affected by external reality. Our capacity to grow, develop, find meaning and fulfilment in our lives depends upon having something supportive and sustaining inside ourselves, the fantasy of benign, helping figures which can be called upon especially in times of difficulty. The astrological counsellor thus aims to encourage the client to enter astrology's fantasy of an ordered, rhythmic, intelligent universe in which we all have our part to play, to imagine that their lives have a plan or purpose which the horoscope can help them discover. This forms the background to the therapeutic process as well as acting as a sustaining unifying symbol.

The client's issues are met, reflected and clarified by means of the horoscope's symbols so that they can be seen as part of their internal world and its fantasy life. This can be compared to the way a young child becomes aware of itself through the experience of being reflected and contained by its mother's loving attention. The client is introduced to the horoscope as a map of the psyche and the notion that their life experience has to do with their internal situation, that what they are grappling with out there somehow reflects what is going on inside. The horoscope symbols are offered as a bridge to experience, a means of coming to identify, face and eventually to integrate those parts of the self which are normally hard to bear. In this way the client can begin to feel stronger, more authentic and complete, more able to appreciate the richness of the psyche which the horoscope portrays and to live more fully and consciously.

Thus the client is helped to discover that there is far more to us than our conscious selves, that we are made up of many parts so that it becomes possible to view ourselves from varying perspectives. This helps to loosen an over-attachment to the ego and open us up to a broader vision which can appreciate that the psyche has its own movement which we can help to shape. This is both humbling and empowering since we are no longer passive victims nor are we at the controls. Rather we are participants, a perspective which increases our sense of self-responsibility, of having creative powers and of belonging.

Time and change

The client is introduced to the notion of 'timing', that things happen in their own time. In other words growth cannot be forced, hurried along or made to serve the ego's purposes. Rather we each have our own internal clock according to which our lives unfold regardless of our more conscious wishes. Yet it is possible to come to respect and cooperate with this and the horoscope can help us to do so. It maps the ebb or flow of our lives, its rhythms and cycles and thus helps us to become more attuned to our own process.

It conveys the sense that there is something 'other' and stronger than the ego and its purposes which is somehow guiding and unfolding our lives. Indeed it may even feel at cross-purposes to our more conscious wishes, something which produces intense pain and frustration until it becomes possible to accept and begin to trust and relate to this 'other'.

This is not however a fatalistic stance which encourages one to become a passive victim of life, but rather an attitude of 'working with' and involving ourselves in life. In the language of alchemy, nature can be tampered with. The alchemists believed that God needed humans to help him perfect or further his creation, to be his co-creators. However this is not the same as controlling and dominating or using nature to serve our own interests. The alchemists did not see themselves as producing gold but as revealing the gold or new life already in potential in the raw materials, just as the sculptor brings to light what is already there in essence in an apparently dead piece of stone or wood. This involved putting the raw ingredients through various processes which would eventually leave them enhanced, more beautiful and evolved.

The alchemist's role in this was to create the right conditions, be in attendance, involved yet without interfering, a sort of active receptivity. This meant setting up the experiments in conditions of seclusion, using a strong, containing vessel and taking note of those times when one could expect the maximum cooperation with nature as indicated by planetary placements. In the same way the astrological counsellor facilitates the transformation of the undeveloped parts of the psyche, the horoscope embodying both the raw ingredients, the processes by which these become transformed and the 'signs of the times', or a means of identifying those processes which are currently needing to be negotiated.

Nature and nurture

Since the horoscope embodies our seed potential or inherent predisposition this suggests that a two way process occurs from the word go. In other words as well as our environment having an impact on us, we too have an impact on it. We meet the world with our own innate patterning and this affects the world's response to us. Whatever our parents are perceived to have done or not done to us, there is something in us which met them halfway or our own behaviour evoked certain kinds of treatment from them. This is not however to discount the impact of the environment and that individuals are often damaged far beyond their powers to evoke it. Thus the astrological counsellor, whilst acknowledging and encouraging expression of unresolved negative feelings, also aims to encourage self-responsibility, to foster the awareness that we are not simply the result of what has happened to us but that we cannot help but have a hand in our fate. The severely deprived child will come in already predisposed to experiencing the environment as rejecting or it will be those times when the mother is not available which will be registered most strongly. And this will be reflected by the horoscope so that it can be identified as part of one's own psychic patterning, a rejected and rejecting part of oneself or internal 'bad' mother.

Thus it is not only a case of recovering from early experiences of rejection but of meeting and owning the part of oneself which tends to evoke such treatment. For, from the astrological perspective, one is already predisposed to meeting that particular archetypal dimension of the feminine in one's life and therefore embodying it in some way. Thus one is encouraged to identify one's own rejecting behaviour towards both oneself and others as well as to see rejection as a necessary part of life. Without it one could not make choices or build a life of one's own. The horoscope conveys such archetypal patterning non-judgementally, a simple statement of the way things are which, if it can be taken on board, allows greater self-acceptance. Accepting something allows it to grow and develop in its own time, just as holding a distressed baby enables it to recover, whereas those things which remain unacceptable go underground, where their growth becomes stunted and we lose their positive potential. What is wounded is also seen to contain something of value if it is allowed to live.

Practitioners

Relationship

The astrological counsellor aims to build a secure, containing environment in which the client can come to feel supported, respected and affirmed. This involves establishing and maintaining regular, usually once weekly, sessions over an open ended period of time in which boundary and separation issues can be brought to light. Listening skills are employed in order that unconscious communication and negative transference can be brought to light and the client begin to feel heard and accepted. In this way a setting is provided in which the horoscope's powerful symbolism can be explored over time in the context of the therapeutic alliance. This takes on the nature of a shared exploration to which the counsellor brings his or her interpretative or map reading skills and the client his or her life issues. The counsellor uses the horoscope symbols to help the client to identify and formulate feelings and experiences so that they can be thought about and explored more fully. This involves a flexible, fluid use of the horoscope more akin to dream interpretation in which the client's reality provides the context and the horoscope serves to amplify this. Thus we have a client-centred approach which does not seek to impose the horoscope but to use it to serve the therapeutic process.

Such an exploratory mode means that the astrological counsellor takes on the role of companion on the journey, a sort of Hermes figure, messenger of the gods and the only Olympian allowed into the underworld. He acts as a mediator between divine and human realms, taking up an 'in between' stance which can offer new possibilities, embodying that reflective mode which can find detachment and perspective. By means of the horoscope the astrological counsellor becomes a mediator of archetypes, making known to the client the symbolic, archetypal dimension so that things can move to a new level. By remaining linked to the horoscope's archetypal dimension the counsellor is less likely to fall into one of the client's complexes so that empathy is balanced with detachment. Horoscope symbols are offered in a suggestive, experimental way so that the client can discover them for him or herself, learn to use them, play with them, relate to them, rather like the messages of Hermes which are always ambiguous and open to interpretation. Thus the horoscope becomes something of a 'transitional object' existing in the space between counsellor and client, linking and separating them and allowing a flexibility of interaction.

Techniques

The astrological counsellor draws upon a variety of techniques from other therapeutic disciplines which are appropriate to the astrological model. For example, subpersonality work may be used to flesh out the planetary symbols and identify inner figures, their needs and potential. Role play and dialogue enable the client to bring their horoscope to life. Free drawing, writing, dream and imagery work encourage access to unconscious material. Thus an active approach is used to help identify conflicts and explore new possibilities, though this will be balanced by periods of listening, empathizing, reflecting, interpreting or just being there in an unobtrusive but attentive way.

Thus both discursive and experiential approaches are used according to the needs of the individual client with the astrological symbolism supplying the ground and framework. This means that the counsellor must be well-trained and fluent in horoscope interpretation skills in order to be able to leave the horoscope behind, only drawing upon it directly when necessary. Rather it needs to remain in the back of one's mind, informing one's thinking, yet leaving one free to relate to the client and really listen to what they are saying. Then it becomes possible to introduce it in the manner of 'free association' or when it arises naturally out of what the client presents. This involves the capacity to convey the horoscope symbols in a grounded and flexible way, adapting oneself to the client's mode of expression, as well as offering them for discussion. In this way the client is given the opportunity to reflect on, explore, challenge, relate to and come to know their horoscope so that in time they can use it and continue to work with it on their own.

To give an example, a client, a woman of 30, began a session by expressing how overburdened she felt, everything was getting on top of her and she was overwhelmed by feelings of inadequacy. What's more all her husband did was to criticize her. My response was to say

> You sound as though you feel very unsupported. In fact this is something which is reflected in your horoscope, a part of you that probably feels almost cast out into the wilderness, Sun with Saturn in an astrological language. How about staying with these feelings and seeing if there are any images which go with them.

My client then remembered her first day at school and how seized up with panic she felt, so lost and alone and afraid of getting it wrong. 'I'm always afraid I've done something dreadfully wrong. Pathetic isn't it? Why can't I just get on with things and stop wallowing in self-pity?' I then suggested that she found it hard to feel compassion for herself, that somehow she ended up abandoning that lost, lonely, frightened child, to which she replied, 'My father used to tell me to stop wallowing. He was very strict with me. I was always expecting him to pounce.' I then pointed out that Sun with Saturn also suggested a rather critical, emotionally unavailable father figure, someone who was unable to boost or affirm her, or help her find confidence in her powers of self-expression and self-reliance.

In this way the horoscope symbols are used to confirm, focus and deepen the client's experience, as well as to highlight its current relevance. For example, in the case just described I then went on to point out that it was her Saturn Return and so it was understandable that she should have such feelings at this time since it was ripe for exploring, understanding and resolving them. In addition to the client's personal experience there is the archetypal dimension which, in the case of Sun Saturn, suggests an inborn tendency for the authoritarian aspect of the father archetype to be a dilemma in life. The Sun is the male principle or the urge to be a self-directing individual, the heroic part of us, and Saturn is the rather fearful, paranoid part of human nature which clings to rules, to oughts and shoulds, Freud's 'superego' and, like the Greed God Chronos, kills off anything new and spontaneous – at least this is the negative pole of the archetype. The positive idealized side is the 'Wise Man' who has all the answers, something my client has tended to search for through the men in her life. Yet each time she has imagined she has found what she is seeking, her 'Wise Man' has a way of turning into the 'Terrible Father'. And while this archetype continues to be projected on to the outside, she remains tied to trying to appease and win over whoever happens to be carrying it for her.

Thus the astrological counsellor seeks to identify and mediate the archetypal level of the complex, to encourage the client to discover this inside themselves, the way that it is driving them. This can be facilitated by drawing, writing, dream work, relating examples from myth and by using the transference. In my client's case she tended to turn my comments into either criticisms or answers, something I was able to point out to her and help her take responsibility for. In time she was able to experience her husband as a more benign figure, as being able to support her up to a point but also as being human, vulnerable and fallible. She was also able to realize her own tendency to provoke his criticism and judgement by investing him with superhuman powers, expecting him to solve things for her, rescue her. Thus by facing and owning her own archetypal image she was able to separate herself from it and begin to embody it in a more conscious and human way, to bring it down to size. Indeed she dreamt of a stern, crotchety old man she felt compassion for and who smiled at her when she put her arm around him. She then discovered that she worked for him and he gave her the afternoon off as well as increased her salary. This coincided with becoming easier on herself.

Once she had relaxed and become more self-accepting she was able to discover positive Saturnian qualities in herself, a realism and patience which enabled her to understand and work with the boundaries of the physical world and be productive, a sort of earthy wisdom which could appreciate here and now, ordinary things, a humility which enabled her to face and accept her failings, leaving her freer to risk taking her own authority. Thus Saturn became more of a supportive rather than a beating stick so that she could use her energies in a more realistic, less driven way. Saturn also embodies separation and the struggle this entails in managing one's own destructive feelings. My client projected her destructiveness out there so that she felt the world to be a very persecutory place, constantly attacking her for not being good enough. Thus the symbolism of Saturn provided the context and key to working with this client, other parts of the horoscope being introduced only in so far as they were relevant to this main theme. By using the horoscope selectively in this way the astrological counsellor can focus the work according to the client's needs.

Does it work?

Pitfalls

If used sensitively and flexibly in the ways described, the horoscope offers the practitioner a creative tool for exploring the psyche. However an overly literal, rigid approach can become a means of distancing oneself from the client and from what is actually happening in the moment. Instead of opening up and deepening the client's experience one ends up reducing it, indeed denying it. This can be compared to an over-literal interpretation of dreams where symbols are forced into common-sense categories in order to try and find answers. Since the astrologer was once seen to possess occult powers there is the danger of using the horoscope omnipotently to avoid one's own failings and limitations. Thus it is important that the practitioner identify any 'oracle' projections with which he or she may be investing the horoscope.

'Oracle' projections can also be a pitfall for the client if the practitioner colludes with this in any way, since it will only lead to their feeling neglected at a deeper level, their real needs untouched. By investing the horoscope with superhuman powers the client will inevitably put pressure on the practitioner to come up with the answers. Thus the practitioner needs to be alert to this in order to be able to tolerate and work with the client's anger and disappointment at there being no magical solution. Otherwise the whole thing is likely to deteriorate into a sort of divination or problem solving activity until the unmet negative transference results in a premature ending.

Another pitfall for both practitioner and client can be an over-fascination with archetypes and images, an attempt at transcendence as a means of avoiding the pain of one's ordinary humanity. The astrological symbols can be very seductive in the face of emerging negativity as a means of taking flight, of holding on to a sense of meaning, rather than risking the chaos and confusion of previously buried infantile states. One may force things into the imaginal realm too soon rather than allowing meaning to emerge in its own time as well as acknowledging and respecting that part of life which feels chaotic and meaningless. The astrological model satisfies our need to feel that there is an intelligent purpose at work in our lives, yet this can become a defence against despair and hopelessness, a faith which is not really grounded in one's own experience. Thus the practitioner needs to be able to abandon the horoscope, demonstrate a willingness simply to be with and hold the client in those darker, more regressed places.

The horoscope can only be used effectively if the practitioner is aware of his or her limitations and those of the astrological model. Though its symbols possess a containing function this is no substitute for the experience of being supported by another human being. Indeed such symbols can be of little help to those whose capacity to symbolize has been wounded, who have insufficient ego strength to relax enough to enter the imaginal realm. Then it is the practitioner's human responsiveness which is the crucial factor.

Research

In 1955 the French statistician, Michel Gauquelin published his first results demonstrating a strong correlation between the planets and the birth times of famous French people. For example, Mars featured prominently for sports champions, military leaders and top executives, Jupiter for actors, politicians and journalists, Saturn for scientists and Moon for writers. Since then these results have been replicated in thousands of cases. Then in 1967 he made connections between the planets and personality rather than career, though implying that a particular personality will naturally lead to a preference for a particular occupation. He gathered more than 50,000 character traits from thousands of biographical texts of famous people and came up with significant results for the Moon, Venus, Mars, Jupiter and Saturn but not for the Sun, Mercury and the outer planets. He found that if one of the significant group of five planets were prominently placed in the chart, that is, close to the Angles, then the individual was likely to show a temperament associated with that planet. For example, those with Saturn strongly placed displayed calm, common-sense, conscientious, reserved, cautious, thoughtful qualities whereas those with Jupiter displayed jovial, opportunistic, warm, self-confident qualities. Indeed his findings confirmed the dictionary definitions of such terms as 'saturnine' 'jovial', 'martial' etc. Though his findings do not vindicate all the claims of astrology it seems that his work has proved that there is something to it, that the planets are meaningful.

Case study

Michele, a woman of 42, came along to me saying, 'My life feels as though it's falling apart.' When I asked her to elaborate on this she described how her marriage and health seemed to be crumbling. Her husband showed little interest in her and she had become infatuated by a man at work. She had such a stiff neck that she was unable to find a comfortable position in which to sleep, and lower back pain which made her tired and irritable. All in all she felt defeated, lost and overwhelmed.

As I listened to her I was reminded of images associated with the astrological Neptune, especially in such words as 'falling apart', 'crumbling' 'defeated', 'lost' and 'overwhelmed', and the world-weary tone of her voice. Neptune embodies the experience of dissolution, disintegration, the loss of one's usual identifications, that longing to find freedom from the world of form and boundaries. When this part of us dominates then the practical business of living feels tedious and hard to manage. One is more susceptible to being captivated by a beautiful sunset, yet also by imaginary fears, a certain paranoia. The barriers are down and what is normally repressed tends to seep into consciousness. Thus one could say that the time was ripe for Michele to undergo some kind of therapy.

On studying her horoscope I discovered that I was on the right track with Neptune, for it was her 'Neptune Square', one of the important mid-life cycles occurring to us all at around the age of 40. It embodies a time of feeling overwhelmed by unfulfilled hopes, dreams, longings, unresolved grievances, unmet fears. Thus it is an opportunity to face these and sort out what is real and what is illusory. People often fall in love at this time in the hope of recapturing what has been lost, only to feel deluded and let down yet again, at least in terms of the idealized images they are carrying. Indeed, the theme of Michele's therapy was the extent to which she was still trying to recover what had been lost, still longing for the idealized parents who would save her from the pain and struggle of living, how this was preventing her from living her own life.

When I related Neptune's symbolism to her she told me of recurrent dreams in which she would search unsuccessfully for her mother and wake up full of desperation and longing. Michele's mother had died when she was five years old and was an unhappy, embittered figure towards whom Michele felt full of both guilt and rage. Perhaps she had been too much for her mother, yet why didn't her mother love her better? I suggested that she felt responsible for her mother's death, to which she replied, 'I feel as though I've been trying to make up for it all my life. I always feel responsible for other people's problems.'

I told Michele that her horoscope revealed her to be a 'feeling type' and therefore very sensitive to and affected by others' feelings and the emotional tone of her surroundings. Consequently she would easily lose touch with her own needs exacerbated by the insufficient mothering she had received. This was reflected in her horoscope by her Moon being 'square' to Pluto, an image of passion and deep suffering which described both her mother and herself. 'Yes, that's how I remember her, a silent yet brooding presence', she said. 'And it sounds like the part of me that I fight against. I always try to put on a brave front.' I suggested that maybe it was time for her to give some space to her suffering, to nurse her wounds so that they could begin to heal. Indeed, once she began to grieve she became more able to let go of the past, give up the idealized mother and learn to care for herself. This created more space between herself and others in a way which improved her relationships and revived her marriage.

Further reading

Alexander, R. (1983) *The Astrology of Choice: A Counselling Approach.* York Beach, ME: Samuel Weiser, Inc. How to use astrological symbolism more effectively by drawing upon the Transactional Analysis model. Illustrated with transcripts from sessions.

Greene, L. and Sasportas, H. (1987) *The Development of the Personality. Seminars in Psychological Astrology.* London: Routledge and Kegan Paul. Includes, 'The Stages of Childhood', 'The Parental Marriage in the Horoscope', 'Subpersonalities and Psychological Conflicts', and 'Puer and Senex'. The theme running throughout is separation and becoming an individual.

Greene, L. and Sasportas, H. (1989) *Dynamics of the Unconscious: Seminars in Psychological Astrology.* London: Arkana. Includes 'The Astrology and Psychology of Aggression', 'The Quest for the Sublime', 'Depression' and 'Alchemical Symbolism in the Horoscope'. These seminars explore the 'shadow' side of human experience.

Both of Liz Greene and Howard Sasportas' books combine astrological symbolism with modern depth psychology and include case history examples.

Pottenger, M. (1982) *Healing with the Horoscope: A Guide to Counselling.* San Diego, CA: ASC Publications, Inc. Divided into Theory, Application and Demonstration sections, this book shows how techniques of counselling and communication skills can enhance one's use of the horoscope. Concludes with an example session.

Valentine, C. (1991) *Images of the Psyche: Exploring the Planets through Psychology and Myth.* London: Element Books. The astrological model is elucidated in the light of the theories of Freud, Jung, Winnicott and Milner and themes from ancient myth. Includes case history examples and a final chapter on working with horoscope symbols and the value of cultivating a symbolic attitude to life.

Appendix A: Glossary of terms

Those new to innovative therapy might find it useful to have an explanation of some terms which are often used when discussing therapies. This list is intended to be helpful but is not exhaustive.

Abuse

It is an abuse of the relationship and of the contract between therapist and client if the therapist seeks personal gratification from the client. This gratification may be sexual, financial or to do with power. Therapists should recognize these needs in themselves and not seek to gratify them with clients.

The therapist should have the intention to recognize sexual arousal in themselves during therapy sessions because repressing and denying it does not help the client. It should be witnessed and noticed as pleasant or otherwise and held as information that could possibly be useful for the client. But it should never be the intention of the therapist to use sexual arousal associated with a client for personal gratification.

Abusive behaviour includes attempts to socialize with clients outside the therapy hour as well as attempts to seduce clients within it. This also applies to ex-clients unless something has happened to establish the ex-client in a suitable identity which would make social interaction safe. It is also abusive for a male or female therapist to gratify themselves by deliberately indulging in sexual fantasies and daydreams about clients. These things are abusive because they break the client's trust that they will not be used to gratify the personal needs of the therapist. Many people come to therapy in the first place precisely because trust in parents, teachers or other authorities has been broken in this way which has led to despair, self-hatred, self-blame, inappropriate seductiveness, inability to say no and the inability to form enduring relationships because of confusion, fear or a tendency to be abusive themselves. Re-enactment of this abuse by therapists is not helpful to these or any other clients.

In the 1960s and 70s some practitioners of innovative therapy emphasized the view expressed by Reich and other psychoanalysts that regular and full discharge of sexual energy is healthy. They took this to mean that a therapist who had sexual intercourse with clients was doing them some good. Nowadays it is emphasized that repression or denial of sexual energy is unhealthy. Being aware of sexual feelings and cravings but choosing not to act on them can be just as healthy as discharging them.

Behaviour therapy

Behaviour therapy uses methods based on the processes of learning which include conditioning, reward, punishment and role modelling. They are applied to concrete acts such as compulsive habits, phobias and the like, sexual 'deviation', aggression and passivity and social skills problems. Behaviour therapy is often practised in medical settings.

Catharsis

Catharsis is the expression of emotion or strong feeling such as embarrassment, fear, anger, grief, joy or love. In innovative therapy this is often done with cushions, for example by hugging them in expressions of love, hitting, twisting and biting them in anger and shying away in fear. In group psychotherapy other members of the group may be spoken to angrily, hugged, shouted at and, when suitably protected, punched.

Clinical psychology

Clinical psychologists are trained in scientific and statistical research about human behaviour. They are mainly employed in medical settings where they run research projects and conduct behaviour therapy with patients. Like psychiatrists they have no training in psychotherapy.

Psychiatry

Psychiatry is a branch of medicine which treats emotion and behaviour. It is based on the concept of mental illness for which physical treatments, especially drugs, are prescribed. In the USA psychiatrists are more likely to be trained in psychotherapy, usually psychoanalysis, than in the UK where many psychiatrists practise psychotherapy without having any training in it at all.

Psychoanalysis

Psychoanalysis is a well established branch of psychotherapy, stemming from the work of Freud which offers insight and understanding based on interpretations given by analysts to the things a patient says about their life, experiences, dreams and artistic expression and of the transference (see below) in the relationship with the analyst. In the USA psychoanalysts must be medically trained. In the UK there is no legislation on this matter and most psychoanalysts complete a training which does not include any component in medicine.

Psychology

Psychology is the study of thought, feelings, experience and behaviour. Most universities offer degrees in psychology. There has been a tendency for them to limit the psychology they teach to facts which can be established by scientific method. Computer modelling of behaviour has become an important part of this. There is a tendency to avoid exploration of the processes involved in psychotherapy.

Regression

Regression is going back to an earlier time of life and re-experiencing events and the feelings associated with them. This sometimes occurs naturally in therapy sessions but can be encouraged by certain techniques. A client who regresses in sessions is also fully open to communication in the present, especially communication with the therapist and does not cease to be in contact in some way with events going on around them. Being unaware of a tendency to regress in everyday life is a cause of suffering.

Role of therapist

The therapist–client relationship is unique and it can be misleading to point to similarities with other helping relationships, such as priests, guides or doctors. It is unique in that the therapist is required to be committed to their own personal awareness to ensure it does not thwart the interests of the client and also to use it for the client's benefit. It is also unique in that the therapist is not paid for what they do but for the time and the place which they offer. There are several aspects of the therapist–client relationship:

- *Authentic relationship*: A therapist should do everything in a genuine way. This requires a commitment to self-awareness already mentioned, but it also means saying and doing things in the therapy room which, in the deepest sense, feel right. They must be genuine and not just acting a part. They must be consistent with the feelings coming from the heart – consistent with the felt sense. Psychotherapists may keep their views and reactions to the client to themselves, at least for the time being, for that is a matter of judgement and timing can be important. But in principle they should not manipulate the client by what they say or do.
- *Reparative relationship*: Sometimes a client missed out on something that was needed at a particular stage in development such as having their sexuality allowed and not denied or abused, or being congratulated and praised for achievements or, in the most broad sense, being held. It sometimes helps for the therapist to provide, at least symbolically, what is being sought. This comes from the client's need to have it and not from the therapist's need to give it.

The deepest changes sometimes occur, however, when the therapist declines to enter into some aspect of a reparative relationship being sought by the client but enables the client to explore the feelings and emotion associated with not having what they missed out on and for which they still crave. The therapist has to use their judgement as to which is best on any particular occasion.

• *Facilitative relationship*: This is the commonest relationship in the innovative therapies. The therapist aims to assist the client's process by suggesting ways in which they can explore it, through talking, bodywork, drawing, guided fantasy, dreamwork etc. but does not direct or structure the work in any way which takes power away from the client.

Transference

This is where one person recreates in a current relationship an important aspect of a childhood relationship, typically that of a parent. The emotions belonging to the previous relationship, usually strong ones of love and hate, are transferred to the ongoing relationship as are expectations that love, hate, nurture or punishment will be received in return. If these transferred feelings are acted out they disturb the relationship. Analysing these feelings and any tendencies to act them out in the psychotherapy relationship is central to psychoanalytic practice. Psychotherapists in the innovative and humanistic traditions used to reject the concept of transference as a part of what they called psychoanalytic mystification. During the last decade they have become less opposed to psychoanalysis and are much more likely to recognize the process of transference and have begun using the term again, as can be seen in this volume.

Counter-transference is the process whereby the therapist recreates in a client an aspect of their own childhood relationships. A therapist who is unaware of their counter-transference is likely to behave and respond to clients in ways which are not helpful. Awareness of the counter-transference opens up the possibility of the therapist sensing what it is that the client is pulling out of him or her and thus an insight into what the client is struggling to gain. This is a potent resource for a therapist.

Appendix B: Related therapies

Bioenergetics

Reich's (1945) innovation in Freudian psychoanalytic theory and practice involved making the body a part of the person to be worked with. He argued that the defensive strategies which we adopt in childhood to deal with experience are also represented in the way we hold our bodies. He called this representation body armouring. Our body armouring is part of our defensiveness and it acts to block and distort our normal body energy, especially sexual energy. Reich began to work on these problems with massage.

Lowen (1958) and Pierrakos (see Chapter 8, this volume) developed Reich's innovation further and it became known as Bioenergetics. The characteristic body structure of the various defensive personality structures, schizoid, burden bearing, rigid, manipulative and so on were investigated and worked on by a combination of exercises and massage to produce physical release and opportunities to use more conventional therapy to bring about integration. Since then Pierrakos has concentrated on the energy aspects of this approach and created Core Energetics, which is described in this book by David Cranmer (Chapter 8). William West's chapter (Chapter 9) on Post-Reichian Therapy tells how these innovations have been further developed.

References

Lowen, A. (1958) *The Language of the Body*. London: Collier Macmillan.
Reich, W. (1945) *Character Analysis*. New York: Orgone Institute Press.

Co-counselling

Co-counselling is a self-help method aimed at discharging distressed feelings so that important decisions about relationships and lifestyle can be made and followed up in a calm and effective way. Two trained co-counsellors take it in turns to be counsellor for one another as client. It was an innovative approach to therapy, especially during the 1970s and 1980s.

Co-counselling was derived from Re-evaluation Counselling developed in the USA by Harvey Jackins. The British version was pioneered by John Heron and others at the University of Surrey in the 1970s. In practice the two systems are the same except that in Co-counselling all rules are, in principle, negotiable between clients whereas Harvey Jackins laid down some rules for Re-evaluation Counsellors which he expected to be followed. For example he stipulated that counsellors should not socialize with one another between sessions. In fact experienced co-counsellors usually find it sensible to make those sorts of choices anyway.

A Fundamentals Training in Co-counselling takes about 50 hours spaced out over a number of weeks. Counsellors learn both the roles of client and of counsellor. They learn a variety of verbal and physical techniques used in other therapies, especially Gestalt, for enabling clients to experience emotional discharge of distressed feelings. Competent decision making can then take place in a calm way without interruption from distressed emotion. This process is intended to lead to what John Heron termed 'emotional competence' – the ability to be fully alive with attention turned outwards towards others whilst also in touch with inner feelings and expressing them in appropriate ways.

Anyone who has completed a Fundamentals Training can join one of the Co-counselling communities that circulate lists of Co-counsellors in most countries that have strong links with Europe and the USA. There are courses for trainers and advanced courses, specializing in social and political areas such as gender, unemployment and sexual abuse.

Many people have found Co-counselling a good starting point for exploring the innovative therapies. The opportunity to express feelings and to explore taboo areas in a friendly and permissive atmosphere is very refreshing. Some use it as a long term tool on their path of self-development, others as a technique for emotional first aid.

Co-counselling requires a strong sense of self-direction, especially between sessions, because you have to arrange the times and venues with other co-counsellors yourself. Those needing help with relationships or with depression often do not have that self-direction. It can also be collusive; two people working together to sustain defences against difficult aspects of their lives instead of overcoming them. Collusion is often against something used as a scapegoat; a person or organization, other therapies, or 'society', to which malevolent social or political forces are attributed – bourgeois, capitalist, oppressive, patriarchal, authoritarian – depicting them as based on fear and therefore disempowering for the individual.

There are other drawbacks to the way Co-counselling can be used. It concentrates, rather mechanically, on the external expression, especially catharsis, of feelings at the expense of learning how to stay with feelings and experience them. And it can 'empty out' feelings only briefly before they 'fill up' again. Catharsis of emotion, especially of rage, can also become addictive. Addiction to catharsis can create a dictatorial atmosphere in a group so that anyone who does not express emotions frequently and noisily is considered not to have started real personal growth. This can lead to poor judgement about appropriateness encouraging catharsis even in situations where it is disruptive, such as in committee meetings. It can also blur the distinction between feeling and emotion, for example between anger which is clear and can be expressed at an appropriate object, and rage which is an endless and unfruitful outpouring of ire.

An experienced trainer or guide can prevent a Co-counselling group developing a collusive or counter-productive subculture. Used in conjunction with other methods Co-counselling is an excellent personal growth tool. It also provides would-be therapists with an introduction to practical methods of helping clients who want to unblock their feelings and discover how to shout, punch, collapse, shake, weep and laugh.

References

Evison, R. and Horobin, R. (1988) Co-counselling. In J. Rowan and W. Dryden (eds) *Innovative Therapy in Britain*. Milton Keynes: Open University Press.
Pyves, G. (1989) *Co-Counselling Manual: A step by step approach to a fundamentals training*. Published by M.G. Pyves, 195 Holcombe Road, Helmshore, Rossendale, Lancs BB4 4NY.

Encounter

The Encounter Group Movement began early in the 1960s and manifested much of the philosophy of that decade. It assumed that society is structured hierarchically which oppresses our real nature and demands roles which are alien to our real selves. An encounter group is very unstructured and participants are invited to be free of these influences and to be fully responsible for who we are and what we do. We can encounter ourselves and others and be encountered as our true selves.

Psychotherapy groups and, since World War II, sensitivity or leadership training groups at the Tavistock Institute in London and T-groups in the USA had concentrated on group process originating from psychoanalytic theory and the developments of Bion and Lewin. Encounter groups sometimes include analysing group process but differ from psychotherapy and T-groups in a number of ways. No distinction is made between personal growth and development and the cure of a mental illness; psychodrama and Gestalt work is done in encounter groups so that individuals can work not only on group process but also on their own problems; the leader does not hide their own thoughts and feelings and they join in group activity; the individual's frame of reference is respected as it is in client centred work; feelings are encouraged more than thought and bodywork is emphasized.

Encounter groups have been of use to a large number of people, usually combined with individual psychotherapy. They have been used to focus on particular social and personal issues such as abuse, drugs, gender and so on. Most people who run encounter groups are reputable but leaders in the past have not always been experienced or trained. The movement used to be against formal training and accreditation so encounter groups have on occasion been misused as a licence for sadistic behaviour by both participants and leaders. A few incidents of this sort made Encounter a frightening idea for many people.

Although the Encounter Movement owed much to psychoanalysis it disowned it and claimed existentialism, phenomenology, the client centred approach of Rogers and the bodywork theories of Reich's followers, especially Lowen, as their main influences. It was also influenced by the practice of psychodrama and Gestalt. Perhaps because it was such a manifestation of the philosophy of the 1960s the movement died out and encounter groups are now rare. The experience of them has however informed the work of many practitioners in the modern innovative therapies who often run unstructured sessions, especially in training groups, which are reminiscent of encounter groups although they do not refer to them by that name.

Reference

Shaffer, J.B.P. and Galinsky, M.D. (1974) *Models of Group Therapy and Sensitivity Training*. Englewood Cliffs, NJ: Prentice Hall.

Gestalt

Gestalt Therapy helps us develop more effective configurations (the German *Gestalten*) of thoughts, feelings, behaviour and spiritual awareness. It is the seedbed model of modern integrative therapies many of which have borrowed from it. All therapists are to some extent trained in Gestalt methods, though they may not see it that way themselves.

The Gestalt model points to the fact that all aspects of our life and experience are patterned in relation to one another. Part of this patterning puts some things as foreground which demand our attention and which are set against a background. Emotions from the past and inadequate ways of dealing with the present are associated with Gestalts which bring us suffering. The aim of the therapist is to help clients get to an edge where these Gestalt patterns dissolve or fracture to be replaced by new and more effective ones.

The methods used in Gestalt are many and varied. They owe a great deal to psychodrama to which Fritz Perls, the founder of Gestalt, paid tribute. The best known are chairwork, which involves role playing to an imagined person or part of a person, including one's self, spouse, parent or other, imagined to be on a chair. In group therapy other group members may have these parts assigned to them by the client who is working on some aspect of their own experience. Cushionwork is similar and allows acting out of affectionate and aggressive fantasies. More subtle methods include concentrating on irrelevant seeming movements in the periphery of the body, especially movements of hands and feet and facial movements. The therapist may physically support or gently resist these movements. The use of touch in Gestalt means that it has a firm link with other therapies which use bodywork. The client's concentration may be attenuated by exaggerating a movement, gesture or sound, such as an habitual laugh, by emphasizing it, contradicting it or inhibiting it. A Gestalt can be broken up in these ways.

Gestalt therapists encourage a first person perspective in their clients emphasizing what is being felt, desired and perceived in the present moment in time – 'in the here and now'. This discourages verbal analysis of the past and discourages statements about people in general. Other people are referred to by name. This encourages direct inner contact with mental process and direct outer contact with other people. Group psychotherapy based on Gestalt is one of the most potent therapies. Gestalt groups counter the belief that group psychotherapy is a sort of watered down individual therapy. Many people find it more potent than any individual therapy precisely because the example, energy and input from other people generates powerful empathy and resonance which is lost if there are no other clients present.

The directness which Gestalt encourages can lead to a superficial, intellectually unfulfilling therapy, always busy doing things and expressing simple feelings in the here and now without contemplation or sensing of the subtle contradictions of our lives. It can also be marred by narcissism leading to overblown egos if the 'here and now, me' aspects of Gestalt are taken literally. 'My needs and wants are fine' is a good Gestalt message to take on board for self-esteem. 'If you happen to be in the way when I am acting on my needs then that is your problem' is not always so good. 'I am a handsome powerful male' is a good self-image. 'I expect you to compete with one another for my attention' is not. These types of uncooperative posture and superficiality sometimes arise and persist in Gestalt work and the overpowering egos which they develop can seduce or inhibit others.

References

Clarkson, P. (1989) *Gestalt Counselling in Action*. London: Sage.
Parlett, M. and Page, F. (1990) Gestalt Therapy. In W. Dryden (ed.) *Individual Therapy: A Handbook*. Milton Keynes: Open University Press.

Hakomi

Hakomi Therapy is the invention of Ron Kurtz. It is based on the ideas which inform most of the modern innovative therapies, notably Reich (see Chapter 9), Gestalt, Focusing (Chapter 7) and Neurolinguistic Programming. Like Core Process Psychotherapy (Chapter 4) it is influenced by the philosophy of Buddhism and Taoism (though the name is a Hopi Indian word meaning *How do you stand in relation to this?*). Hakomi therapy aims at compassion, acceptance and mindfulness. The therapy involves gentle exercises and discussion in which attention is paid to the processes of the mind and body as an indivisible system which functions as a whole. By doing this a greater awareness is achieved of Self and the way we construct and use this concept. This in turn leads to a better feel for the meaning of life and how it may be fulfilled, a greater acceptance of the nature of the world and our experience of it, more equanimity and more loving kindness.

Reference

Kurtz, R. (1988) *Hakomi Therapy*. Boulder, CO: Hakomi Institute.

Information and literature available in Britain may be obtained from Prue Rankin Smith, 18 South Street, Lewes, Sussex BN7 2BP.

Neurolinguistic Programming (NLP)

Neurolinguistic Programming was developed in the early 1970s by John Grindler, a professor of linguistics and Richard Bandler, a Gestalt therapist and computer scientist both in the USA. They analysed the behaviour of several psychotherapists, especially Virginia Satir and Milton Erickson. This led them to build up a model of how therapists create rapport with clients, which in turn enables them to influence them.

NLP practitioners create a rapport by mirroring and resonating with their clients. Adopting their body postures and gestures, tone of voice and speed of speech and synchronizing their breathing with a client enables the practitioner to sense much of what is going on internally for him or her. The mirroring is done gently and subtly, unobtrusively so that it does not distract the client. In this way the practitioner discovers many things about how the client responds to and processes the world, in NLP terms, how the client models the world. Part of this involves attending to eye movements. Equally important is the attention given to emotion, metaphor and the framework of assumptions used by a client.

Once rapport has been established between two people, a gradual change in either of them will produce a change in the other. The NLP practitioner can then influence the client by gradually changing their own breathing, posture, metaphors, frameworks and so on. In this way the client's perspectives are opened up for revision and change, giving the client an opportunity to resolve the problems which lead them to therapy.

Because NLP was based initially on analysis of successful psychotherapists it is not surprising that it shares with them the concepts of mirroring and resonance which experienced therapists come to do naturally and unself-consciously. Other therapies do not describe these processes as fully or put them as centrally as NLP does but a number of therapies described in this book, Core Process Psychotherapy (Chapter 4) is an example, note that clients access their mental life in different ways. Some begin to address a problem by thinking, some by sensing an emotional state, some by getting a body-sense as in Focusing (Chapter 7). Having accessed material in one way or another a client may change to another modality for working on it. The therapist resonates with the change. Gradually a therapist gets a feel for the client's feelings and emotion.

The techniques for establishing rapport in NLP make it a powerful system for influencing clients. If this enables clients to get what they want in terms of change in themselves and in their lives then it is successful. A pitfall is that it can be used manipulatively so that the practitioner gets the client to behave in the way the practitioner wants at the expense of the client gaining power to resolve their own problems successfully in their own way. Some training schemes in NLP are dominated by trainees who appear to want to develop their own skills at manipulating others rather than in helping other people therapeutically, giving the impression that NLP is a system for controlling other people in ways which would be considered fair for sales staff or lawyers but not for counsellors or psychotherapists.

Reference

Robbie, E. (1988) Neuro-Linguistic Programming. In J. Rowan and W. Dryden (eds) *Innovative Therapy in Britain*. Milton Keynes: The Open University Press.

Object Relations Theory and Therapy

Object Relations Theory was an innovation developed from psychoanalytic theory by Melanie Klein and others and is a distinctly British development of the work stemming from Freud. It posits that our consciousness develops from birth as an interplay between what we take into ourselves about the nature of the world of people and things and what we project of ourselves on to the world which we see as outside of ourselves.

As a baby grows it develops a concept of object which then begins to differentiate and split into good and bad things (usually people or aspects of people), as those that satisfy its needs and those that do not or are threats. The baby begins the process of introjecting into its own self what it experiences as external aspects of objects or of people. It also begins to construe its own self as an object containing good and bad bits. It then begins projecting its experience of its good and bad self out on to the environment which it is beginning to see as separate from itself.

The process of projection and introjection never ceases and in adulthood we continue with it. As adults our individual set of object relations is a complex pattern of projections and introjections built on the basis we constructed in childhood and retaining the structures which we developed when we were very young. The patterning of emotional response and behaviour which results from this process is essentially defensive in that it reflects neediness for gratification and the avoidance of threats. So it colours the way we perceive our friends at work and people at home and how we view the social and political world around us. It also determines the cues and messages which we present to others and prompts their projections on to us.

We cause ourselves to suffer if our pattern of object relations, or people relations, is in line with our environment as a child, when it started to develop, but out of line with the realities of other people in the world in which we now live as adults. Developing a better set of projections, or ideas about others, and introjections, our ideas about our self, and communicating them better is the goal of

Object Relations Therapy. The crucial question is how to achieve this and recent innovations have been useful in this respect.

The pitfall of Object Relations Theory is the pitfall of psychoanalysis in that it can be used to offer no more than verbal insight because psychoanalysis is basically a structured conversation between therapist and client. The patient talks about himself or herself. The analyst interprets this in order to give the client insight. Insight is of course useful, even essential, just as conversation is, but it can feed a type of intellectual defence in which a distressed client heaps more and more distress on themselves by struggling to know more and more and in particular to know why they feel the way they do, and why they do what they do, and why the supposed causes work in the way they do, and why other people do what they do, and on and on as if a resolution to their situation can be based exclusively on understanding answers to the question 'why?' Defensive intellectualizing of this sort avoids contacting difficult feelings and integrating them. It also avoids developing the part of us which is beyond words. Object Relations Therapy shares with the rest of psychoanalysis a tendency to get stuck in this way.

Recently, experts in many of the innovative therapies have taken a great interest in Object Relations Theory. Training centres teach it, study groups have been set up by practitioners and there is a general buzz around the subject. These therapists are applying their skills in working with it in a less word-dependent way than the psychoanalysts who initially developed the theory. Exercises to create families from group members who assign each to a family position, character, personality, lifestyle and so on and group sculpts doing the same thing can leave people with a profound feeling for their own pattern of projections and also a great respect for Object Relations Theory. It opens up for them an exploration of what they believe and do which gets them into particular situations. It also enables them to explore how they characterize and react to what they see in others. This leads clients to refresh their object relations so they are less patterned to generate misery for themselves and more effective at getting their needs met.

Reference

Cashdan, S. (1988) *Object Relations Therapy*. London: Norton.

Person centred psychology

Shortly after World War II Carl Rogers began to publish his work on person centred, or client centred psychology. The basic idea is that our energy and effort after development is healthy. We do not need treatment for how we feel or what we do. We need instead the unconditional positive regard of other people. This enables us to develop a positive image of ourselves which enables us to live lives fully free from disturbance.

In childhood our natural healing process becomes disturbed because we discover we are accepted only if we fit the wishes of other people, usually our parents. We take on the image of ourself which this creates and try to live as if we were that image. The remedy in counselling and psychotherapy is for the therapist to offer us non-judgemental positive regard so that we can discover who and what we really are. A client centred therapist spends a lot of time encouraging a client to talk and showing them that they have been heard and understood – not agreed or disagreed with but understood and in that sense accepted. This helps people detach themselves from the conditioning of childhood.

The client centred approach has had a great influence on group leaders, although there is no client centred theory of groups, and on training in work and educational settings.

Someone who espouses the client centred way of life is open to experience, not threatened by life and able to live in the moment and accept feelings as they arise. Therapy based on this approach is slow and it works best with people who are verbally fluent. People who access their inner life emotionally or through the body and who prefer to work on it in those modes find it harder to use a client centred therapist.

Reference

Thorne, B. (1990) Person Centred Therapy. In W. Dryden (ed.) *Individual Therapy: A Handbook*. Milton Keynes: Open University Press.

Psychodrama

Psychodrama is one of the root innovative therapies. It was developed earlier this century by Jacob Moreno and other therapies, notably Gestalt, Transactional Analysis (TA) and Co-Counselling owe a lot to it.

Jacob Moreno trained in medicine and psychiatry and introduced theatre and active role playing into therapy. He worked in Vienna after the First World War and emigrated to the USA in 1925. His work foreshadowed the work of Fritz Perls and Eric Berne who developed Gestalt Therapy and Transactional Analysis (TA) respectively. They borrowed from Moreno or rediscovered some of the things he had already tried out.

Well worked out training programmes in psychodrama have been available in Britain since the 1970s, notably at the Holwell Centre in Devon, run by Marcia Karp. Since then professionals with an interest in therapy, health care, education and training have often been influenced by psychodrama.

Moreno looked upon human beings as essentially 'spontaneous and creative' with intelligence that enables us to make a fresh and appropriate response to whatever situation we are in. As children we develop ways of responding to situations which become patterned according to how other people, especially parents and teachers, react to us. The way we respond to a new situation as adults depends on this conditioning and we tend to lose our creative skills. Pent up feeling and restrictive role patterns inhibit our spontaneous creativity. Instead of taking appropriate risks with ourselves we tend to react to situations in unnecessarily rigid and defensive ways.

Psychodrama offers a wide variety of active ways for individuals to work with others in a group. Past events, memories, dreams, crises, relationships at work and at home are acted out. The insights and integration of emotion and action are especially prominent in the effects of psychodrama.

Reference

Brazier, D. (1991) *A Guide to Psychodrama*. London: Association for Humanistic Psychology.

Transactional Analysis (TA)

Transactional Analysis was developed in the 1960s by Eric Berne, a Canadian psychiatrist who was trained in psychoanalysis. Berne put the way we experience ourselves and communicate with others as central and his model of a person is a model of ego states and how they communicate. He was influenced by Object Relations Theory. The system of therapy known as Transactional Analysis is organized on a professional basis world wide.

Although Berne recognizes that people can think and do evil things he assumes that we are driven by processes which seek health. We are in his term basically OK. Our experience of life is shaped by our childhood experience, embodied in the present by the regressed subpersonalities of free child, rebellious child (innovative therapies have sometimes manifested that aspect) and other ego states remaining from that time. It is also shaped by our authority figures such as our nurturing, controlling and other parent states. Our adult personalities are lived in the here and now.

Learning to recognize when we are in adult, child or parental states, expressed in voice, words, gesture, posture, reactions and attitudes and evoking particular memories is useful. It reduces confusion and contamination of one way of being by another.

Eric Berne stresses the importance of love and recognition, intimacy in human development and anything which gives us these things he termed 'strokes'. Early on in our lives we pick up messages about strokes and how to manage them. These messages become our 'scripts' for the roles we play with other people. These are defensive and in protecting us actually limit our spontaneity and reduce the joy we get from relating to others for they lead to 'games' and 'rackets'.

The group of innovative therapists who worked with Berne have developed his system further. Our different subpersonalities play games with other people and set up rackets which rob us of long term pleasure in the interests of short term defences.

TA enables people to become more autonomous by dropping the scripts and messages from the past and becoming better able to relate to other people by being more aware of our mental states and needs. Its drawbacks are mainly to do with its appearance of simplicity, especially when described in writing. A tendency to use jargon and slogans which has instant appeal at a popular level, such as 'I'm OK, you're OK' has given it a misleading appearance of superficiality. In the hands of trained and experienced therapists it offers a fluid and effective means of personal growth and development in adulthood.

Reference

Clarkson, P. (1993) *Transactional Analysis: An Integrative Approach to Psychotherapy*. London: Routledge.

Transpersonal Therapy

Earlier this century attempts were made to reintroduce ideas about identity previously embodied in religious practice which had been ignored in the prevailing therapies of psychoanalysis and behaviourism. The idea of the self as an entity which develops through a journey and which is grounded in something bigger (see psychosynthesis), Maslow's ideas about self-actualization, Jung's ideas about archetypes and the collective unconscious and astrological counselling (see Chapter 14, this volume) are all important in Transpersonal Psychology. Guided fantasy and other methods, especially ones involving symbols, are used to explore them. The development of other psychotherapies based on religious ideas, such as psychosynthesis (Chapter 5) and Core Process Psychotherapy (Chapter 4) has made the need for Transpersonal Psychology, always something of an umbrella term, less necessary.

Reference

Gordon-Brown, I. and Somers, B. (1988) Transpersonal Psychotherapy. In J. Rowan and W. Dryden (eds) *Innovative Therapy in Britain*. Milton Keynes: Open University Press.

Women's therapy

Men's therapy (see Chapter 13) and women's therapy are both linked to the imbalance of power, wealth and prestige embedded in society and culture. The work of anthropologists and sociologists suggests that all societies have this imbalance to some degree. In the earliest hunter and gatherer societies it may have been important for survival to have it this way. Men, having more aggression, louder voices, faster running and more powerful arm and chest muscles were good for defence against predatory animals and hostile people, hunting for food and stockading. Women, not having aggression except in defence of their bodies and babies, with soft voices and subtle intuitive minds well attuned to the mystery of creation, change and development were good at running encampments. Such a division might have been to the advantage of all, at least from the point of view of survival.

The hunting and gathering mode of existence began to die out a long time ago and most parts of the world are now inhabited by people who aspire to live an increasingly urbanized life based on industrial division of labour in the creation and distribution of goods and services. This includes modern farmers who have replaced hunters and gatherers. These changes have meant that people in the richest countries are not predominantly concerned with day to day survival. Many in the poorer countries hope to live like this as well.

Modern division of labour brings with it an imbalance in power, wealth, respect and prestige which has become a major mental health hazard. This hazard led women to develop forms of therapy for themselves to remedy the problems it gave them. Men have been slower to see that they are also the victims of this imbalance. Andrew Forrester (Chapter 13) describes some of the innovations that are now happening in that area.

Both women's and men's therapies start from the premise that there is no reason to suppose that men and women should not have equal opportunities to command the same social and political power as each other and to enjoy equal respect with one another in domestic arrangements, careers and in society generally. Women's therapy arose from the consequences of denying this premise through the images of female inferiority coded into language, the mass media and the major social institutions of family, religion, education, law, medicine, military defence and social class.

Here are some examples of coded assumptions about gender. It is common English usage to refer to machines such as ships, cars and planes as 'she' which codes in the idea that women are powerful but also in need of control by a skilled male person at the controls. The mass media frequently present women as satisfiers of domestic needs giving non-threatening support at work and as objects for male sexual gratification. Christianity used to deny women priestly abilities and opportunities. Until 50 years ago the most prestigious British universities awarded women diplomas for passing the same exams that earned men a degree. It was 1950 before female doctors were not expected to resign from positions in a hospital when they married. And it was only in 1991 that a husband ceased to be responsible for paying his wife's income tax.

The effect of these arrangements regarding women are a threat to self-esteem and can broadly speaking be met by women in three ways. Accepting them as valid, conforming to them outwardly without believing in them and rebelling against them, seeking to change the situation and not to re-enact it. These responses are those of the oppressed whether the basis of the oppression is sex, race, class, religion or whatever other tag is used to divide people up into categories.

Women's therapy seeks ways to work on power, esteem and perceptions of women, by women for women in the world as it is, largely controlled by men to the detriment of both. Issues about power, role, sexuality, eating and sexual, physical and verbal abuse are central to it.

Reference

Ernst, S. and Goodison, L. (1981) *In Our Own Hands*. London: The Women's Press. This book describes many of the older innovative therapies and emphasizes how to avoid assumptions about gender in using them.

Index

COUPLE THERAPY: A HANDBOOK

Douglas Hooper and Windy Dryden (eds)

This handbook reviews therapy and counselling with committed couples. Although the emphasis is on married and cohabiting heterosexual couples the book also deals with homosexual couples. It explores centrally how the problems of closely involved couples are assessed and tackled in different circumstances and in different ways. It places couple therapy in its theoretical and institutional contexts, analyses important therapeutic concerns such as gender and ethnic issues, working with an individual in a couple, sex therapy, crisis intervention, conciliation and mediation; and examines the wider issues of agency provision, couple education, research and therapeutic training.

Contents

Contributors
Patricia d'Ardenne, David Barkla, Ian Bennun, Michael Butler, Jeremy Clarke, Jean Collard, Windy Dryden, Andy Farrington, Sarah Gammage, Waguih Guiguis, Bridget Hester, Mary Hinchliffe, Douglas Hooper, Brigid Hulson, Adrian James, Penny Mansfield, Lisa Parkinson, Robin Russell, Thomas Schröder, Shoshana Simons, Eddy Street, Anni Telford, Kate Wilson.

336pp   0 335 09892 4 (Paperback)   0 335 09893 2 (Hardback)

CHILD AND ADOLESCENT THERAPY: A HANDBOOK

David A. Lane and Andrew Miller (eds)

Major changes are happening in child and adolescent therapy. The contexts in which the work is done, the range of problems tackled, and the models of intervention adopted are all in flux. This book is an overview of current developments. It presents diverse practice in multiple settings; it looks at the changing agenda for therapy, and the evaluation of interventions. It explores the challenges in play therapy, with non-speaking children, for the management of trauma, in child abuse, bullying and school phobia. In terms of settings, contributors cover the residential therapeutic community, the child guidance clinic, multidisciplinary approaches to support the school, and therapy in the community. In general, it reflects the excitement (and confusions) in current child and adolescent therapy, and is an important resource for trainee and practising professionals in, for instance, social work, the health services, therapy and counselling, educational psychology and special educational needs.

Contents

Part I: The changing agenda – Child and adolescent therapy: a changing agenda – Evaluation of interventions with children and adolescents – Part II: Practice – An interactive approach to language and communication for non-speaking children – The barefoot play therapist: adapting skills for a time of need – Abuse of children – School phobia – Bullying – The management of trauma following disasters – Part III: Settings – The residential community as a therapeutic environment – The Child Guidance Clinic: problems and progress for the 1990s – School support: towards a multi-disciplinary approach – Change in natural environments: community psychology as therapy – Index.

Contributors

Nigel Blagg, Maria Callias, Phil Christie, Danya Glaser, Peter Gray, Neil Hall, Roy Howarth, David A. Lane, Monica Lanyado, Andrew Miller, Elizabeth Newson, John Newson, Jim Noakes, Wendy Prevezer, Martin Scherer, Ruth M. Williams and William Yule.

272pp   0 335 09890 8 (Paperback)   0 335 09891 6 (Hardback)

INTEGRATIVE AND ECLECTIC THERAPY: A HANDBOOK

Windy Dryden (ed.)

This reports and reflects upon the burgeoning interest in and activity of integrative/eclectic approaches to therapy. The first chapter reviews the field and introduces the subsequent chapters which cover: some specific integrative/eclectic approaches; a number of specific therapeutic arenas or modalities; the research literature; and the training of integrative therapists. This is an essential sourcebook for practising and trainee therapists and counsellors.

Contents

The evolution and current status of psychotherapy integration – Systemic Integrative Psychotherapy – Cognitive-analytic therapy (CAT) – Multimodal therapy – Counselling skills: an integrative framework – Behavioural-systems couple therapy: selecting interventions according to problems presented – Sex therapy: an integrative model – Family therapy: evolving an integrated approach – Integrative encounter – Research on integrative and eclectic therapy – Systemic Integrative Psychotherapy training – Appendix – Index.

Contributors

Hal Arkowitz, Michael Barkham, Petruska Clarkson, Pauline Cowmeadow, Michael Crowe, Sue Culley, Roy Eskapa, Waguih R. Guirguis, John C. Norcross, Jane Ridley, John Rowan, Anthony Ryle, Andy Treacher.

320pp   0 335 09337 X (Paperback)   0 335 09338 8 (Hardback)